OUR LADY STAR OF THE SEA PARISH
1513 6TH STREET
BREMERTON, WA 98337

YOU CAN UNDERSTAND THE BIBLE

PETER KREEFT

YOU CAN
UNDERSTAND
THE BIBLE

*A Practical Guide to Each
Book in the Bible*

IGNATIUS PRESS   SAN FRANCISCO

The chapters in this book first appeared in article form in issues of
The National Catholic Register during 1989, 1990, and 1991

Original book editions:
You Can Understand the Old Testament: A Book-by-Book Guide for Catholics
© 1990 by Twin Circle Publishing Company
Published by Servant Publications, Ann Arbor, Michigan
and
Reading and Praying the New Testament: A Book-by-Book Guide for Catholics
© 1992 by Twin Circle Publishing Company
Published by Servant Publications, Ann Arbor, Michigan

New, combined and revised edition printed by permission of Peter Kreeft

Cover art: Raphael (1483–1520)
The Crossing of the Red Sea
From *The Story of Moses.* Fresco.
Location: Logge, Vatican Palace, Vatican State
Photo Credit: Scala / Art Resource, NY

Cover design by Riz Boncan Marsella

CONTENTS

Part Two: The New Testament

AUTHOR'S NOTE

I am not a biblical scholar, and this is not an authoritative and exhaustive introduction to the Bible. It is a popular overview, intended to pique the reader's interest in reading and studying God's Word. It is a book for amateurs. It tells the reader not the things only scholars care about, like arguments about dates and authorship, but what everyone (except fools) cares about: life-changing wisdom. The first comes from man's mind, the second from God's.

Unless otherwise indicated, I quote from the Revised Standard Version (RSV) of the Bible. I have chosen this particular version of Scripture because it is both literal and literary, both accurate and beautiful.

GENERAL INTRODUCTION TO THE BIBLE

There are thousands of books about The Book. Why another one?

This Book itself says, "Of making of many books there is no end, and much study is a weariness of the flesh" (Eccles 12:12). (This is the favorite Bible verse of lazy students.) How is this book different?

First, it is for beginners. It is needed because biblical literacy is declining in Western civilization, as is literacy in general.

Second, it is especially (but not exclusively) for Catholics. Ironically, biblical literacy has declined among Catholics too since Vatican II, even though that Council strongly called for a renewal of it. A book like this on Bible basics would have been superfluous fifty years ago.

Third, it is short and simple. Each chapter can be read over a cup of coffee and a doughnut. It is not full of the latest theories in professional biblical scholarship. I am not a professional Bible scholar, but a teacher and an amateur. (*Amateur* means "lover".)

It is also designed to be practical. It is not a short-cut to reading the Bible itself. It is like a lab manual rather than a textbook. (So is the Bible itself: its Author intends reading and thinking to be preliminary to doing: see Mt 7:24–29.)

***

Reading the Bible should be a form of prayer. The Bible should be read in God's presence and as the unfolding of His mind. It is not just a book, but God's love letter to you. It is God's revelation, God's mind, operating through your mind and your reading, so your reading is your response to His mind and will. Reading it is aligning your mind and will with God's; therefore it is a fulfillment of the prayer "Thy will be done", which is the most basic and essential key to achieving our whole purpose on earth: holiness and happiness. I challenge each reader to give a good excuse (to God, not to me, or even just to yourself) for not putting aside fifteen minutes a day to use this fundamental aid to fulfilling the meaning of your life.

Both prayer and Bible reading are ways of listening to God. They should blend: our prayer should be biblical and our Bible reading prayerful.

In Catholic theology, the Bible is sacramental: it is a sign that is an occasion for grace. The Bible fits the two classic definitions of a sacrament: (1) a visible sign instituted by Christ to give grace and (2) a sign that effects what it signifies. However, unlike the seven sacraments, it does not work *ex opere operato*; it does not give grace by itself, but is dependent on our use of it.

How do you get grace? The same way you get wet. You don't make the rain, and you don't make God's grace. But to get grace you have to go outside yourself, you have to go where God is, just as you have to go outside to get rained on. If you stand in the street, you'll get hit by a car. If you stand in the Bible, you'll get hit by God's kiss. The Bible is a big sprig of His mistletoe.

Though it is not a sacrament, it has power. Its power comes from two wills, God's and ours. It is the Spirit's sword (Eph 6: 17) that cuts our very being apart (Heb 4:12), though we must give it an opening by exposing our minds and hearts and wills to its cutting edge. When we do that, God's Kingdom comes to earth. For it first comes to that tiny but crucially important bit of earth that is your mind and will. Then it transforms your life, which your mind and will control. Then, through your life, your world.

What strange kind of a book is this, anyway?

The word *Bible* means "book" (singular). But the Bible is in fact seventy-two different books (sixty-six in the Protestant canon) from many different authors and times and in many different literary styles and forms: history, poetry, prophecy, drama, philosophy, letters, visions, practical advice, songs, laws, and much more. This is not a book, this is a world.

Yet there is a unity in this diversity. Most essentially the Bible is a story. Unlike the holy books of other religions, the Bible's basic line is a story line. It narrates real events that really happened to real people in real history. G. K. Chesterton said, "There are only two things that never get boring: stories and persons." The persons involved here include the three most important Persons of all: the Father, the Son, and the Holy Spirit. The Bible is "stories of God". But it is also stories about us, about our relationships with God and each other. (The word *religion*, from the Latin *religare*, means essentially "binding relationship".) The horizontal (man-to-man) and vertical (man-to-God) relationships meet here and form a cross.

But there are many kinds of stories: war stories, love stories, detective stories, and many more. What kind of story is this? It tells us what kind of story we are in; that is how it tells us the meaning of our lives.

It is a love story, because it is history, and history is "His story", and He is love. Love is God's plan and purpose in all that He does.

The story unfolds in three acts, which theologians call creation, fall, and redemption. Every story ever told fits this pattern, because this is the basic pattern of all human history.

We could call the three stages setup, upset, and reset. First a situation is *set up*; then it is somehow *upset* by a problem or conflict or challenge; and then it is *reset*, when the challenge is confronted, either successfully or unsuccessfully. Paradise, Paradise Lost, and Paradise Regained are the three acts of the cosmic human drama, and we are now in the third act, which began as early as the third chapter of Genesis, when God began to "redeem", or buy back, fallen mankind.

This third act, in turn, has three scenes. First, God reveals Himself as Father, in the Old Testament; then, as Jesus the Son in the Gospels; finally, He sends the Holy Spirit to be the soul of His Church for the rest of time.

***

The books of both Old and New Testaments are divided into three main categories: history, wisdom, and prophecy. Thus the Bible encompasses past, present, and future. But its history books are more than records of the past; they tell us truths that are just as true and operative for the present. And its wisdom books tell timeless truths that are not just for the present time but for all times. Finally, its prophets do not merely foretell the future, but "forth-tell" God's truth for all times. The whole Bible is God's permanent prophet continually telling forth the truths we need to know to guide our road on earth to a happy eternity.

***

There are two fundamentally different ways of reading the Bible: as God's Word to man or as man's word about God; as divine revelation or as human speculation; as God's certain "way down" to us or as our groping and uncertain "way up" to Him. It claims to be the first of those two things: divine revelation, "the Word of God". But it is the Word of God in the words of men. For God is a good teacher and therefore gives us not only everything that we need but also only what we can take. He reveals Himself more and more, progressively, as we progress through our story. Stories are not static. At first, it is simple, even simplistic and crude—"baby talk", if you will. But it is true, even perfect, baby talk. We should expect the Old Testament to be more primitive than the New, but no less true. For instance, good and evil are revealed first primarily as justice and injustice, right and wrong; then, gradually, the primacy of charity is revealed. For a charity that has not first learned justice is only sentiment.

***

The Bible claims to give us four things that we need and want most, four things God has to give us: truth, power, life, and joy.

First, the Bible claims to give us *truth*—truth about God that we could not have discovered by ourselves (and also truth about ourselves that we could not have discovered by ourselves).

But what kind of truth? Not just abstract correctness but something more solid, the kind of truth that we say is "tried and true" (see Ps 12:6), the kind that is "*made* true" or performed (see Ezek 12:25), the kind that "*comes* true" as the fulfillment of promises (see Mt 5:17–18). This is the kind of truth we find in a person, not just in an idea—in a person who is totally faithful to his word. God is that Person, and the Hebrew word for that kind of truth is *emeth*. If you let this Book speak to you, you will find that it shows you the true character of God and of yourself. It is a mirror.

Second, the Bible claims to have *power*. It uses images like a hammer and fire (Jer 23:29) for itself. It calls itself "the sword of the Spirit" (Eph 6:17).

But what kind of power is this? It is not physical power but spiritual power, which is infinitely greater, for it is the power to change spirit, not just matter, power over free hearts and minds, which the Chinese call *te*. It is the power of goodness, and of love, and even of physical weakness and suffering and sacrifice.

Third, the Bible claims to give *life*. Jesus calls it a *seed* (Lk 8): a living, growing thing. Hebrews 4:12 says that "the word of God is living and active, sharper than any two-edged sword, piercing to the division of soul and spirit ... discerning the thoughts and intentions of the heart." Physical swords only give death; this gives life. Physical swords only cut bodies; this cuts open souls and heals them. For a sword, though in itself a dead thing, can come alive in the hands of a swordsman; and this is "the sword of the Spirit". What happened in Ezekiel 37, when the dry bones came to life, can also happen to you as you read this Book, if you let it—that is, if you read it prayerfully, in the presence of God, talking to Him as you read it. For this is no trick or gimmick of human imagination; He is really there! And "He is not the God of the dead but of the living" (Mt 22:32).

But what kind of life is this? It is spiritual life, eternal life, supernatural life, a sharing, by grace, in the very life of God (see 1 Pet 1:4). The Greek word for this in the New Testament is *zoe*. When you read the Bible, beware: it will *do things* to you. For when you read it, it is reading you. Its Author is reading you, from within. It is like looking into a mirror and seeing another face there looking at you. Or like sitting on a rock that suddenly moves and turns out to be a large and alarming animal. "Look out! It's alive!" Bibles should come with warning labels.

Fourth, the Bible claims to give *joy*. The Psalms are chockfull of expressions of joy in God's Word (e.g., 1:2, 19:8, 119:

97, 119:103). Jeremiah says to God, "Thy words became to me a joy" (15:16).

But what kind of joy is this? It is the joy that does not depend on anything earthly, anything in this world; the joy that is apparently without a cause, because its cause is bigger than the universe: it is God's love. This Book is a love letter from God with your name on it. God doesn't send junk mail or spam. He says, "I have called you by name, you are Mine" (Is 43:1). The words *I love you* are magic words: they change us, they bring wonder and inner surprise, they bring us the greatest joy our lives can contain on earth. How much more when we hear them from our Creator!

***

The Bible calls itself "the Word of God". But it points beyond itself to the "Word of God", Jesus Christ. Every word in this book is part of His portrait. The words man can utter are not alive, but the Word God utters eternally is not only alive but divine. He calls Himself "the Son of God". Meeting Him is the point of the whole Bible (see Jn 5:39) and the whole point of our lives.

***

Here are ten tips for reading the Bible profitably.

1. At first, forget commentaries and books that try to tell you what the Bible means. Read the Bible itself. Get it "straight from the horse's mouth". Data first. The Bible is the most interesting book ever written, but some of the books about it are among the dullest.

2. Read repeatedly. You can never exhaust the riches in this deep mine. The greatest saints, sages, theologians, and philosophers have not exhausted its gold; you won't either.

3. First read through a book quickly, to get an overall idea; then go back and reread more slowly and carefully. Don't rush. Forget time. Relish. Ponder. Meditate. Think. Question. Sink slowly into the spiritual sea and swim in it. Soul-surf its waves.

4. Try to read without prejudice. Let the author speak to you. Don't impose your ideas on the book. Listen first before you talk back.

5. Once you have listened, do talk back. Dialogue with the Author as if He were standing right in front of you—because He is! Ask Him questions and go to His Book to see how He answers. God is a good teacher, and a good teacher wants his students to ask questions.

6. Don't confuse *understanding* with *evaluating*. That is, don't confuse *interpretation* with *critique*. First understand, then evaluate. This sounds simple, but it is harder to do than you probably think. For instance, many readers *interpret* the Bible's miracle stories as myths because they don't *believe* in miracles. But that is simply bad interpretation. Whether or not miracles really happened, the first question is what was the author trying to say. Was he telling a parable, fable, or myth? Or was he telling a story that he claimed really happened? Whether you agree with him or not is the second question, not the first. Keep first things first. Don't say "I don't *believe* Jesus literally rose from the dead, therefore I *interpret* the Resurrection as a myth." The Gospel writers did not mean to write

myth but fact. If the Resurrection didn't happen, it is not a myth. It is a lie. And if it did happen, it is not a myth. It is a fact.

7. Keep in mind these four questions, then, and ask them in this order: First, what does the passage say? That is the *data*. Second, what does it mean? What did the author mean? That is the *interpretation*. Third, is it true? That is the question of *belief*. Fourth, so what? What difference does it make to me, to my life now? That is the question of *application*.

8. Look for "the big picture", the main point. Don't lose the forest for the trees. Don't get hung up on a few specific points or passages. Interpret each passage in its context, including the context of the whole Bible.

9. After you have read a passage, go back and analyze it. Outline it. Define it. Get it clear. *Don't be satisfied with a nice, vague feeling.* Find the thought, and the structures of thought.

10. Be honest—in reading any book, but especially this one, because of its total claims on you. There is only one honest reason for believing the Bible: because it is true, not because it is helpful, or beautiful, or comforting, or challenging, or useful, or even good. If it's not true, no honest person should believe it, even if it were all those other things. And if it is, every honest person should, even if it weren't. Seek the truth and you will find it. That's a promise (see Mt 7:7).

PART ONE

THE OLD TESTAMENT

ONE

Introduction to the Old Testament

The first and longest half of the Bible is called by Christians the "Old Testament" (or "Old Covenant"). Jews call it simply their Bible, or sacred Scriptures. They too believe it is divinely inspired, but they do not believe this about the New Testament, unless they are "Messianic (Christian) Jews". Jews worship the same God Christians worship, but not the same Messiah (Christ).

The Old Testament story distinguishes Judaism (and Christianity) from all other religions of the world in two main ways. First, we find here a religion based on historical facts, not just abstract ideas and ideals or mystical experiences. Second, the God of the Old Testament differs from the gods of other religions in at least four important ways:

1.   Only a few individuals in the ancient world, like Socrates in Greece and Ahkenaton in Egypt, rose above their society's polytheism (belief in many gods) to monotheism (belief in one God) like the Jews.

2.   Only the Jews had the knowledge of a God who created the entire universe out of nothing.

3.   Other peoples separated religion and morality. Only the God of the Bible was perfectly good, righteous, and holy

as well as the Giver of the moral law, demanding moral goodness in all men.

4. These differences are accounted for by a fourth one: although other peoples sometimes arrived at profound truths about God by their imagination (myth), their reason (philosophy), and their experience (mysticism), they mixed these truths with falsehoods because they did not have a word from God Himself. Other religions tell of man's search for God; the Bible tells of God's search for man. Other religions tell timeless truths about God; the Bible tells of God's deeds in time, in history.

God reveals Himself both through words (especially the law given to Moses and the words of the prophets, God's mouthpieces) and deeds. These deeds are both supernatural (miracles) and natural (providence: God providing for His people).

Throughout the Old Testament story, God selects His special instruments: Abel (not Cain), Noah (not the rest of the world), Abram (not Lot), Isaac (not Ishmael), Jacob (not Esau), Joseph (not his brothers), and, in general, the Jews (not the Gentiles)—until Christ the Messiah finally comes. Then Christ's Church, the "New Israel", spreads the knowledge of the true God, the same God of Israel, throughout the world.

Until that time, God's providential care created, preserved, and educated the nation of Israel to be like a womb, like a mother for the coming Messiah. When Jesus was born from Mary's womb, she became the fulfillment of all that Israel was about.

Yet God is not finished with Israel, even now, according to the New Testament (see Rom 10–11). The Church as the New Israel does not simply displace the old, any more than a daughter can displace her mother. For the New Testament is not a mere addition to the Old, nor is it the setting aside of the Old. Jesus says in Matthew 5:17, "Think not that I have come to abolish the law and the prophets; I have come not to abolish them but to fulfil them." The Old Testament, like the New, is about Jesus. It is the beginning of the story of salvation, the same story Jesus completes, the same story we are in now.

TWO

Begin at the Beginning:
Genesis 1–2

We begin with Genesis because we want to follow the Red Queen's advice to Alice when she asks how to tell her story: "Begin at the beginning. Then proceed until you come to the end. Then stop." The Bible is the only book ever written that has fulfilled that admirably simple instruction to the letter.

Genesis means "beginning". The Hebrew title, *Bereshith*, is taken from the first word, "In the beginning". Genesis is the book of beginnings—of the universe, of man, of sin, and of salvation (which is the main theme of the whole Bible). Only God has no beginning: "In the beginning, God".

Genesis is the first book of the *Pentateuch*, a Greek word meaning "five-volume book" (Genesis, Exodus, Leviticus, Numbers, and Deuteronomy). Jews call these five books the *Torah* (law).

According to the earliest Jewish and Christian traditions, Moses wrote Genesis. Many modern scholars doubt this, but the Bible contains many references to Moses as an author, though he probably used and edited older sources.

Like the whole Bible, Genesis is history but not scientific history. This does not mean that it is myth or fable, but that its style is often poetic and that its content is selective. The author is like a photographer who points his camera only at the subjects that are important for his purposes, from his point of view. The purpose of the Divine Author of the Bible, the Holy Spirit, is to tell us about God and His acts of "salvation history".

Thus Genesis, like salvation history itself, and like every story, has three parts: creation, fall, redemption; generation, degeneration, and regeneration; Paradise, Paradise Lost, and Paradise Regained.

The action moves from the Garden of Eden to Egypt, from man in innocence and paradise to the chosen people in sin and slavery, hoping for deliverance. The time span of Genesis covers more years than all the rest of the Bible together. It is divided into eleven sections, each beginning with "This is the list of the descendants of . . ." (*elleh toledoth* in Hebrew).

Since the beginning is so crucial and since Genesis covers the beginning of all three stages of our story—creation, fall, and redemption—we will take three chapters to explore Genesis, one for Exodus, and one for the next three books.

The God Who Creates out of Nothing

Genesis begins not just with the beginning of something, but with the beginning of everything. Its first verse uses a word for which there is no equivalent in any other ancient language. The word is *bara'*. It means not just to make but to create, not just to re-form something new out of something old, but to create something wholly new that was simply not there before. Only God can create, for *creation* in the literal sense (out of nothing) requires infinite power, since there is an infinite gap between nothing and something. Startling as it may seem, no other people ever had creation stories in the true sense of the word, only formation stories. The Jewish notion of creation is a radically distinctive notion in the history of human thought. When Jewish theologians like Philo and later Christian theologians (who learned it from the Jews) told the Greeks about it, they were often ridiculed.

Yet the consequences of this notion of creation are incomparable. They include radically new notions (1) of God, (2) of nature, and (3) of human beings and human life.

1.   A God who creates out of nothing is radically different from any of the gods of paganism. (a) Having infinite power, He must be one, and not many, not limited by others. (b) Further, to create this entire universe requires not just infinite power but also infinite wisdom (the wisest men on earth have never been able even to make a lasting peace or a perfect society, much less a universe), (c) It also requires a fantastic sense of beauty ("poems are made by fools like me, but only God can make a tree"), and (d) infinite generosity (for one who does not even exist cannot possibly deserve to be created).

2.   (a) Without the notion of creation, nature is either denied or worshipped. Ancient Gentiles, lacking the notion of creation, saw nature either as an illusion (in the Orient) or as something sacred (in the West), as the local habitation of the gods. Creation frees nature from nothingness and from godhood.

(b) Further, if God created nature, it is not only real rather than illusory, it is also good rather than evil. Genesis repeats the point with liturgical emphasis: at the end of each of His six days of work, God chants, "Good, good, good". This is why the problem of evil is more crucial for a Jew or a Christian than for anyone else: he is stuck with a theology of delight and cannot blame evil on the primal glop God was stuck with, since God created the very glop out of which He formed the worlds. That's why Genesis 3 has to come after Genesis 1 and 2: to answer the obvious question raised by the creation account: If an all-good God is in charge here, where did evil come from?

(c) The doctrine of creation also means that nature is rational. It is not the arbitrary, fallible wills of many gods, or the primal chaos before the gods, but the all-knowing, all-wise will of the one God who designs and controls nature. The doctrine of creation is thus the basis for science. It is no accident that science grew up almost entirely in the West, not in the Orient, where nature was seen as a shifting veil of *maya* (illusion).

3. Finally, human beings and human lives get a radically new meaning by the doctrine of creation. If God created my very existence, I simply have no being, no essence, and no rights apart from or independent of God. My relationship to God is not an addition, however precious, to my being; it is my very being, my essence. Man is not man and then related to God; to be a human being *is* to be God's creature, God's servant, God's son or daughter. Not a second of my time, a cent of my money, a drop of my blood or my sweat, or a thought in my head can I truly call my own unless I first call it His. I owe Him my all because I owe Him my being. The Bible thus does not present a "religion" as a department of life. It presents life itself as essentially, totally, and inescapably religious, that is, God-relational, from its very center.

How did God create? It was strictly a no-sweat operation. He simply spoke His Word. Christ is present in Genesis, for Christ is "the Word of God": "All things were made through him, and without him was not anything made that was made" (Jn 1:3).

The Key Question Is Why, Not How

Did God use evolution? He may have. Genesis is not a science text, so it does not tell us *how* so much as *why*. But
there are hints. Only three times in the creation account is
bara' used: for the creation of matter (1:1), life (1:21), and
humanity (1:27). The other times, God said, "let the waters
bring forth . . ." or "let the earth bring forth . . ." That is, for
most of His acts of "creation", He *made* rather than *created*.
For example, He used the pre-existing material of "the dust
of the earth" to make man. Was that an ape body? Perhaps.
Why not? Our "image of God" distinctiveness, our person-
ality, is grounded in the soul, not in the body. We are "rational *animals*". God is not an animal.

Catholics have seldom had the difficulties and embarrass-
ments many Protestants have had about creation vs. evolution. Ever since Augustine, they have interpreted Genesis'
"days" non-literally. (The Hebrew word there, *yom*, is often
used non-quantitatively in Scripture.) Purposes, not clocks,
measure God's time.

Genesis also goes a long way to resolve the current fem-
inist furor. On the one hand, it clearly says that "the image
of God" is "male *and* female" (1:27), and that males' present
kind of "rule" over females is a result of the fall (3:16). On
the other hand, it is equally clear that sexual differentiation
is God's natural design, not our artifice.

In fact, God creates everything by differentiating. Form,
species, differentiation—this feature of the world is due to
accident according to materialism and illusion according to
pantheism, but it is due to divine will and design according
to theism. God *distinguishes* being vs. nonbeing, light vs. darkness, the "waters above" (the heavens) vs. the "waters below"
(the earth), seas vs. land, living vs. nonliving, plants vs. animals,

birds vs. fish vs. land animals, species vs. species, each "after its kind", animals vs. humanity (in God's image)—and Adam vs. Eve, man vs. woman. Masculinity and femininity are not a sinister trick of nature or society but a wise and benevolent gift of God, and cause for rejoicing, not for embarrassment, except to the fallenness that leads us to hide from God and from each other.

No one has ever told this story better. When our first astronaut ventured into space, this was what he read, in awe. It is literally inexhaustible.

Primitive tribes often recite their "creation epics" over the body of a sick or dying person, to bring the person back to the time of beginnings, when God touched time and matter firsthand. Without buying into superstition or magic, I think it is not too much to say that there seems to lurk that kind of mysterious power in these words. Next time you feel confused, try reading Genesis 1. Somehow, it seems to clear away a lot of fog.

THREE

Our Free Fall into Sin: Genesis 3

We will devote an entire chapter to Genesis 3, because the event narrated in these thirty-one verses, the event we call the fall, is one of the three most important events that have ever happened. The other two are the creation and the Incarnation. These are the two "big bangs" and one big thud in our history.

No greater or more far-reaching tragedy has ever happened than the fall. A nuclear holocaust is a minor inconvenience compared to the primal divorce from the source of all our joy, our goodness, our peace, our wisdom, and our very identity.

If we were to meet unfallen Adam and Eve now (as we may if we find an unfallen race on another planet), we would either worship them or totally misunderstand and despise them. We would not feel comfortable with them as something like ourselves. The imagination boggles when it tries to conceive the state of original innocence. That is why such a challenging and fascinating theme has hardly ever been tackled by our poets and storytellers, and never with any real success. (Milton's *Paradise Lost* and C. S. Lewis' *Perelandra* come closest.)

Why the Fall Need Not Have Happened

The first lesson obviously taught by the story of the fall is that it was a free fall. It need not have happened. One way of stating this doctrine is C. S. Lewis': if there are other intelligent and free beings on other planets (as seems possible considering the size of the universe and of God's imagination), they need not have fallen. To be a person is not necessarily to be a sinful person. To be in God's image is not necessarily to be in a defaced image. To be married to God is not necessarily to have sued for divorce, as we did in this disastrous rebellion.

There are only three basic explanations for evil. It is to be blamed either on God above us, nature below us, or us. Genesis 3 rejects the two convenient excuses that either God or evolution made us this way. The message of Genesis 3 is that the buck stops here. The finger that points blame is curved one hundred and eighty degrees.

Jews, who have and believe this Scripture just as Christians do, say they do not believe in "original sin" because they think of that doctrine as Calvinism, as a denial of the goodness of God's creation even when defaced by sin. But Genesis 3 does not teach Calvinistic "total depravity" (except in the sense that we are totally unable to save ourselves without divine grace, which is also taught in Orthodox Judaism). Rather, the forbidden fruit was "the knowledge of *good and evil*", not pure evil. There's still a little good in the worst of us, but also a little bad in the best of us.

By the way, the word *knowledge* here means "experience". God wanted to keep us from the knowledge of good-and-evil that comes from experiencing and tasting it (thus the image of eating fruit), not from the knowledge that understands it. The same word is used in Genesis 4 for sexual intercourse: Adam "knew" Eve, and the result was not a book but a baby.

We Are Morally Bad, Not Bad in Our Being

Genesis 3 does not teach that man is now *ontologically* bad, bad in his *being*, but *morally* bad, bad in his *choices*. God made our being; we make our choices. Yet it is our state of sinfulness, or separation from God (our state of original sin), that leads us to make sinful choices (actual sins). The word *sin* comes from the German *Sünde*, which means "separation." We sin (actual sin) because we are sinners (original sin), just as we sing because we are singers. Sin is not our essence (that remains ontologically good), but it is more than our day-to-day choices; it is our habit, our character. Yet this habit or character in turn was caused by Adam and Eve's first "actual sin" or evil choice, symbolized by the eating of the forbidden fruit.

How are we to blame for what Adam and Eve did? We aren't; we are to blame for what we do. But what we do is conditioned by what they did, just as a baby who is born a drug addict because its mother took drugs during pregnancy, is conditioned by what its mother did. The mystery of heredity is only the biological dimension of the greater mystery of solidarity, of interdependence among persons, that goes all the way up into the Trinity itself.

The Bible never says we are punished for Adam's sin, but rather that we sinned "in" Adam. There in that innocent little preposition is the mystery of solidarity. Premodern thinkers, less individualistic than we, saw the human race as an organism, like a tree, not an anthill. Each individual (leaf) gets bad sap because the tree as a whole has bad sap. Adam was the first bad sap. Our sin is not a matter of *imitation*, of ant-like "follow the leader", but of *incorporation*, just as our salvation through Christ is not a matter of our imitating Christ from without but of being incorporated into Christ from within by faith and baptism. (It's all in Romans 6.)

The account of the fall in Genesis 3, like the account of the creation, is couched in highly poetic, symbolic language. The talking snake and the two trees are, by any intelligent literary standards, meant to be interpreted symbolically, not literally and physically. But what they symbolize is real and literal. The event of the fall must have really happened at some point in real time. For if not, if the fall is merely a timeless truth about our sinfulness projected into the form of a before-and-after story, then there never really was a time of innocence; and in that case, we are sinful not because we freely chose to make ourselves that way, but because God created us that way from the beginning. In that case, God is on the hook and we are off the hook for sin. We are simply His instruments, His smoking gun. If God, not Adam, started the fall, then God, not Hitler, started the Holocaust.

Faith and Works Go Together from the Beginning

Why did we fall? What could have motivated our first ancestors to exchange the joy of walking with God in the garden of pure paradise for anything else at all? Genesis 3 holds the clue. The first step in the fall was a weakening of faith. Saint Paul says, "Whatever does not proceed from faith is sin" (Rom 14:23). The devil's first temptation to Eve was for her to doubt God's word that eating the forbidden fruit meant death (3:2–3). Once Eve let the demonic lever of doubt find a fulcrum in her soul, her will and her acts soon followed. Faith and works from the beginning go together, neither is ever apart from the other. This is why the very first step in the war against sin and for sanctity is to "take every *thought* captive to obey Christ" (2 Cor 10:5).

What is the connection between sin and death, sin's punishment—i.e., between spiritual death of the soul and physical death of the body? It is not an arbitrary one decreed by an angry God, like, "I'll smack your hands if you steal those cookies!" Rather, it is a natural and inevitable necessity of human nature in its situation of dependence on God as the Source of all life, spiritual and physical. Once this Source of life was gone from the soul by sin (separation), the necessary consequence was that the body also died. For the body is one with the soul, not another *thing*. Body and soul are related like the words and the message of a poem, or the color and the shape of a painting, not like a horse and a cart. Once the soul freely cut its lifeline to God, the body necessarily and unfreely fell with it, like two mountaineers bound together by one rope. Before the fall, our bodies received life from God, through the obedient soul; thus there was no reason we should ever die. Now our bodies are dependent on subsidies from finite nature instead, a source that soon runs dry.

After the fall, Adam and Eve used the two defense mechanisms that we've been using ever since: hiding and passing the blame. First, they hid from God and from each other, covering themselves, probably their sexual organs, with clothes. Why their sexual organs? The fall was not a matter of sex. God had commanded them to "be fruitful and multiply". Probably because they had hoped, by eating the forbidden fruit, to fulfill the devil's false promise to be like God, complete and independent. But their sexual differentiation revealed their incompleteness as individuals and their dependence on each other.

Their (and our) second escape was to pass the blame. Adam blamed Eve (v. 12) and Eve blamed the devil (v. 13). God, of course, accepted (and accepts) neither excuse. The blame is on us, and God puts it on Christ on the Cross.

The Great War Begins

Christ is present in Genesis 3 as well as in Genesis 1 (as the creative Word of God). Verse 15 is the Bible's first prophecy of redemption. It is an outline of all future history. That history is to be a spiritual war between the children of Eve (ultimately, Christ, the son of the New Eve, Mary) and the children of the devil. Christ shall bruise Satan's head, destroying his power. But Satan shall bruise Christ's heel, on the Cross, shall wound God's "Achilles' heel" or weak spot, His assumed humanity.

Saint Augustine's masterpiece *The City of God* interprets all human history according to Genesis 3:15, as spiritual warfare between "the City of God", God's children through Eve and Mary and Christ, and "the City of the World", Satan's children. Ever since Cain vs. Abel, mankind has been at civil war with itself because half of it is still at revolutionary war with God. There are only two kinds of people. We are either God's children or Satan's. Jesus reaffirmed this terrifying truth many times, for example, in John 8:41–47 and in John 3:3.

Genesis 3:15 interprets all human history as a battle. It is neither a mere doom nor a mere blessing. It is neither black nor white, but a checkerboard. Between the old Paradise of Eden lost and the new Paradise of Heaven to be gained, this world must always remain, for all the sons of Adam and daughters of Eve, full of pain in childbirth and thorns and thistles in sweaty work: neither a snake pit nor a hot tub, but a battlefield.

God's exile of Adam and Eve from Eden is like death itself: a punishment but a mercy, a "severe mercy". If God had not sent the cherubim with the flaming sword to bar the gate of Eden, Adam and Eve may have crept back in to eat the fruit of the other tree, the Tree of (Eternal) Life and established themselves in their sinful nature eternally. That would have been literally hell on earth, eternal hopelessness.

Death is now God's anesthesia. It is needed to complete His healing operation on us who have contracted the deadly disease of sin. Only in death do we stop wiggling about on the operating table. Then God can penetrate into our deepest heart with His loving but terrifying scalpel.

The perennial temptation is to creep under the angel's flaming sword, to try to create a heaven on earth. The two most popular forms of this are the Oriental form of ignoring real physical evils by creating a mystical inner paradise through yoga and meditation, and the Western form of ignoring real spiritual evils by building a technological heaven on earth. Both are doomed to failure, of course, but the failure is the greatest *not* when it is obvious, and leads to repentance, but when the failure is masked by apparent success. The thorns and thistles are sent to jolt us awake and remind us of our necessities, of where we are, of the battlefield. Since the peace we are seeking comes from God alone, "Woe to those who cry, 'Peace! Peace!' when there is no peace" (Jer 6:14).

FOUR

The Divine Rescue Operation:
Genesis Continued

The three stages of history—creation, fall, and redemption—
are reflected in the three parts of Genesis. This third chapter
explores the third and longest part, God's "redemption" or
"buying-back" of His creatures who sold themselves into
Satan's slavery.

This began immediately after the fall in chapter three, when
God pronounced the "curses" on Satan (vv. 14–15), on Eve
(v. 16), and on Adam (vv. 17–19). All these punishments are
also mercies for us. These are like tourniquets, stemming the
flow of blood, or like quarantines, stopping the spread of disease.

Death is the most obvious example. We know little about
many of the names in the genealogies, but we know with
certainty the one thing repeated about every single one: "And
he died . . . and he died . . . and he died".

The next event narrated, after the fall, is a death—in fact,
a murder. Not every death is a murder, but all death is a
consequence of sin. Thus murder shows the meaning of death
more clearly than a so-called "natural" death does. Cain's
murder of Abel is the Fall flowing out, like Abel's blood. It
is a kind of icon of our whole fratricidal history of violence,
both inner and outer, both small and great.

God's Radical Surgery

Such a radical disease requires a radical surgery. "Without the shedding of blood there is no forgiveness of sins" (Heb 9:22).

"The City of God" and "the City of the World" began to exist side by side as opposite movements of the human heart as soon as Adam and Eve fell into "knowing" good and evil rather than good alone. But with Cain and Abel these two "cities" begin to exist as two groups of people. Cain and Abel are the fathers of the two spiritual races that subsequently divide all human history: the damned and the saved, the once-born and the twice-born.

When we come to Abraham in chapter 12, the style of narrative changes. Historians can pin down specific dates, places, names, and cross-references in secular history from Abraham onward, but there is no way of knowing when Noah lived or perhaps even whether he and his flood are meant to be archetypal symbols or literal facts. Between the symbolic style of the first three chapters and the literal history of the story of the chosen people, which begins with the call of Abraham in chapter 12, there are eight borderline chapters that could reasonably be interpreted either way.

When God changes Abram's name to Abraham and Jacob's to Israel, He does something only God can do, because for the Hebrews your name means not your social label but your divinely ordained nature, character and destiny. That's why Jesus was implicitly claiming divinity when He changed Simon's name to Peter (Jn 1:42).

The call of Abraham in Genesis 12 comes right after the Tower of Babel in chapter 11 to contrast man's way with God's way. The tower symbolizes all proud human attempts to conquer heaven and happiness by force, or to create a heaven on earth by our own cleverness (language, reason, science, technology). Throughout the Bible, the symbolism remains the same: all human towers to Heaven tumble, and all divine descents succeed. Our "way up" always turns out to be a "way down", and all divine "ways down" turn out to be the "way up". The Messiah is the prime example.

How reasonable the Tower of Babel sounds, and how silly the call of Abraham seems! What a way to fight the serious battle against evil—to pick out one man, flawed like all of us, for a lifelong trek into the wilderness with no road map and no guarantees, only promises. Yet this is the beginning of history's most public miracle: the Jewish people. Their survival and continued rejuvenation, their unparalleled flourishing and achievements, out of all proportion to their tiny size and strength, violate every known law of history and sociology. The more we consider their history, the more we are in awe at divine providence. The more we open our eyes to see, the more we open our mouths to gasp.

Consider just one incident in the long Joseph story, found in chapters 37 to 51. If one Egyptian tailor had not skimped on the thread of Joseph's mantle, no Jew would be alive today. That mantle came apart in the hands of Potiphar's wife, who was thus able unjustly to accuse Joseph of attempted rape and get him imprisoned, where he met Pharaoh's butler and baker and interpreted their dreams, thus coming to Pharaoh's attention, interpreted *his* dreams, and saved Egypt from famine by his divine gift of prophecy. Only the grain preserved by Joseph's prophetic gift saved his family in Palestine who had sold him into slavery, when he finagled their coming to Egypt. Thus, generations later, we have hordes of healthy Jewish slaves in Egypt, ripe for Moses' liberation in the Exodus, and all their subsequent history.

In international diplomacy that divine technique is called brinkmanship. In chess, it's called a wild gambit. In gambling, it's called going against the odds. God's style is *not* conservative!

Notice how God uses His own enemy, evil, against itself and for good. The obvious lesson of the whole long story of Joseph and of all human history miniaturized here, is providence (see Rom 8:28). Or, as Joseph tells his brothers about their having sold him into slavery, "You meant evil against me, but God meant it for good" (50:20). "God writes straight with crooked lines." He used Satan, Judas, Pilate, and Caiaphas to crucify Christ and thus redeem the world!

God has nothing but flawed instruments to work with. There is a striking contrast between the heroes of Genesis and the heroes of pagan mythology. The men of the Bible are real: flawed, weak, stupid, sinful. Adam, Noah, Abraham, Isaac, Jacob, Moses—every one of them is a spiritual klutz, learning only through repeated mistakes. What makes them heroes is not their strength but their faith. They believe: that is, they let God be God, they open the door to the real power, the real success, which is God's activity, not their own.

We can all do that. Thus we can identify with these heroes, as we can't identify with Hercules (unless we're Rambo) or Aphrodite (unless we're Marilyn Monroe).

A God of Infinite Justice and Infinite Love

It's often said that the Old Testament, especially Genesis, teaches a God of justice, in stark contrast to Jesus, who teaches a God of forgiveness and love. It is a lie, of course. The God of the Old Testament does all that He does out of love; and the Father of Jesus needs to satisfy justice as well as love; that's why Jesus had to die. I used to think that only those who never read the Bible could fall for this fallacy. But experience has taught me otherwise. Why is it so common? I think it comes partly from misunderstanding the literary style of Genesis. It is not meant to be *psychology*, either of God or humanity. The modern style of storytelling emphasizes psychological motive and scrutinizes inner consciousness. This is simply not the style of premodern writing. Augustine's *Confessions* is the only personal introspective autobiography in premodern literature.

Thus the "wrath of God" is not meant as a description of God's own private feelings, but of His public deeds, of how those deeds look to fallen, "wrathful" man. Psychologically, this is "projection". When God gave Lady Julian of Norwich a "showing" of His wrath, she said, "I saw no wrath but on man's part."

God is indeed a God of justice and thus of punishment, which is part of justice. But love is the motive behind all His deeds of discipline. "For the Lord disciplines him whom he loves. . . . If you are left without discipline, then you are illegitimate children and not sons" (Heb 12:6–8).

Genesis is the book of beginnings, and no subsequent change in all human history ever has or ever will alter the essential pattern of the story begun here. Even a nuclear holocaust would be only Cain and Abel on a worldwide scale. Even the fall of Rome (i.e., of civilization) was only the Tower of Babel on a larger scale. God remains faithful, man remains faithless; God remains patient, man remains fickle, to the end—and God triumphs in the end. Paradoxically, the most human, humane, humanistic, humanly fulfilling thing man can say to God is: "Arise, O Lord! Let not man prevail . . ." (Ps 9:19). For we are our own worst enemies, and our divine opponent against whom we strive is our best friend and only hope.

Genesis ends with the chosen people in slavery, but it ends in hope. The Old Testament ends with a prophetic warning and a curse (Mal 4:6), but with hope for the Messiah. The New Testament ends with an apocalypse, but with hope: "Amen. Come, Lord Jesus!" No book is more severe *and* no book is more hopeful than the Bible, from Genesis on. Not the slightest compromise is made either with the optimistic pride that tries to recreate Eden or with the pessimistic despair that refuses to believe, to hope, and to love. Genesis destroys our two great illusions, if we let it. It is utterly unsparing. You cannot read it without being changed, if you let it interpret you before you interpret it.

FIVE

God's "Liberation Theology": Exodus

Supernatural Liberation from the Deeper Slavery of Sin

Genesis was about a genesis: of creation, fall, and redemption. Exodus, not surprisingly, is about an exodus: of God's people from Egyptian slavery. The exodus was the event that, more than any other, forged the identity of the Jewish people, the event they looked back to for the next 3,500 years as the decisive one in their history.

It is enlightening to contrast the way an orthodox Jewish or Christian theologian looks on this event with the way liberal or modernist theologians look at it. For this difference about the past is reflected in a difference about the present, about what God is doing for us today, and how, essentially, we are supposed to work with Him; what the essential *opus dei* or work of God is.

For the modernist, all the supernatural elements in the exodus, all the miracles, all the divine initiatives, are the Jewish people's retrospective interpretation of the historical facts, not historical facts themselves. Piously desiring to give God credit for their liberation, the Jews invented specific miracle myths to symbolize the general truth of divine providence, such as the ten miraculous plagues or the miraculous parting

of the Red Sea (or Reed Sea). They read their present subjective faith back into their past objective history.

This view is self-defeating, for it does not really give God
credit for anything much at all. Not miracles, for one thing.
And not for choosing the Jews. The Jewish notion of the
"chosen people" is indeed the proud and elitist one that it
seems to most modern egalitarians *if* it was the Jews' interpretation rather than God's literal choice—*if* they only used
God as a mythic way of speaking about themselves. It is the
supernatural idea that is the only humble idea.

The same dispute concerns contemporary "liberation theology". This is the issue: What is God doing, most fundamentally, in the world today, and what are we supposed to
be doing to cooperate with Him? The liberal answer is that
He is inspiring political leaders to liberate oppressed peoples, as He inspired Moses to liberate the Jews from Egypt.
In other words, the earthly manna of political freedom,
power, and prosperity—liberation from their opposites of
slavery, weakness, and poverty—is the most important thing.
The heavenly manna is only a manmade myth or symbol
for that.

This is the orthodox answer of both Jews and Christians
to the same question: God is giving us heavenly manna of
divine grace. That is our primary need. Man can liberate
man from slavery to man, but only God can liberate man
from the deeper slavery to sin.

In the orthodox interpretation of the exodus, it was Moses'
faith, not his political shrewdness or power, that opened the
gate to God's miracle-working liberation. Machiavelli, who
was probably an atheist as well as one of the first modernists,
goes so far as to imply that Moses must have had superior
arms to accomplish his remarkable success! (This involves a
radical "reinterpretation" of the text, of course; but far be it

from a modernist to bow in superstitious slavery before objective data!)

The Symbolism of the Exodus Story

However, there is symbolism in Exodus. Catholic theologians ever since the Fathers of the Church have seen in the historical, literal events of the exodus also an allegory. Christ, the new Moses, liberates His people, the Church, the new Israel, from the spiritual slavery of sin and from the power of the world (symbolized by Egypt), which is under the dominion of Satan (symbolized by Pharaoh), through the sea (death) and the wilderness (Purgatory) to the promised land (Heaven). This symbolic reading of eight elements in the exodus story does not replace the literal and historical one, but presupposes it.

Tragically, this rich, double-level way of thinking has nearly disappeared from modern consciousness and biblical scholarship. It is either/or, literal *or* symbolic today. Modernists favor symbolic interpretations, but only of the embarrassing (to them) miracle stories. The orthodox reaction to modernism, especially among Protestants, has been not only to defend the truth of literal miracles and the accuracy of biblical history but also to suspect symbolism. But it can be both. Saint Thomas Aquinas explains the reason: "The author of Holy Writ is God, in whose power it is to signify His meaning not by words only (as man also can do) but by things themselves. So, whereas in every other science things are signified by words, this science [theology] has the property that the things signified by the words have themselves also a [symbolic] signification ... the spiritual sense, which is based on the literal and presupposes it" (*Summa Theologica*, I, 1, 10). Since God writes history as man writes words, the literal events of history can be signs of other truths just as human words are signs of things other than themselves.

Symbolic interpretation of historical facts was not invented by Aquinas; it is biblical. For example, Saint Paul sees the exodus as a symbol of baptism (Rom 6:2–3; 1 Cor 10:1–2), and the Passover (Exodus 12) as a symbol of Christ (1 Cor 5:7). Though Christ is called the *Paschal* Lamb and Easter the *paschal* feast in the liturgy, most Catholics do not make the connection to the Passover because they do not think symbolically about real historical events.

The Law: The Very Heart of It Is Love

The giving of the law in Exodus is as important as the exodus itself. The law is the center of Judaism, which is more a practical religion than a theological or creedal one; orthopraxis (right action) is more central for Jews than orthodoxy (right belief).

Orthodox and modernist accounts of the giving of the law differ. The text, which gives the orthodox account, credits *God* with inventing and giving the Ten Commandments. In fact, His was the very hand that chiseled them in Moses' stone tablets. The modernist instead credits *Moses* with these ten "good ideas" (which is like crediting the mail carrier with writing your letters).

We can distinguish four different levels or areas of the law. The law is like an onion; strip away the outer layers and you find the inner. Most publicly and externally, there are many *civil* laws regulating public social life. Second, there are detailed *liturgical*, ceremonial laws regulating worship. Both of these levels of the law are specified in Leviticus, the next book.

Third, the *moral* law, the Ten Commandments, given in Exodus, is a far deeper level of law. Unlike the specifically

Jewish civil and ceremonial laws, such as kosher foods and tithing, the commandments are for all people, all societies, and all times. Thus, though Christians are in no way bound by the Jewish ceremonial or civil laws (because they were all in some way preparatory for Christ), we are still under the Ten Commandments in one way, though not in two other ways.

We are under them in that they express God's changeless demands for all of us, God's blueprint, God's idea for human living. But we are freed from the *curse* of the law by Christ's atoning death; that is, we are freed from God's eternal punishment for our disobedience. And we are freed, gradually, from our impotence to obey it, from our slavery to sin, by the Holy Spirit. In other words, the Son justifies us and the Spirit sanctifies us. These are two new relationships to the law.

The heart of the law, its fourth and deepest aspect, is love (see Deut 6:4–5, the most familiar of all Jewish prayers, and Mt 22:35–40). Christianity did not invent the idea that "love is the fulfillment of the law." Christ's law of love is not new, but old. He says so Himself. Many Christians believe the implicitly anti-Semitic idea that Judaism is a religion of law, not love, and Christianity a religion of love, not law. No, Christ only fulfilled what is already the heart of Judaism.

The good Jew *loves* the law (see Ps 1:2; 119:97). The psalmists frequently express this spontaneous emotion, something we do not easily understand. For we think of the law only as an abstract formula, a verbal command. How can you love that? Furthermore, any law necessarily threatens us with punishment for disobedience, so we naturally fear it rather than love it. How can the law be loved?

The answer is that the law expresses God's will and is thus the glue that binds us to God. It is *God* we love *via* the law.

The good Jew, like the good Christian, sees behind the law to the Lawgiver, whose will is perfect love. Since God gave the law out of love, we can obey it and desire to obey it out of love. Law and love are not enemies but allies.

Moses: The Most Complete Prefigurement of Christ

Exodus centers on Moses, greatest of all Jewish prophets, the man who spoke with God face to face and lived. Moses is as prominent and primary in Judaism as Mohammed is in Islam or as Confucius is in Confucianism. Yet his deepest significance is beyond Judaism: Moses symbolizes and foreshadows Christ. Let's look at some of the ways he does, some of the parallels between Moses and Christ.

1. Both were outsiders (Ex 3:1–10; Jn 3:13).
2. Both received long training before their public ministry (Ex 2:10; Lk 3:23).
3. Both performed many miracles (Ex 7–14; Jn 3:2 and 21:25).
4. Both were preserved from an evil king's plot to murder them as babies (Ex 2:2–10; Mt 2:14–15; and Rev 12:1–6 and 13–17).
5. Both stood up against masters of evil (Ex 7:11; Mt 4:1).
6. Both fasted for forty days (Ex 34:28; Mt 4:2).
7. Both controlled the sea (Ex 14:21; Mt 8:26).
8. Both fed a multitude of people (Ex 16:15; Mt 14:20–21).
9. Both showed the light of God's glory on their faces (Ex 34:35; Mt 17:2).
10. Both endured rebellion from their people (Ex 15:24; Jn 5:45–47).

11. Both were scorned at home (Num 21:1; Jn 7:5).
12. Both saved their people by intercessory prayer (Ex 32:32; Jn 17:9).
13. Both spoke as God's mouthpiece (Deut 18:18; Jn 7:16–17).
14. Both had seventy helpers (Num 11:16–17; Lk 10:1).
15. Both gave a law from a mountain (Ex 20; Mt 5–7).
16. Both established memorials (Ex 12:14; Lk 22:19).
17. Both reappeared after death (Mt 17:3; Acts 1:3).
18. Both did the work of prophets, priests, and kings— the three most important positions of authority in the ancient world.
19. Both conquered the world, the flesh, and the devil.
20. Finally, both brought their people from slavery to freedom and to the Promised Land.

Moses is the most complete symbol or prefigurement of Christ in the Bible.

God Reveals His Own Essential Name

Exodus contains what is perhaps the most profound verse in the Bible, the most profound thing human ears have ever heard: the verse that reveals the essence of ultimate reality, the nature of God as expressed in His own true name. Remember that for the ancients your name revealed your nature, your essence. Exodus 3:14 is the only time God ever revealed His own essential name. All the other names for God in the Bible are our names for Him, or designate His relations to us. Once and once only does God use His own name for Himself, what He is in Himself: when He tells it to Moses from the burning bush.

Why only to Moses? Men and women had been wondering what was the true name of God for centuries; why did only Moses find out? A rabbi once told me the answer to that question: because Moses was the only one practical enough to go straight to the horse's mouth: he asked! God was waiting for centuries for someone to ask Him; instead, they only speculated!

The divine name is simply "I AM", or "I AM WHO AM". It is the name Jesus appropriated for Himself in John 8:58, thus clearly and uncompromisingly claiming divinity and inviting execution for blasphemy. For no Jew will ever even try to pronounce the divine name. In fact, no one even knows how to pronounce it correctly since it has not been pronounced for millennia. It was written only in consonants, omitting the vowels. Thus it is called the sacred Tetragrammaton or four-consonant, four-letter word, JHWH.

The reason no Jew will speak it is that, unlike any other name, you cannot say it without claiming to bear it. You can say "John" or "Mary" in the second or third person, but "I" only in the first. You can say "Hi, John" or "Have you seen Mary?" but you can't say "I" unless you *are* "I". God thus asserts His incommunicable, unique being, the divine subjectivity. He is not object but subject. As Buber says, "God cannot be expressed, only addressed", for "He is the Thou that cannot become an It."

That's why He always initiates rather than responding, questions rather than answering, knows rather than being known, wills the law rather than being under it, and impregnates our souls rather than vice versa. That is why "she" is a wrong symbol for Him and "he" a right one. To the feminists' seemingly reasonable protests against the apparent male chauvinism in the Bible's language about God, we must reply, as C. S. Lewis says, simply: "God himself has taught us how to speak of him."

SIX

God's Law, Israel's Wanderings, and Moses' Farewell: Leviticus, Numbers, and Deuteronomy

These three books, coming after Genesis and Exodus, complete the Pentateuch, the five Books of Moses on which all of Judaism is based. Though not as richly varied as Genesis or Exodus, they contain priceless and unforgettable gems.

Leviticus: The Book of Laws

The Hebrew title for this book is its first word, *Wayyiqra*, "and he called". God, not man, called into being these laws and their administrators, the Levites. The English title *Leviticus* means "the things of the Levites". Leviticus is the book of laws God gave Israel through Moses.

As Israel's law book, Leviticus contains hundreds of regulations extending to exact and tiny details of Israel's social life and temple worship. It is obviously *not* exciting reading, unless you happen to be a lawyer. Yet it is, when you realize that some extremely important lessons pervade all these minutiae:

1.   God's loving care of His people reaches down into even the tiny details of their lives. Nothing is too small to be an occasion for His care or our obedience.

2.   Law is good. It is not "repressive" of good, only of evil. God is the author of law and good order, not of confusion. He gives us law out of love for us, for our instruction, discipline, and protection.

3.   The key word and idea in the book is *holiness*—a word that occurs over eighty times. The key text is 11:45: "I am the Lord who brought you up out of the land of Egypt, to be your God; you shall therefore be holy, for I am holy." That gives us our essential motive for sanctity.

4.   The laws in Leviticus were God's gracious provision for sinful man to approach a holy God. Like the New Testament, Leviticus unites two apparently opposite ideas: law and grace, justice and mercy, the demand for obedience and the promise of forgiveness for disobedience. The God of Leviticus is both absolutely holy and absolutely loving, uncompromisingly just and uncompromisingly merciful.

5.   Most important of all, Leviticus foreshadows Christ. The New Testament Epistle to the Hebrews interprets these laws messianically and symbolically. Hebrews should be read together with Leviticus as companion books.

Saint Paul calls Israel's law "our tutor to bring us to Christ" (Gal 3:24, NKJV). Christ's sacrifice on the Cross and the presentation of this sacrifice in the Mass are symbolized and foretold by the offerings that made up Israel's temple liturgy: the holocaust or burnt offering foretold Christ's death; the peace offering foretold the peace Christ would make between God and rebellious man; and the sin offering foretold Christ as bearing the punishment for our sins.

Yom Kippur, the "Day of Atonement", was the most important day in the Hebrew calendar. On this day alone the high priest entered the Holy of Holies to make (or rather to foreshadow Christ's making) atonement (reconciliation) with God for the sins of his people (16:30). Aaron, the temporal high priest in Leviticus, foreshadows Christ our eternal high priest who offers Himself to the Father for our salvation.

Why must Christ die to save us? Because the necessary penalty and consequence of sin, from the beginning, was death (Gen 3:2). The bloody sacrifices in Leviticus were based on the principle that "the life of the flesh is in the blood; and I have given it for you upon the altar to make atonement for your souls; for it is the blood that makes atonement, by reason of the life" (17:11; see Heb 9:22). "For the wages of sin is death, but the free gift of God is eternal life in Christ Jesus our Lord" (Rom 6:23).

Numbers: Israel's Wanderings in the Wilderness

"In the wilderness" (in Hebrew, *Bemidbar*), the fifth word of the book in Hebrew, is the usual Hebrew title of this book, because it is the story of Israel's wanderings in the wilderness, the desert of Sinai, between Egypt and the promised land. Moses kept a diary of these wanderings, according to 33:2, which leads many traditional Jews and Christians to believe that he was the author of this book, and of the rest of the Pentateuch, though many Scripture scholars doubt this.

The English title, "Numbers", refers to the two times Moses took a numbering or census of all Israel. In chapter 1 he numbered the old generation that left Egypt, and in chapter 26 he numbered the new generation that was born in the wilderness and would enter the promised land. Only Joshua and Caleb span both generations. They are the only Jews born in Egypt who were allowed to enter the promised land. The rest all refused to trust and obey God in the wilderness and when He commanded them to go ahead and conquer the land (chapter 14).

This is a painful book. In it Israel learns the hard lesson of the unavoidable consequences of unbelief and disobedience. It is a purgatorial education and purification, necessary for a people not yet mature in faith and obedience. It is fools, they say, who learn by experience.

Like Leviticus, Numbers teaches both the justice and the mercy, both the severity and the kindness, of God. Despite its painful lesson, it is an optimistic, upbeat book, for it teaches that God's people (now as well as then) can move forward to inherit God's promises (the promised land, symbol of Heaven) if and only if they learn the exceedingly simple and therefore exceedingly difficult lesson to trust and obey.

Christians find a number of symbols of Christ in Numbers, including the following:

1. the bronze serpent on the stake (21:4–9), which symbolizes Christ on the Cross (Jn 3:14);
2. the rock that quenched the people's thirst, which Saint Paul interprets as Christ (1 Cor 10:4), for Christ and Christ alone satisfies all our heart's desires, that are restless till they rest in Him;
3. the manna that came down from Heaven (11:7–9), which symbolizes the Eucharist, Christ as the Bread of Life (Jn 6:31–33); and
4. the cities of refuge (chapter 35), which symbolize the sacrament of reconciliation.

Deuteronomy: Moses' Farewell Speeches

The Hebrew title, *Haddebharim*, "the words" (1:1), indicates the central contents of this book: three long speeches by Moses (1:1–4:43; 4:44–26:19; and 27–34) to prepare Israel for the climax of the story of the exodus and their wanderings in the wilderness: the conquest and inhabiting of the promised land.

Moses is 120 years old and about to die. This is his swan song, his farewell to the new generation written down for all generations. These are sermons not only for Israel but for all the "people of God", for the Church. As Leviticus is the lawbook, Deuteronomy is the essential book of sermons. But while the laws were for Israel alone, the sermons are for all times and peoples.

The word *Deuteronomy* comes from the Greek word meaning "second law" because in this book the Ten Commandments are repeated a second time (chapter 5).

The essential point of all Moses' sermons is simple. It is the message of Psalm 1, the message of the two ways. Two and only two ways are open for us in this life: the way of obedience to God and the way of disobedience. These roads lead to two different destinations just as surely as two different physical roads lead to two different physical destinations. The way of obedience is divinely guaranteed to lead to inheriting all God's promises. The way of disobedience is equally guaranteed to result in misery and failure.

The history of Israel as recorded in the next twelve historical books of the Bible repeatedly and consistently illustrates and proves the truth of this central lesson. So does the history of every other nation and of every individual life throughout the history of the world.

The two most memorable and precious verses are the following:

1. The "shema" (6:4–5), the prayer that is to a Jew what the "Our Father" is to a Christian: "Hear, O Israel: The LORD our God is one LORD; and you shall love the LORD your God with all your heart, and with all your soul, and with all your might." Nothing, in time or eternity, is more important than that.

2. The fundamental challenge and choice that Moses presents to Israel and that life presents to us: "I call heaven and earth to witness against you this day, that I have set before you life and death, blessing and curse; therefore choose life, that you and your descendants may live, loving the Lord your God, obeying his voice, and cleaving to him; for that means life to you" (30:19–20).

Because of Moses' disobedience (Num 20:7–13), God did not allow him to enter the promised land that he so longed for. Or rather, God postponed it until later, for when Moses appeared with Christ on the Mount of Transfiguration (Mt 17:3) he was clothed with heavenly glory. The fact that Joshua (whose name is the same as "Jesus") rather than Moses led Israel into the promised land symbolizes the fact that Moses is only a preparation for Christ, a kind of John the Baptist. Christ alone fulfills all the Old Testament symbols and types, especially that of Moses.

Moses was one of the greatest men who ever lived. The last three verses of Deuteronomy are a beautiful epitaph to this spiritual giant. (This epitaph, and the account of Moses' death in chapter 34, were obviously not written by Moses, even if the rest of the Pentateuch was, but probably by Joshua.) Yet even this giant was a sinner and a failure without Christ. There's no more hope for Moses than for us; no less for us than for Moses.

SEVEN

From Conquest to Chaos:
Joshua and Judges

Lessons from Sacred History

Unlike *all* the other sacred scriptures in the world, the Bible is *essentially* history. Though often interrupted by long stretches of sermon, song, poetry, prophecy, parables, wisdom, or laws, the unity and continuity of the Bible is its historical "story line". That story runs from the very beginning of time itself, in Genesis, to the end of time, in Revelation.

We are still in this same story. History is our story. It is also "His-story". God reveals Himself and His wisdom not only through the words of the Bible but also through the events of history, as well as through the things in nature. Since we are in this same story today and since it is "His-story", the principles and lessons that held true in the past eras, chronicled in Old Testament historical books like these, are just as true today. The lessons of these books are lessons of life-and-death importance for the survival of America, of Russia, of Upper Volta, as much as for ancient Israel. For the laws of history do not change, any more than the laws of nature do.

The Bible is "sacred history". That does not mean anything less realistic than secular history, as some modern theologians imply—as if "Bible stories" belonged to the category of myths or fairy tales. Rather, "sacred history" means history from a double point of view, the divine as well as the human. It has two natures. Like Jesus, the Bible is the Word of God in the words of man. Its human nature is not suppressed but fulfilled by its divine nature.

The history of God's chosen nation is full of divinely revealed secrets about national life and death, about the secret of survival and salvation socially as well as individually. No book of social, political, or historical science has ever shown more clearly how nations rise and fall, succeed and fail, by using or refusing their lifeline to God, the source of all life, this-worldly as well as other-worldly and social as well as individual. For Israel's history is the key to the world's. Israel is not God's exception but God's rule, God's paradigm case.

Joshua: A Call to Follow Our Commander and Engage in Spiritual Warfare

The Book of Joshua is the end of one story and the beginning of another. It is the happy ending to the long epic of Israel's deliverance from Egypt and slavery and the fulfillment of God's promise to Abraham back in Genesis: the "promised land". It is also the beginning of the hard tale of the conquest of that land.

As such, it is a warlike, grisly book, full of blood and violence. We tend to turn away from such a warlike book today, giving the apparently good reason that the Prince of Peace has come, and God no longer commands His people to fight bloody wars as He did then. True, but we are just as much at war now as then. Spiritual warfare will never end until the end; and this warfare is just as real, just as awful and as awe-full, as physical warfare. For who, after all, are more formidable—Canaanites or the demons they worshipped?

Yet this idea of spiritual warfare, so prominent in Scripture and the lives of the saints, is rarely taught today. We forget that "we are not contending against flesh and blood, but against the principalities, against the powers, against the world rulers of this present darkness, against the spiritual hosts of wickedness in the heavenly places" (Eph 6:12). The life-or-death battles in the Old Testament, especially in this most warlike book, are apt symbols of the no less life-or-death spiritual warfare of the New.

The simple success strategy of God's people in Joshua is the old lesson of "trust and obey" (Good military wisdom, if your commander is perfect!). Whenever Israel trusts and obeys her Divine Commander, she triumphs, even against apparently unconquerable obstacles, such as the Jordan River, which is miraculously crossed (chaps. 3–4), and the walls of Jericho, which "come tumblin' down" (chap. 6).

Like any general, God leads through different paths. Sometimes He leads His people through miracles, sometimes not. Sometimes His orders make human, rational sense, like the military strategy of "divide and conquer"; but sometimes they seem sheer folly to human prudence, like the command to march seven times around Jericho blowing trumpets. Why does God act in such an apparently arbitrary way?

The appearance of arbitrariness and irrationality is an echo, a projection of our own expectations and categories onto God. God acts in humanly irrational ways for a very good reason: to test His people and teach them the crucial lesson that "some boast of chariots, and some of horses; but we boast of the name of the LORD our God. They will collapse and fall; but we shall rise and stand upright" (Ps 20:7–8); the lesson that "unless the Lord builds the house, those who build it labor in vain" (Ps 127:1). God is never arbitrary; He always has good reasons, but they appear arbitrary to us because they are so much better than ours.

The Book of Joshua centers around the hero of its title. It traces his life from the beginning of his public leadership, which he inherited from Moses, right up to his final farewell speech and death, which are strikingly similar to Moses' final speech and his death at the end of Deuteronomy. Joshua is the new Moses.

But isn't it Jesus who is the new Moses? Yes. And the Hebrew spelling of *Jesus* is *Yeshua*, which is the same as *Joshua*. Moses gave him this name (Num 13:16), changing his original name, *Hoshea*, which means "salvation", to *Yehoshua* (Joshua), which means "The Lord is salvation".

The Church has traditionally interpreted Joshua as a type or symbol of Jesus for at least six reasons:

1. The name and its meaning are the same.
2. Jesus, like Joshua, is the new Moses.
3. He is the commander of God's chosen people and the conqueror of God's enemies.
4. He is the one who leads his people even through the waters of death (symbolized by the Jordan River in Joshua and the water of baptism in the New Testament—see Romans 6:4).
5. He does what Moses could not do: he brings his people into the promised land (symbolic of Heaven).
6. Further, the conquest and division of the land into the twelve tribes symbolizes and foreshadows the expansion of Christ's Church into the world by His twelve apostles.

But the thing symbolized is always more than the symbol. Christ, the new Joshua, did what the old Joshua could not do: save His people forever, not just for a time; and from spiritual defeat (sin), not just from military defeat.

There are many memorable events in this book, so vivid that children remember them almost as well as the events in Genesis, once they hear them. But two passages stand out as especially significant. In the first, a heavenly figure appears who is called "the commander of the Lord's army" (5:13–15). Some commentators think this is not just Michael the archangel, but Christ Himself in pre-incarnate form.

In the most important passage of all (24:15), Joshua calls upon all Israel to make *the* great choice, the single greatest choice every individual and society must make in his, her, or their life, because this choice determines the meaning and purpose and point of life itself, and even determines life or death for eternity: "Choose this day whom you will serve, whether the gods your fathers served in the region beyond the river, or the gods of the Amorites in whose land you dwell; but as for me and my house, we will serve the Lord."

It is a perfect echo of Deuteronomy 30:15–19, where Moses, in *his* farewell sermon, confronts us with the same choice. All the war and militarism of Joshua boils down to this Mosaic wisdom: "Choose life".

Judges: Israel's Repeated Failures and God's Repeated Deliverance

During the four centuries between the death of Joshua and the age of the kings (beginning with Saul, David, and Solomon), Israel was ruled by a series of seventeen judges. These were not just judges in the modern sense, that is administrators of legal justice, but also political governors and military leaders. Most were warriors (for example, Samson and Gideon), one was a priest (Eli), and one was a prophet (Samuel). Prophets, priests, and kings (rulers) were the three most important offices God appointed for His people, and all three point to Christ, who is the ultimate prophet (the very Word of God), priest (mediator and Savior), and king (ruler of the whole cosmos). The Hebrew word for "judge", *shophet*, also means "savior" or "deliverer", just as "Jesus" does.

If Joshua is the book of repeated successes, Judges is the book of repeated failures. Israel's history during this time is a dark age full of corruption, a large black sky with only a few bright stars. For after Joshua and the generation that had conquered the promised land with him had died out, "There arose another generation after them, who did not know the Lord" (2:10).

Judges contains seven cycles of Israel's disobedience and repentance, infidelity and return to fidelity to God. Again and again, Israel compromises and worships the gods of the native Canaanites—just as we, the New Israel, worship the gods of our society (consumerism, control, comfort, power, prestige, pleasure). Again and again, the loss of Israel's inner, spiritual strength results in a loss of outer, material strength socially, politically, and militarily; and they are defeated and oppressed. Compromise always leads to chaos.

Then they repent, and God raises up a new judge each time to deliver them. (No amount of human folly can exhaust the divine patience.) But each new judge-deliverer is different. The monotony of Israel's (and our) sins contrasts with the creative originality of God's methods of deliverance: Samson, Gideon, Samuel.

Alas, as soon as Israel is delivered, prosperity leads to pride and disobedience once again, and the endless cycle repeats itself:

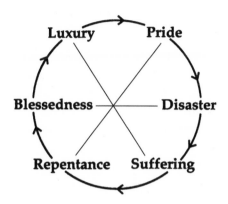

All human history, individual and social, follows this pattern. The story is utterly up-to-date. The history of nations ever since Israel has continued to teach the sad results of "playing God". The last verse of the book sums it up and reveals the root cause of Israel's ills: "Every man did what was right in his own eyes" (21:25).

How relevant is this old book to us? The degree of its relevance is exactly proportionate to how little we fear "every man doing what is right in his own eyes". Does this sound to us like a recipe for disaster or for mental maturity, health, and wholeness? Is this not the basic advice of nearly all our psychological "sages" today? Are there many leaders in our society who believe, preach, and practice the opposite of "every man doing what is right in his own eyes"?

That unfashionable opposite is summarized simply in Proverbs 3:5–7:

> Trust in the LORD with all your heart,
> and do not rely on your own insight.
> In all your ways acknowledge him,
> and he will make straight your paths.
> Be not wise in your own eyes;
> fear the LORD, and turn away from evil.

There's no other way than these two.

EIGHT

National Happiness from Personal Holiness: First and Second Samuel

The historical books of the Bible were not designed, either by men or by God, merely to satisfy our natural curiosity about past events, but to guide our present lives and choices to ensure our future supernatural blessedness. To look for "lessons" in these books, therefore, is not an arbitrary imposition of an external, alien point of view. For God, unlike man, writes lessons not only in words but also in events. He is the primary Author of the book of history as well as of these historical books.

There are many memorable "lessons" in First and Second Samuel (How naive, unfashionable, and "moralistic" the very word "lesson" sounds to our modern ears! In that psychological fact itself there lies a lesson.) Among them, one of the most prominent and relevant to our own time is the dependence of a nation's happiness on its leaders' personal holiness.

First and Second Samuel contrast the personalities of good but weak Eli with good and strong Samuel, strong but selfish Saul with idealistic David, David as obedient with David as disobedient; and they show how these contrasts, these choices, will determine all of Israel's subsequent history. The difference between a two-degree angle and a three-degree angle is perhaps only a fraction of an inch in the beginning, close to its origin. But when the lines are extended through space, as history is extended through time, the difference becomes a matter of many miles.

First Samuel traces Israel's history from the birth of Samuel, last of the judges, to the death of Saul, Israel's first king. Second Samuel traces the rule of David, Israel's greatest king.

First Samuel: The Age of Kingship Emerges

Samuel, the last judge, anoints Saul, the first king. A new age emerges through this transition. "Anointing" was a quasi-sacramental, symbolic pouring of oil onto the head of the man God chose. It publicly signified and certified God's choice. The title *Christ* or *Messiah* means "the anointed one" or "the chosen one". The Jewish kings as God's chosen ones and the Jews as God's "chosen people" foreshadow and prepare for Christ, God's Chosen Person.

Before the transition from Samuel to Saul, we see a transition from Eli, the old priest, to Samuel, the young prophet. At a time when "the word of the LORD was rare in those days; there was no frequent vision" (3:1), God called Samuel, dramatically but quietly, in the night. And Samuel gave the perfect, classic response to God's call, just as Mary was to do a thousand years later with her *fiat*. Samuel said simply, "Speak, Lord, for thy servant hears" (3:9). Only because Samuel first listened to God, did Israel listen to Samuel: "When Samuel spoke, all Israel listened" (3:21, TEV). This is *the* key to all effective preaching, pastoring, and priestly work.

The people asked Samuel for a king, "like all the nations" (8:5). Like us modern Americans, they didn't want to be different. This disappointed God (God is not an American), but God let them have their foolish way (8:6–9) to teach them—the hard way.

They chose Saul as their king, not for his wisdom or holiness but for his "image", as we would put it today: "There was not a man among the people of Israel more handsome than he ... he was taller than any of the people" (9:2).

The time of Saul, like most times, was full of corruption. Eli's wicked sons, ruling at Shiloh, were so bad that God sent terrible judgment on the nation. Israel was defeated in battle by the Philistines (chap. 4). Eli's sons were killed. And Eli died in grief and horror at hearing that the ark of the covenant, God's visible throne in Israel and the holiest object in the world, was captured. It was almost as if a Satanist were to steal the Eucharist for a Black Mass. Eli's daughter-in-law died in childbirth upon hearing the news, and named her son Ichabod, which means "the glory has departed".

But Saul was not the answer to the departed glory. Though for a time he gave Israel military glory and victory, he proved to be an evil king (13:8–14; 15:10–23; 28:3–17). He was envious of David and sought to murder him, even though David was God's anointed.

David was protected from Saul by his friend Jonathan, Saul's son and heir. The friendship between David and Jonathan is a classic, model friendship. Jonathan gave up to David his legitimate claim to be king (20:30–31) because of his loyalty to David and because of his loyalty to God, for he knew God had chosen David to be king (chap. 18).

The crisis and culmination of Saul's dissolution and self-destruction came when he played with the occult—something God had forbidden with frightening strictness (Ex 22:18; Deut 18:9–12). Once Saul conjured up the spirit of the dead prophet Samuel through the mediumship of the Witch of En-Dor (chap. 28), it was too late: Saul lost his kingdom, his life, and probably his soul. Samuel told him, "The LORD has turned from you and become your enemy" (28:16; compare Mt 7: 23). Saul's story is a story of crime and punishment, a moral tragedy.

Second Samuel: Israel's Brief Golden Age

But David's story is one of glory. David is Israel's model king, the standard by which all subsequent kings are judged. David is one of the primary Old Testament types or symbols for Christ:

1. He is a king.
2. He is born in Bethlehem.
3. He is anointed ("Christ").
4. He is "a man after God's own heart" (1 Sam 13:14).
5. He experiences rejection and danger, and out of it composes some of the great messianic psalms, such as the one (Ps 22) Jesus quoted on the Cross.
6. He is the literal ancestor of Christ, who is frequently called "the son of David" and "descended from David according to the flesh" (Rom 1:3).
7. Like Christ, David forgives and spares his enemies. On two occasions, he spared Saul's life when Saul was seeking his (chaps. 24–26).

King David is a type of Christ the King. It is difficult for us Americans to love kings, for our nation was born in a rebellion against a bad king. Yet Christ *is* a king as well as prophet and priest. The Church has not designed for us "the Feast of Christ the President", but the Feast of Christ the King. Christ did not preach "the administration of God", but "the Kingdom of God".

God promised David through Nathan the prophet that the Messiah would be descended from him. This hope for an even greater king than David was kept alive in Israel during the dark times of decline, corruption, civil war, exile, and captivity that were to follow for many long generations after David. The New Testament refers to Nathan's prophecy and Christ's fulfillment of it three times (Acts 2:30; 2 Cor 6:18; and Heb 1:5). David is the connecting hinge between Abraham, who first received the promise, and Christ, who finally fulfilled it; he is halfway between Abraham (about 2000 B.C.) and Christ.

David wanted to build God's house, the temple, but God decreed that it should be built instead by David's son Solomon, a man of peace. David wanted to build a house for God, but instead God built a house for David. The "house of David" is a dynasty divinely guaranteed to produce not just a great temporal kingdom but an eternal one (see Lk 1:32–33). The prophecy was fulfilled: David's dynastic line was preserved right down to the time of the Messiah, who was David's great-great-great-etc.-grandson. In the northern kingdom of Israel, there were nine different family dynasties, but in Judah only one. Judah and Benjamin were the only tribes that remained until the time of Christ; the other ten were scattered and lost.

The characters of Eli, Samuel, Saul, Nathan, and David are vivid and memorable because they are realistic. Though David is Israel's greatest king and a type of Christ, Second Samuel does not idealize him or gloss over his sins.

Second Samuel tells David's story as both history and biography. For the fate of the nation and of David are intertwined. The spiritual law of cause and effect is not only individual but also social. David's spiritual success brought about God's blessing not only in his private life, but also in the life of the nation; and David's spiritual failures necessarily brought down God's judgment not only on him and his family, but also on his nation.

David's remarkable political "rags to riches" story (from shepherd boy to king) and his remarkable military success in quenching civil war and enforcing peace stemmed from his personal friendship with God and obedience to God's will. Then came the turning point in his life: his adultery with Bathsheba and his arranging the murder of her husband Uriah. The book then chronicles the tragic consequences of these sins for his family and for the nation.

These consequences start to unravel when Bathsheba's new baby by David dies shortly after birth. Later one of David's sons, Amnon, commits incest with his half-sister Tamar. Then David's beloved son Absalom, the full blood-brother of Tamar, murders his half-brother Amnon to avenge his sister, leads a military revolt against his father David, and is killed by David's general Joab. One of the most poignantly agonizing passages in the Bible is David's grief over Absalom: "O my son Absalom, my son, my son Absalom! Would I had died instead of you, O Absalom, my son, my son!" (18:33).

Nathan's prophecy is fulfilled: God sends a sword into David's house. Not only family disaster but also national disaster come: famine, war with Philistia, and, later, the renewed civil war under Solomon's sons that would split Israel forever.

The brief "Golden Age" Israel enjoyed lasted only one or two generations: part of David's rule and part of Solomon's. The rest is troubled times. Saul began in glory but ended in ruin. So did Solomon. Only David remained God's man, through repentance. David did not attain the best thing, personal purity and perfection, but he attained the next best thing, repentance. This was crucial for the nation. David's repentance held Israel together and staved off God's judgment for another generation.

One of the most arresting passages in Scripture is the scene of this repentance. Nathan the prophet confronts David with his crimes by his parable of the rich man who stole the poor man's single sheep. David is impaled by its stunning punch line: "You are the man." After reading 2 Samuel 12:1–15, read Psalm 51, the great prayer of repentance that David wrote after this sudden self-knowledge. It is a favorite of many of the saints, for all saints know themselves to be sinners, and this is the great sinner's Psalm.

Here are four short and simple lessons for our time and our nation from First and Second Samuel.

1. *Most* times are times of trouble. Prosperity and peace are the exception, not the rule.

2. Personal sins produce national tragedies. Just as the sins of the fathers have consequences in the lives of their children (Ex 20:5–6), the sins of the rulers have consequences in the life of the nation. This law does not change when kings change to presidents.

3. There exists an unavoidable law of spiritual cause and effect, as universal and as objective as the law of gravity: the only road to blessing is obedience, and the road to judgment is disobedience to God's laws.

4. But it's never too late. David's repentance restored him to God's favor, and although the sword remained in his house as a purgatorial punishment, David remained God's man. He weakened his relationship with God by sin, but did not destroy it, and restored it by repentance. If even a murderer and adulterer could be a great king and a great man of God, what can you be?

NINE

From Israel's Golden Age to Decline and Fall: First and Second Kings

The two Books of Kings, originally one in the Jewish canon, trace the history of Israel from its peak, the reign of Solomon, through its decline, division, civil war, corruption, exile, and destruction.

First Kings: Solomon's Reign as the Summit of Israel's Golden Age

The Bible calls Solomon the greatest king and the wisest man in the world, for his wisdom was not just from humanity, but from God. This is clear at the beginning of his reign (chap. 3), when God promises Solomon any one gift, and he asks for wisdom—such a wise choice that it proves that he already has the wisdom he asks for: "I am but a little child; I do not know how to go out or come in. . . . Give thy servant therefore an understanding mind to govern thy people" (3:7, 9).

God is so pleased that He gives Solomon not only the wisdom he asked for, but also the riches, power, and honor he had not asked for. Under Solomon, Israel amassed unsurpassed riches and territory from the border of Egypt to the border of Babylonia. Best of all, an oasis of peace prevailed between the constant warfare before and after Solomon.

C. S. Lewis speaks of "Solomon—the bright solar blend of king and lover and magician which hangs about that name". But it is wisdom for which this archetypal king is most renowned. Immediately after Solomon asks for and receives the gift of wisdom from God, this wisdom is tested and shown by his judgment between two women who have equal claims on the same baby (chap. 3). Solomon turns the situation around: instead of being tested by the situation and the women, he tests them to discover which one is the real mother, just as Jesus did whenever He was apparently trapped by His interlocutors. Compare 1 Kings 3:16–28 with John 8:2–11.

This is the kind of wisdom we expect from God, who is the Questioner, not the questioned, the First Person Singular ("I AM"). It is a wisdom mere human reason and education cannot teach, and it produced awe and wonder. "And Israel heard of the judgment which the king had rendered; and they stood in awe of the king, because they perceived that the wisdom of God was in him" (3:28). Just as Solomon's wisdom was first manifested in his asking God for wisdom, Israel's wisdom is manifested in their recognition of Solomon's wisdom.

For centuries after Solomon, anonymous Jewish writers often signed their books "Solomon". Solomon probably wrote most of Proverbs. But the writers of Song of Songs, Ecclesiastes, and Wisdom of Solomon, all of whom call themselves Solomon, all very probably wrote centuries later, using Solomon's name to indicate their teacher and model.

A Jewish tradition has it that Solomon wrote Song of Songs in his youth, Proverbs in middle age, and Ecclesiastes in old age, for Song of Songs idealistically exalts young love,

Proverbs is the practical wisdom of maturity, and Ecclesiastes manifests the disillusionment of Solomon's old age when he had lost his wisdom and turned away from its source, "the fear of the Lord, the beginning of wisdom".

One of the most remarkable aspects of Solomon's wisdom was his ability to handle wealth without being corrupted by it. This is certainly an art that is rare and relevant today.

The first thing Solomon did with his wealth was to build God's house, the great temple. Like a medieval cathedral, it was a labor of love. Into it was poured a great deal of time and money, and (much more important) great passion and commitment. The Israelites considered this the richest and most beautiful building in the world, the best that man could do, for it was not for man but for God, like the great Gothic cathedrals of the Middle Ages. The destruction of this temple was more traumatic to the Jews than most of us can realize. The second, rebuilt temple was also destroyed, by the Romans in A.D. 70. Only the "Wailing" (West) Wall is left: the most sacred place on earth for Jews. The rebuilding of the temple (of which we are now beginning to hear the first faint rumblings and hints) is supposed to be a sign of the end of the world and/or the coming of the Messiah.

In God's providential plan, Solomon's temple had to be great because it was a symbol of Christ, who compared His body to the temple when He said, "Destroy this temple, and in three days I will raise it up" (Jn 2:19). The temple had to be perfect because it was to receive the Messiah. It was like Mary's womb that way.

The symbol pales, however, before the reality symbolized. Thus Christ also said, "I tell you, something greater than the temple is here" (Mt 12:6). In Heaven, He will be our temple: "And I saw no temple in the city, for its temple is the Lord God the Almighty and the Lamb" (Rev 21:22).

In his later life, Solomon's pagan wives turned his heart away from worshipping God to worshipping idols, and the king with the divided heart left behind him a divided kingdom. Solomon sank into an orgy of idolatry pandering to all his wives; he worshipped all their gods as well as the Lord. He had a harem of three hundred wives by one count, seven hundred by another. Solomon made three mistakes: (1) too many women, (2) too many gods, and (3) most importantly, he let his women choose his gods rather than letting his God choose his women.

After Solomon's death, civil war split the nation in two under his unwise son Rehoboam. (Unfortunately, wisdom is not hereditary.) Never again would Israel attain peace, glory, riches, or even unity as it had under Solomon. It was split forever, and eventually taken captive and enslaved. Like Camelot, Israel's golden age was like one brief summer.

First Kings is not a biography of the kings, nor is it a political history, but a spiritual history. Politically important kings, like Omri, are sometimes passed over quickly. Like First and Second Samuel, First and Second Kings are a prophetic interpretation of the invisible spiritual causes that led to the visible political decline and fall of Israel. They are a historical commentary on the first, greatest, and most practical commandment (Deut 6:5; Mt 22:38). Once Israel favors other gods, God favors other nations. Nations can no more escape the moral and spiritual order than individuals can. God has no double standard.

Second Kings: A Divided Israel Loses Its Way

First Kings ends with Israel divided into two nations, after the civil war between Solomon's sons. Second Kings traces the history of both kingdoms down the slippery slope to destruction. Chapters 1 to 17 are confusing because they trace *two* sets of kings, alternately, in the two kingdoms of Israel and Judah. The northern kingdom was destroyed by Assyria in 722 B.C. (chap. 17), and Judah by Babylon in 586 B.C. (chap. 25).

Nineteen consecutive evil kings rule in Israel. All worship idols at Bethel. There are nine separate dynasties, and eight of them come to power by murdering the previous king.

In Judah there is only one dynasty, the house of David, which God promised would last until the Messiah. Eight of Judah's twenty kings are good, and Judah lasts 136 years longer than Israel. These two facts are interpreted as cause and effect by the prophetic author (who, by the way, may well have been the great prophet Jeremiah; the literary styles are similar).

But even Judah's good kings did not abolish idol worship. Therefore God abolished temple worship by allowing Nebuchadnezzar to destroy the temple and the holy city of Jerusalem. Once the temple no longer hosted the worship of the true God, it was no longer divinely preserved.

The remnant of the Jews, having lost their nation, their freedom, their holy city, and their temple, are marched 900 miles away into exile in Babylon. Read Psalm 137 to see how they felt.

During the period between Solomon and the exile (the period of the divided kingdom), most of the great prophets lived and taught: Elijah, Elisha, Amos, and Hosea in Israel; Isaiah, Jeremiah, Joel, Obadiah, Micah, Nahum, Zephaniah, and Habakkuk in Judah. The nation's spiritual health depended on heeding the Word of God through these divine mouthpieces, and the nation's bodily, political health, in turn, depended on its spiritual health. The same must be true today of the Church and the world—unless the Church is *not* God's mouthpiece, God's public prophet.

Two Great Prophets Foreshadow John the Baptist and Christ

In First Kings and Second Kings, we see the ministry of Elijah, one of the greatest prophets of all time. In the New Testament he is a type or symbol of John the Baptist, whom Jesus calls the greatest of all (Mt 11:11, 14). Like Christ, Elijah ascended to Heaven (in a chariot of fire) and appeared on the Mount of Transfiguration with Moses (Mt 17). Moses' death was also unusual since God buried him and his body was never found (Deut 43:6).

But Elisha, Elijah's successor, was more like Christ. Elijah lived alone like John the Baptist; Elisha lived among the people like Christ. Elijah emphasized law, repentance, and judgment, like John the Baptist; Elisha spoke more of faith, grace, and hope, like the gospel.

Even when sin seems to have the last word, it does not. God does. As Saint Thomas More said, in a tumultuous time like Israel's and like ours, "The times are never so bad that a good man cannot live in them."

Among the many striking incidents in the lives of these two prophets, I am especially struck by Elisha's ability to see angels, the army of the Lord surrounding the army of Israel's enemies which surrounded Israel (2 Kings 7:13–17). It is a vision we certainly need to recapture today.

Second Kings ends on a note of hope, despite the terrible final chapter that describes the utter destruction of Jerusalem and the temple. Though God's chosen nation is ruined, God's plans are not. As in Noah's time, a small faithful remnant always remains. The Jews have a legend that there are twelve good men alive at every time in history; they save the world from God's judgment. God would have spared Sodom for only ten; perhaps just one more is all that is needed to spare America. Perhaps that one is you.

TEN

A Different Perspective on History: First and Second Chronicles

The last time I tried to read the Bible straight through, I bogged down somewhere in Chronicles. I think other readers have often had the same experience. And thereby hangs a tale—a fascinating tale about why we do not find Chronicles fascinating, as did those who wrote it and read it in premodern times.

The Four Aspects of the Author's Point of View in Chronicles

First and Second Chronicles (originally one book, in the Jewish canon) tells the same story as the two books of Samuel and Kings: the story of all the kings of Israel, from Saul to the exile and captivity. But it tells the story from a different point of view and perspective, one we moderns find it hard to "identify with". There are four distinctive features of this point of view in Chronicles.

First, it is a more divine, less human and empirical point of view. It is a more "judgmental" book than Samuel or Kings because God has a right and a power to judge events beyond the little bit we have.

Second, it is a priestly point of view rather than a prophetic one. The prophet Samuel is traditionally thought to have written Samuel but the priest Ezra may have written Chronicles. That would explain why Chronicles emphasizes the building of the temple, in excruciating detail, and why its standard of judgment for evaluating each of the kings is whether he fostered, neglected, or opposed temple worship according to the levitical priestly laws.

Third, it begins with nine whole chapters of genealogies.

Fourth, it idealizes. It emphasizes the good kings more than the evil ones, the two best kings, David and Solomon most of all, the virtues and successes of David and Solomon rather than their faults and failures, and it tells only of Judah, the more faithful and longer-lasting kingdom, which contained the temple and had at least some good kings, while ignoring the history of the northern kingdom of Israel, the apostate and therefore shorter-lived kingdom, which had no temple and no good kings.

The Modernity of Chronicles

Now the fact that these four distinctive features of Chronicles make it less interesting than the previous historical books to the typically modern mind, even the modern Christian mind, tells us four interesting things about us and our mind. Becoming aware of these four typically modern habits of mind by contrast with this ancient book, criticizing them, and perhaps even reversing them (if we are both willing and able to do so), might go a long way toward healing four spiritual ills of our age and our mind. Thus the very irrelevance of Chronicles may turn out to make it extremely relevant to us. Let's explore how.

First, I wonder how much we Christians are unconsciously affected by the modern suspicion of the claim that the Bible is divine revelation, not just human wisdom; God's

Word to man, not just man's words about God. If we did *not* share that suspicion, at least unconsciously, why would we not *prefer* a book like this, written from a more divine and heavenly point of view, over one written from a more earthly and empirical point of view, like Samuel or Kings?

Second, we favor the prophetic over the priestly point of view and emphasis. Perhaps this is because we like to emphasize morality, the special province of the prophet, more than liturgy and worship, the special province of the priest. We like to emphasize our "horizontal" duties to each other (ethics) more than our "vertical" duties to God (religion). Modernity tends to reduce supernatural religion to natural morality.

Why? I can think of at least two reasons. First, the moralities of the world are essentially the same, but the religions of the world are essentially different. Thus the belief and practice of one religion entails the unpopular judgment that other religions are false, or at least less true. Second, we know that morality concerns us, but we are not as convinced that temple worship concerns us. If the details of the building of Solomon's temple in Jerusalem, which tend to bore us when we read Chronicles, were details of our own home, or vacation cottage, we would be fascinated. This means that we do not really "identify with", and perhaps do not understand, the importance of the temple in Jerusalem, and its connection with Christ and thus with ourselves. (More about this later.)

Third, we are bored with the genealogies of Chronicles because we are out of touch with history, tradition, and our roots in the past. Or perhaps because we no longer believe that individuals (the names in the genealogies) can make much of a difference to history. The "Great Man" theory of history is nearly always scornfully rejected today. Christ Himself is often seen as limited and conditioned by His times and culture.

The first nine chapters of First Chronicles consist of a long list of names going back to Adam. The ancients were fascinated with this sort of thing because they loved to remember and venerate their ancestors, from whom they had received a tradition they thought precious, even divine; also because they saw names as sacred words, not mere labels. Remember the scene near the end of Alex Haley's *Roots*, where the freed Blacks, entering their new "promised land" recite their history and genealogy, beginning with their African ancestor Kunta Kinte.

The genealogies in Chronicles focus on Judah, not Israel, because God's promise, as far back as Genesis 49:10, was that the Messiah would come from that tribe. In the Hebrew Bible, Chronicles is the last book. That's why the New Testament opens, in Matthew, with the genealogy of the Messiah: to show Christ as the fulfillment of the Old Testament prophecies and promises. This promise kept the Jews' spirit alive even when the body of their nation was dead or dying.

Finally, our fourth reason for disliking Chronicles is its idealism. We are more convinced of evil than of good. Certainly, we find evil more *interesting* than good. Virtues seldom make headlines; vices do. We demand "realism" in our histories and biographies, not "idealism".

Chronicles is idealistic, positive, and hopeful even though its times were miserable. Its readers were a poor, small, weak, straggling remnant of Jews just returned from captivity in Babylon to a ruined homeland and temple. It was probably written by Ezra, the priest-scribe, to encourage the people of Judah to rebuild the temple and to hope for a restoration of her past glories, to look back to their golden age and to look up to David and Solomon as imitable models, recoverable ideals—to be proud of their national heritage.

The Practicality of Chronicles

The pride was not to be national first of all, but spiritual. Ezra wanted to make sure his people's hope was in the proper order, the only truly practical and workable order: namely, that material hopes and glories are consequent and dependent on the spiritual. Thus Chronicles repeats the constant, and constantly forgotten, lesson of all Old Testament history: the nation's political health depends on its spiritual health, and the nation's spiritual health depends on the spiritual health of its leaders.

The gospel, or good news, of Chronicles, is the same as that of Moses: the covenant is a divinely guaranteed light even in the worst darkness, a hope beyond worldly wisdom. This hope was not a mere *wish*, but a "*sure and certain* hope of resurrection" of the glory of the Jewish nation, for it was based on *God's* guarantee, the promise of the one who cannot but keep His promises.

But the covenant has two parts. The promise is conditional. God fulfills His part only when His people fulfill theirs. The prophetic and moral lesson Ezra the priest finds in his people's history implicitly appeals to free will, free choice. Yes, there is a guarantee: "All things work together for good"—but only "for those who love God".

David and Solomon attained goodness and greatness because they had the wisdom to put first things first. Most of Judah's kings and all of Israel's lacked the wisdom of Solomon, who knew that "the fear of the Lord is the beginning of wisdom" (Prov 9:10). With a few notable exceptions (Joash, Josiah, the boy king, and Hezekiah), Solomon's successors did not understand that the true glory of Judah was her spiritual mission, her mission of mediation, her mission to bring men to God and God to men. They did not understand that apart from this mission as the instrument of *God's* Kingdom, *their* kingdom had no calling, no destiny, no distinctiveness, no purpose, no meaning, and no hope of greatness.

The Temple and Its Liturgy Foreshadow Christ

The significance of the temple is its messianic mission. Nothing in Scripture is significant apart from the Messiah, for nothing in the universe is significant apart from Him (Col 1:15–20)! The significance of the temple was to foreshadow Christ's salvation in its liturgy. Its ritual lambs were pictures of the Lamb of God. Also the temple was literally and physically to receive the Messiah when He came.

Thus the temple foreshadowed the Eucharist, which is the temple in which God continues to be really present with His people—a temple of flesh rather than of stone, but just as concrete. The tabernacles on our altars are not little images of the great Solomonic temple in Jerusalem; Solomon's temple was a mere image of the tabernacle that we know.

The climax and conclusion of Chronicles sets up the rebuilding of the temple in Ezra and Nehemiah. It is the decree of King Cyrus to allow the Jews to return home from their Babylonian captivity and rebuild their temple. Chronicles begins with Solomon building the original temple and ends with Cyrus authorizing the rebuilding of the second temple four centuries later.

This second temple, after being enlarged by Herod, was destroyed by the Romans, together with virtually the entire city of Jerusalem, in A.D. 70, and has never been rebuilt since then. The rebuilding of the temple is believed to be one of the signs of the end of the world and the second coming of Christ according to some Christians, and of the (first) coming of the Messiah according to some Jews. Even though this belief is not universally held, except among most Fundamentalist Christians, it is certainly an arresting fact that for the first time in nearly two thousand years some Jews are now openly speaking of plans to rebuild the temple, according to a story in *Time* magazine. Perhaps *Time* here unwittingly points to eternity.

In its fulfilled, eucharistic sense, the temple has already been rebuilt. It is "rebuilt" thousands of times every day throughout the world. The symbol may or may not be rebuilt, but the reality it symbolizes is indestructible, for it is not an "it" but a "He", and He has promised, "Lo, I am with you always, to the close of the age" (Mt 28:20).

ELEVEN

God Brings His People Back to the Promised Land: Ezra and Nehemiah

Ezra and Nehemiah are companion books. They tell the story of the "second exodus": the return of the Jews to their homeland after seventy years of exile in Babylon.

There were three waves of deportation of the Jews to Babylon: in 606, 597, and 586 B.C. Then there were three waves of return. The first, in 538, was led by Zerubbabel; the second, in 457, was led by Ezra; and the third, in 444 B.C., was led by Nehemiah.

A Momentous Time in World History

The period of time covered in Ezra and Nehemiah was crucial in world history. The philosopher Karl Jaspers calls it "the axial period" in the history of the world. About the same time the Book of Ezra was written (between 457 and 444 B.C.), Guatama Buddha lived in India (around 560–480 B.C.), Confucius (551–479 B.C.) and Lao Tzu (dates unknown) in China, and Socrates (470–399 B.C.) in Greece. All over the world at this time, great founders of spiritual traditions are calling their people to reconstitute their traditions on more inward and moral foundations. All over the world, spiritual history is turning a corner.

Yet only a small remnant of Jews returned from exile: a little less than fifty thousand out of the two or three million who were permitted to go. Imagine freeing three million prisoners and over 2,950,000 stay in their comfortable cells! During the first exodus, most of the Jews complained to Moses that life in Egypt had been more comfortable than the purgatorial wandering through the wilderness. We usually prefer comfort to freedom. Life in Babylon had been comparatively easy, but the trek to Jerusalem was 900 miles long—and there were no buses or trains. Not only that, but once they arrived, they faced a ruined land, city, and temple, along with the formidable task of rebuilding.

Those who returned were from the southern kingdom, the tribes of Judah, Benjamin, and Levi. The ten tribes of the northern kingdom are "the ten lost tribes of Israel". But a few representatives of these tribes probably returned as well; the "lost tribes" were not totally lost.

The Second Exodus under King Cyrus of Persia

This second exodus took place when King Cyrus of Persia overthrew the Jews' conqueror, Babylon, and issued a decree freeing them to return home. A prophecy of this event appears in Isaiah (44:28–45:4), which even mentions Cyrus by name.

The return of many Jews from all over the world to the new homeland created for them again, for the first time in 1,900 years by the United Nations in 1948, has sometimes been called the third exodus. It has often been seen as a sign of the last days.

The second exodus was far less dramatic and impressive than the first exodus from Egypt. And today's third exodus is less dramatic than Ezra's 900-mile trek from Babylon to rebuild the holy city and the temple.

Though Israel's days of glory seemed to be behind them in Ezra's time, and though this was true politically (the monarchy was never reestablished), yet their true and greatest glory was still ahead of them. For their true glory was the spiritual glory (see Rom 3:1–2), which in the past had been their role as prophet to the world, especially as prophets of God's coming Messiah. Now in the future their greatest glory would be their role as the home and the people of God incarnate.

God's providential control over history and His care for His people are seen in His keeping His people safe even in exile. Both the second and the third exodus fulfill the promise made through Jeremiah: "You will seek me and find me; when you seek me with all your heart, I will be found by you, says the LORD, and I will restore your fortunes and gather you from all the nations and all the places where I have driven you, says the LORD, and I will bring you back to the place from which I sent you into exile" (Jer 29:13–14).

Christ is symbolized in Ezra in the same way He is in Exodus. As Moses is a Christ-symbol, leading God's chosen people out of captivity and Egypt (sin and worldliness) and to the promised land (Heaven), so Ezra, Nehemiah, and Zerubbabel do the same. (Zerubbabel was also part of the direct Davidic messianic line: see 1 Chron 3:17–19 and Mt 1:12–13.)

One reason why the Jews had to return from captivity was that in God's providential plan, Israel, not any other land, was to be the land of promise, that is, the land of the Messiah. The promised land does not mean merely the land God promised to give to the Jews for them to live in, but also the place God had prepared for *Him* to live in

when He came to save the world. The Old Testament prophecies of the Messiah concerned Jerusalem and Bethlehem
(Mic 5:2), not Babylon. The Messiah was not to be born in
Babylon. That is the deeper reason why the Jews had to
return.

The People Rebuild the City Wall and Bind Themselves
to the Law

The story of Ezra and Nehemiah is one of solidarity and
recommitment in a time of trial. Ezra was a priest, in fact, a
direct descendant of Aaron, the first high priest. He was also
a scribe; thus he collected most of the books of the Old
Testament. Tradition also ascribes to him Psalm 119, the longest psalm and the one in which the law is mentioned in every
verse.

Nehemiah had been the cupbearer of Artaxerxes, king of
Persia. (A cupbearer tasted the king's wine to prevent him
from being poisoned.) This position meant that Nehemiah
was a trusted official of the Persian court. He was allowed to
leave Persia and lead the last group of Jews home from exile.
(Ezra had already returned with the second group of exiles
thirteen years earlier.)

Once home, Nehemiah challenged and organized the Jews
to rebuild the wall of Jerusalem, for a city without a wall was
hardly a city at all. It could be conquered easily. Like most
saintly people, Nehemiah had to overcome opposition from
his enemies and even from his friends. Yet the task was completed (the wall rebuilt) in only fifty-two days—a feat that so
impressed Israel's enemies that they knew God had to be on
Israel's side.

Ezra and Nehemiah made up a team. While Nehemiah
rebuilt the city wall, Ezra rebuilt his people's spirit. When

he discovered that the people and even the priests had intermarried with Gentile women, he put a stop to this practice and led the people in repenting and recommitting themselves to the law. This separation from the other peoples was important because Israel had been chosen by God to be holy (the word means to be "set apart"), different from the world, to accomplish God's plan of salvation for the world.

Rebuilding the spiritual health of the people within the city wall was capped by the providential, nearly miraculous finding of a copy of the Scriptures, the Book of the Law. (The story of the preservation of all the books of the Bible makes one of the most amazing and exciting stories in literary history.) Nehemiah read this book to the people during a marathon, all-day session, and the people wept with joy. (Contrast our reaction to an even slightly long Scripture reading at Mass!)

The reaction of the people to the reading of the law was freely to bind themselves to it, to their covenant with God. Now everything was restored except the king: the people were back, their commitment to be set apart as God's chosen people was restored, the covenant was restored, the law was re-revealed, the city wall and the holy city of Jerusalem and its temple were all rebuilt. The kingly line was intact, but the true king who was to spring from that line, the Messiah, would not be a political ruler, as most of the Jews, even His own disciples, expected. (See the disciples' foolishly political question to Him even after the Resurrection in Acts 1:6.)

Nehemiah and Malachi, the last Old Testament prophet, lived at the same time, and both spoke against the same evils, especially cold-hearted indifference. There were to be over four hundred years between the time of Nehemiah and Malachi and the time of John the Baptist, Jesus' cousin and forerunner, who is the last prophet of the Old Covenant—four hundred years with no revelation from God. God used this period to prepare a hunger and an expectation in His people's hearts for the Christ to come. We can celebrate our easy Advent of four weeks because the Jews endured their hard Advent of four centuries.

TWELVE

Biblical Heroines of Friendship and Courage: Ruth and Esther

The Bible's view of women is not that of male chauvinism. Nor is it that of modern so-called "feminism", which is really an attack on all things feminine. Rather, without losing their feminine identity, heroines like Ruth and Esther and Deborah perform feats that the narrow-minded would restrict to men—much like Saint Joan of Arc centuries later.

Ruth and Esther are the central characters of two little gems of short stories (short only in space, not in content) that are named after them. They come at two very different times: Ruth, before the era of kings, during the time of the judges; and Esther, after the era of kings, during the time of the exile. Both times are bad times, hard times. It is usually in such times that God raises up special saints.

Ruth: A Woman of Faithfulness and Friendship

The inner beauty of the character of Ruth and the beauty of her story are like lights shining against the dark background of sin, corruption, chaos, violence, and war during the time of the judges. It is a story of very ordinary people (the stuff saints are made of)—Ruth, Naomi, and Boaz—who remain faithful to God and to each other in faithless times and in a faithless nation. Once again, we are reminded of the truth of Saint Thomas More's saying, "The times are never so bad that a good man cannot live in them."

The "good man" here is a woman. Ruth and Esther, along with Judith, are the only books of the Bible in which a woman is the central character.[1] Ruth is not a Jewish woman by birth or race, but a Moabite. The Moabites were descended from Lot, Abraham's nephew, not from Abraham. They were even less closely connected with the Jews than the Arabs, who are descendants of Abraham's son Ishmael. The Moabites worshipped not God but pagan idols, and were the military enemies of Israel, both before and after the time of Ruth. One of the lessons of this book, then, is universalism: God accepts Gentiles as well as Jews if they only believe in Him. It is the same lesson as the one implied in Jonah and in the parable of the Good Samaritan.

Good stories with a happy ending must have an unhappy beginning. Ruth and Naomi begin in great misfortune: famine and the deaths of Naomi's husband and two sons. (Ruth was the widow of one of Naomi's sons.) Naomi probably thought God had abandoned her, but His providential plans surprise and surpass her expectations as they unfold in the events of the story (as they always do: cf. Eph 3:20; 1 Cor 2:9). They include a husband and a son for Ruth.

The name *Ruth* means "friendship" from the Hebrew *reuit*. The story of Ruth is a story of friendship rewarded. Ruth's friendship with Naomi and with Naomi's God is

---

[1] However, the most important merely human character of the whole Bible and of all human history, and the most perfect was a woman: Mary, the Mother of God.

the moving force behind the events of the story. This friendship and fidelity are expressed in the key verse, the most famous verse in the book (1:16). This is Ruth's choice to leave her pagan culture and religion and follow Naomi to Israel and to God: "Where you go I will go, and where you lodge I will lodge; your people shall be my people, and your God my God." The choice for God brings reward as surely as the morning brings the light.

The reward in Ruth's case is not only her continued friendship with Naomi and her escape from famine in Moab by accompanying Naomi to Israel, but also an unlooked-for happiness in meeting, loving, and marrying Boaz, and thus becoming the great-grandmother of David, Israel's greatest king, and through him the ancestor (the great-great-etc.-grandmother) of Christ Himself, the Son of David and Son of God.

This family connection becomes especially significant when Boaz is factored into the equation. Boaz is a figure or symbol of Christ because he is the *goel*, or "kinsman-redeemer", the relative who saves Ruth from her state of widowhood and aloneness by redeeming her, buying her back to be his own, as prescribed by Jewish law. Christ did the same to all of us, of course. He was our Redeemer and also our kinsman, our relative. We are in His family physically because He is the Son of Man and mankind is one family through Adam.

It is said that no one on earth is more than seven steps removed from blood relationship to anyone else on earth. There have been only fifty-eight generations since Christ. Suppose you learned that you were the direct blood descendant of James, Christ's "brother" (i.e., cousin). But you are just as much a part of this same literal blood family. Christ redeemed His whole family, human "kind". He can be our

Redeemer only because He is the Son of Man (our kinsman) as well as Son of God.

In Jewish law, the *goel* had to be (1) a blood relative of those he redeemed, (2) free and in no need of redemption himself, thus *able* to redeem, and (3) *willing* to pay the price to redeem. Boaz fulfilled all three requirements. So did Christ. In Boaz's case, the price of redemption was finite; in Christ's case, infinite: the very blood of God as the redemption of those of His blood relatives (humanity) who also choose to be His spiritual relatives, or adopted children, born "not of blood but of God" (Jn 1:13).

Like Mary, Ruth was a kind of co-redeemer, for without her cooperation it could not have been done in this way. Ruth's bond "where you go, I will go. . . . Your God shall be my God" expresses the same state of soul, the same essential core of the spiritual life, the same secret of sanctity, as Mary's *fiat*: "Be it done unto me according to thy word."

Esther: A Courageous Woman Saves Her People

Here is another little gem of a book: a beautifully written story about a beautiful queen. Her name, *Esther*, is Persian, and means "star". But she is a Jewess, in exile with her people in Susa, the great capital city of Persia. Her story is full of drama and suspense.

The evil Haman, a Jew-hater like Hitler, attempts genocide, just as Hitler did. Apparently, nothing can stop his plans, because he gets King Xerxes (Ahasuerus) to sign an edict to destroy the entire Jewish population in the whole Persian Empire, and any "law of the Medes and the Persians" that had been enacted by the king could never be changed. Such was Persian law. (For this reason, tradition says, the Persians would never enact a law unless they agreed on it twice: once while drunk and once while sober.)

The story tells how God raised up this Jewish girl to become the queen of the most powerful empire in the world in order to save His people from Haman and extinction. God uses ordinary people (Esther and her wise uncle Mordecai) to overcome apparently impossible obstacles to protect His people and keep His promises to Abraham many centuries before: "I will bless those who bless you, and him who curses you I will curse; and by you all the families of the earth shall bless themselves" (Gen 12:3).

God's name is not mentioned even once in the original Hebrew version of this book (though it is in the later, Greek version, "Second Esther", which is part of the Second Canon or Deuterocanonical Books). But His providential hand is clearly seen by any attentive reader, just as it is in the long story of Joseph in Genesis 37 to 50. God's *supernatural* intervention is rare, whether in the form of verbal revelation or miraculous deeds; but God's providential control of the natural causes in history is omnipresent, as He is.

He works through human instruments and human wisdom, like Mordecai's, and even uses evil men, like Haman and Hitler, to contribute in the long run, against their own will, to His outcome, for He is the author of the story. He used even Satan in the Book of Job to fill a role in His plan, and also, more crucially, in the Gospels: even Judas turned out to be only a pawn in God's hands, which brought good ("Good Friday") out of evil.

In our own day, we can see how the modern Haman, Hitler, brought about *not* the extinction of the Jews, as he planned, by his holocaust, but the creation of the Jewish homeland, which, in the opinion of most historians, would not have happened without the Holocaust. Thus God can bring good even out of the worst of circumstances. Throughout history, God consistently blesses all who bless Abraham's people and destroys those who try to destroy them. For He blessed all people through this people by being born from them.

Read the exciting plot of this story yourself, and you will stand in awe of how thin was the thread on which God hung the survival of His people. For if Esther had not had the courage to face the Persian king and confess she was a Jew, and if Mordecai had not had the wisdom to escape Haman and counsel the king, there would be no Christmas this year.

THIRTEEN

Job Confronts Life's Darkest Problem and Encounters God Himself

It is universally recognized that Job is one of the greatest books ever written, an all-time classic. It is terrifying, beautiful, haunting, mysterious, tender, yet powerful as a sledgehammer—if only we read it with empathy and openness and not try to "figure it out" as if it were a detective story.

Though bottomlessly mysterious, its main point, or lesson, is very obvious. It lies right on the surface, in the words of God to Job at the end. Only a philosopher (like Rabbi Kushner, in his bestseller *When Bad Things Happen to Good People*) can miss the message. If the problem of Job is the problem of evil, then the answer is that *we do not know* the answer. We identify with Job in his ignorance, not in his knowledge.

The problem of evil, of suffering, of injustice in a world ruled by an all-powerful and all-just God, is life's darkest problem. Job offers us no clear solution, no philosophical formula, no bright little concept, but an infinite mystery. God Himself, rather than any idea God teaches, is Job's answer. He is the God Rabbi Abraham Heschel describes as "not an uncle, but an earthquake".

Much of the dramatic interest in Job comes from the ironic contrast between Job's point of view and God's. The reader is allowed to share God's point of view too because of the preface (chap. 1), but Job is not. Thus there is a constant irony, a contrast between what seems to Job and what really is. God seems to be on trial; Job is really on trial. Job seems to be questioning God; God is really questioning Job.

Five Levels of Understanding Job

Job is a many-layered book. Peel away surface layers and you find more underneath. Five of these layers are the following:

First, there is the problem of evil. How can a good God let bad things happen to good people? The solution of Job's three friends is simple: Job is not "good people". Faced with the apparent alternative between doubting God's goodness or Job's, they doubt Job's. It is a reasonable conclusion, but wrong, as we know from God's own words describing Job as "a sound and upright man, one who fears God and turns away from evil".

Second, there is the problem of the conflict between faith and experience. Job's faith tells him to expect just rewards; Job's experience shows him undeserved suffering. One of God's most important attributes in the Old Testament is His fidelity (*emeth*, "truth"), His trustability; and Job's experience seems to prove God untrustworthy. In fact, Job is on trial, not God, and he is proved trustworthy. God plays brinkmanship with him, but Job passes the test. As Saint Paul says of God centuries later, He does not let us be tested beyond what we are able to endure (1 Cor 10:13).

Third, there is the problem of the meaning and purpose of life, expressed in Job's question to God, "Why didst thou bring me forth from the womb?" (10:18). The question turns a different color when asked from agony. It is here not the philosopher's detached speculation but the sufferer's cry, "Why do you let this happen to me?" Job is like a small child's tear-stained face looking up at Daddy who has apparently let his child down.

Fourth, there is the problem of identity. When Job's three friends come to comfort him, they cannot recognize him at first (2:12), so disfigured he looks, sitting on his dung heap covered with sores. This is the Job who formerly sat in the city gates solving everyone's problems and shining forth as an example of justly rewarded righteousness. Has Job lost his identity? Just the opposite: his suffering brings him his deepest identity, as the sculptor's chisel strokes bring identity to a great statue.

Fifth, and deepest of all, there is the problem of God. Neither Job nor anyone in the Bible ever denies God's existence (except "the fool" in Ps 53:1). But God's purposes and God's character and God's reliability are the mystery revealed throughout the Bible and throughout Job. The question is not what God is in Himself (the theologian's question) but who God is to me, to Job. This is the key to open the doors to solve the other problems as well, for it is God who gives Job his identity, his purpose, and his solutions.

Job's three friends are not fools. Readers often omit reading their speeches and concentrate only on Job, but this is a mistake. Their arguments are very strong. (1) Their faith premise states that God is all-good and all-powerful and rules His world with perfect justice. (2) Their ethical premise adds that justice means rewarding the good and punishing the evil. (3) Their common-sense premise further reasons that rewards are in the form of happiness and punishments in the form of misery, not vice versa. (4) Their experiential premise is that Job is very miserable. (5) Their logical conclusion is that Job is very wicked. They do not argue in exactly that logical form, but with much more poetry and power, but that is the gist of their argument. Job cannot answer it.

Seeing God

The answer the book suggests is, first, that God's goodness and justice are far more mysterious than we think. Second, our blessedness is also far more mysterious. Long-range blessedness is purchased with short-range miseries. Suffering makes for wisdom, which is the heart of blessedness. That part of the solution is well known to all the sages.

What Job adds to the sages is that the essence of this long-range happiness is the vision of God Himself, whom Job asked to meet face-to-face even if he must die (13:15). We must appreciate the Jews' deep fear of God and conviction that no one could see God's face and live, if we are to appreciate the drama of the ending of Job, where God shows Job His face and Job not only survives but is satisfied. "I had heard of thee by the hearing of the ear, but now my eye sees thee" (42:5).

This ending answers another problem in Job: Why is Job satisfied even though God does not answer a single one of Job's agonized and very good questions? Job is not a meek, humble, easily satisfied man. He's from Missouri. Fr. George Rutler is right: we must not speak of the "patience of Job", but of the *impatience* of Job.

Job is satisfied by the only possible answer that would satisfy such a man. If God had offered words, Job would surely have questioned those words again, and the verbal battle would have gone on eternally, as it does among philosophers. Instead of answers, Job got the Answerer. Instead of words, Job got the Word. Job got what Saint Thomas Aquinas asked for shortly before his death, when the Lord, speaking from the crucifix, said to him, "You have written well of me, Thomas; what will you have as a reward?" Thomas gave the world's best possible answer: "Only yourself, Lord."

God the Questioner

Another problem is that of timing. Why does God hang Job out to dry for thirty-seven chapters? Why does Job have to go through his long and agonizing dark night of the soul? "Seek and you shall find"—but Job seeks and fails to find for a long time. Why?

Because God is the Finder, not the found; the Subject, not the object; the Questioner, not the answer man; the Initiator, not the responder. A God who would have showed up in response to Job's questions would not have been the true God, but a divine computer programmed to supply the answers if only we press the right buttons. When God does show up, the first thing He says is, "Now it is my turn to ask, and yours to answer." Just as Jesus hardly ever answers a question directly, but answers the questioner instead of the question, thus reversing the relationship and making the questioner the one who is challenged, so God reverses the roles in Job. Job learns that he is not asking God, "What is your meaning?" but God is asking Job "What is *your* meaning?" in and through the events of his life. It is true for all of us. Whenever we are led to ask, "What is the meaning of my life?" we are *being asked* exactly that question by God. We answer it not merely by words or thoughts only, but by deeds, choices, responses to life's challenges and sufferings.

Thus another problem is solved: *for whom* does God let Job suffer so? It certainly is not for the sake of the accuser, Satan, who is a mere instrument in God's hands, like a dentist's drill. Nor is it for God's sake, as if God were ignorant of the future and had to set up an experiment to find out whether Job would pass His test of fidelity.

So it must be for Job's sake.

It must be out of God's love for Job. This would sound totally absurd to Job on the dung heap, of course, but it is perfectly understood by Job when he sees God face-to-face. God carved out a great hollow place for Himself in Job with all these sufferings. Yet the hole made no sense until God came and filled it, as a lock makes no sense until the key comes.

Speaking Truth vs. Speaking Truly

Finally, there is a deep puzzle in 42:7. God says that Job— who (by his own admission) uttered "wild words" of challenge to God, full of mistakes and even heresies (for example, that God is unjust)—spoke "rightly" about Him, but that the three friends, who said nothing but pious orthodoxies, did not! But everything the friends say can be found in the rest of the Bible. How can this be wrong? Job contradicts it; how can this be right?

The friends spoke the truth, but not truly. Job spoke untruths, but truly. For the friends, God was an absent, indifferent object; for Job, God was a present, involved person. The three friends had a polite correspondence with God; Job had a stormy marriage with God, including fights but no divorce. The biggest difference between Job's speeches and those of the friends is that they only speak *about* God, while Job speaks *to* God. Prayer is the most accurate theology, for God is the I AM, not the IT IS. As Rabbi Martin Buber said, "God can only be addressed, not expressed."

Job is a Christ-figure. He is a "suffering servant", chosen by God to suffer not because he is so bad, but because he is so good. And he suffers for others. At the end, God accepts the three friends only because Job prays and sacrifices for them. In Job we see the christological drama of death and resurrection played out not on the hill of Calvary outside the soul, but in a mirror-image of it, a hole in the heart where the words "My God, my God, why hast thou forsaken me?" go up as a precious and redemptive offering to heaven. What happens in the Book of Job is the Mass, and Job is the altar.

FOURTEEN

Our Primary Prayer Book: The Psalms

The Bible is the world's most popular book, but it is not one book but a whole library of books. In this library, Psalms is the most popular and most widely used book. Thus Psalms is the most popular book in the world.

Psalms spans the ages. When we pray the Psalms we pray in union with David and the other ancestral composers of these prayers; in union with Christ and the apostles, who used them, as all Jews did and still do, as their favorite prayer-book and songbook; and in union with Jews and Christians in every age and place.

Psalms bridges the gap between Jews and Christians better than any other book can, for Psalms is not just Scripture, but also liturgy. Though Jews and Christians worship in different temples, they pray the same prayers to the same God. No theological cleverness, compromising, or negotiating is needed to bring us together: we are side by side as we pray these words.

Christians love the Psalms no less than Jews, from whom we inherited the book. But Christians add a messianic level of meaning to many of the psalms. A Christian sees Jesus' face in these words, as in the whole of the Jewish Scriptures.

Yet this deeper, Christocentric level does not lessen or remove the other levels of meaning.

How the Psalms Are Meant to Be Used

Psalms are songs as well as prayers. They are meant to be used, not just read. Prayer and singing are actions. The Psalms are more like instructions in a laboratory manual than like sentences in a textbook. We must perform them. They are more like sheet music than like a tape or CD: we must play them on our own spiritual instruments.

Prayer was often *chanted* by ancient Jews and Christians, and still is by many peoples throughout the world. We should try this old, "tried and true" method of praying by chanting, I think, both in private and in public, using either chants that are given to us or those we improvise ourselves. Even chanting a psalm in a monotone gives an effect that merely speaking it does not. Further, speaking it aloud gives an effect that reading it silently does not. It is like an echo; different walls of the soul add to the sound.

Most of us do not, and many of us can not, attend Mass daily. But everyone can pray a few psalms daily. And this is liturgy. Many of the psalms were and are used as part of the Jewish temple liturgy. The early Church's liturgy was heavy with them, from the time of Christ and the apostles to the present day.

Today their role has shrunken, unfortunately, both in liturgy and in private devotions. In the liturgy, they are largely confined to the "responsorial psalm", which I think I have *never*, in attending about five thousand Masses, heard the congregation sing robustly.

The Psalms should be the foundation stone of every Christian's daily prayers. For to pray them regularly, to become familiar with them so that their phrases spring to mind spontaneously, is to shape our minds and hearts according to God's mind and heart. Here is the prayerbook God Himself inspired for us to use. Next to the "Our Father", they are the closest that human words will ever get to God's own answer to anyone who asks Him, "Teach us to pray."

The Psalms were written from the widest possible range of feelings and situations, and *for* the widest possible range of feelings and situations. The Psalms are like the sabbath: "The sabbath was made for man, not man for the sabbath" (Mk 2:27). We find here a world as wide as we find in our own souls and lives: we find joy and despair, praise and complaint, certainty and doubt, defeat and success, suffering and liberation. We should become familiar enough with them to be able to go to the one that is appropriate to the present occasion and need. At least we should make a list or an index so that we know to use the one that fits. The locks of our hearts and lives are constantly changing, but the Psalms provide keys to fit all the locks. We just need to know where the keys are; we need to classify them. Simply "going through" them from beginning to end, while good, is not the best way to use them.

We will develop favorites that we come back to dozens of times, more often than we use other, less favorite ones. This too is good. It is like choosing personal friends.

Since the Psalms are poetry, the translation matters more here, I think, than in most of the books of the Bible. Our prayers need to be strong and clear and simple and intelligible. But they also need to be moving and beautiful. I heartily discourage the use of flat, pedestrian, colloquial translations without a sense of height, awe, reverence, and holiness.

In the original, the Psalms are stylized and poetic, not prosaic. The old Douay or King James versions were more accurate and more literal than most modern ones. The original (not New) Revised Standard Version is a good blend of modern clarity and ancient beauty.

Though the Psalms span the range of a multitude of human attitudes, one stands out as their primary theme, the one they keep coming back to: praise, worship, adoration. If our prayers are not largely praise, they fail to conform to God's prayer pattern. Praise is our rehearsal for heaven. Praise is tremendous therapy for self-absorbed, worried, and self-pitying souls, for praise is self-forgetful—one of the things we need the most. Praise looks at God, not at self. We praise God simply because He is God, because He is praiseworthy. Nothing else can free us from the terrible slavery to the thousand little tyrants of the modern world—our cares, worries, worldly responsibilities, and diversions—as perfectly as self-forgetful praise of God. It need not be accompanied or motivated by *emotion;* merely *doing* it works healing within.

The Divisions in the Psalter

The Psalms are divided into five books, each ending with a psalm of pure praise (41, 72, 89, 106, 150). They can also be divided into psalms for each of the four main purposes of prayer: (1) adoration, (2) thanksgiving, (3) repentance, and (4) petition. Or they can be further divided as follows:

1. psalms of praise (e.g., 18, 100, 103);
2. liturgical psalms (e.g., 120, 135);
3. psalms for pilgrimage, sung by pilgrims traveling up to Jerusalem (120–134 inclusive);
4. royal psalms, for the reign of the King of Kings (2, 20, 21, 28, 45, 72, 89, 101, 132, 144);
5. psalms of repentance (e.g., 32, 51, 130);
6. didactic, or moral teaching psalms (e.g., 1, 37, 119);

7. psalms for personal use (e.g., 23, 27, 34);
8. cursing psalms (7, 35, 40, 55, 58, 59, 69, 79, 109); and
9. messianic psalms (e.g., 2, 22, 45, 110).

The cursing passages cannot, of course, be used by Christians unless we interpret them spiritually and remember that "we are not contending against flesh and blood, but against the principalities, against the powers, against the world rulers of this present darkness, against the spiritual hosts of wickedness in the heavenly places" (Eph 6:12). We must hate sin, as these psalms and psalmists do; but we must not hate sinners, even if the psalmists did, failing to distinguish the two. Everything in Scripture is for our instruction, but not everything is for our imitation.

Many passages in the Psalms, as well as whole psalms, are messianic. If we had none of the rest of the Old Testament but only the Psalms, we would still be able to "check it out" and see that Christ fulfilled the Old Testament patterns and predictions. For instance, compare:

1. Psalm 2:7 with Matthew 3:17;
2. Psalm 8:6 with Hebrews 2:8;
3. Psalm 16:10 with Mark 16:6–7;
4. Psalm 22:1 with Matthew 27:46;
5. Psalm 22:7–8 with Luke 23:35;
6. Psalm 22:16 with John 20:25, 27;
7. Psalm 22:18 with Matthew 27:35–36;
8. Psalm 34:20 with John 19:32–36;
9. Psalm 35:11 with Mark 14:57;
10. Psalm 35:19 with John 15:25;
11. Psalm 40:7–8 with Hebrews 10:7;
12. Psalm 41:9 with Luke 22:47;
13. Psalm 45:6 with Hebrews 1:8;

14. Psalm 68:18 with Mark 16:19;
15. Psalm 69:9 with John 2:17;
16. Psalm 69:21 with Matthew 27:34;
17. Psalm 109:4 with Luke 23:34;
18. Psalm 109:8 with Acts 1:20;
19. Psalm 110:1 with Matthew 22:44;
20. Psalm 110:4 with Hebrews 5:6;
21. Psalm 118:22 with Matthew 21:42; and
22. Psalm 118:26 with Matthew 21:9.

(This list was compiled by Dr. Kenneth D. Boa.)

The Psalms are like an ocean fed by many rivers, many writers. They are for wading in, bathing in, swimming in, surfing in, boating on, and even drowning in (for the mystics have loved and used them too). Their authors include David (about half), Moses (90), Ezra (119), Solomon (72 and 127), Asaph, and many others. They were written during a period of perhaps a thousand years, from the time of Moses, about 1400 B.C., to the return from exile, about 430 B.C. They will last forever.

FIFTEEN

Our Road Map to Practical Wisdom: Proverbs

Let us begin with an embarrassing problem about this book. Almost always, the more intelligent, clever, and original you are, the more bored you are by Proverbs. It tells you nothing you didn't know before. It is a book of platitudes, of old, well-worn truisms. It is, simply, dull.

Yes, that is how the most "advanced" minds see Proverbs. And our nation, our civilization, and our world are today threatened with destruction precisely because of the ideas of those "advanced" minds, because we have departed from the old platitudes. If there is anything our civilization needs in order to survive the threat of moral and spiritual and perhaps physical destruction, it is to return to these "safe", "dull" platitudes. For they are *true*. They are a road map to life, and we are lost in the woods.

That is what wisdom is: practical truth, truth for living, a road map. Another book of well-known practical wisdom very similar to Proverbs is the *Analects* of Confucius. The Western reader often finds them as tedious and uninteresting as Proverbs. Yet they were the blueprint for a society that lasted for over two thousand years, arguably the world's most successful social experiment, at least in terms of longevity.

Just as "you can't fool Mother Nature" ecologically, you also can't depart from nature's ways socially. Proverbs points out the two ways of life summarized by Psalm 1: the way that leads to life and health, and the way that leads to destruction. Even the most "advanced" and original minds cannot change that, for the maps come from God and from human nature itself, which He designed. Unless we somehow manage to be less bored by Proverbs, we will not be around much longer to be bored.

The Value of Practical Wisdom

We are the first society in the history of the world that is losing its store of traditional proverbs. The older generation remembers hundreds; the younger generation, almost none. Every society in history has educated its young partly by proverbs. What is the significance of this fact? I think we can find at least four assumptions behind the use of proverbs that are so important that no society can survive without them.

First, the assumption that practical wisdom is a real, true, objective thing, not just one man's "personal opinion". Consequently this thing, wisdom, is democratic rather than elitist; it is attainable by everyone, not just by the clever, the original, or the "experts".

Second, the assumption that most important things in life, which are the subjects of Proverbs, are knowable, are intelligible, at least partly. The great mysteries of life—life itself, and death, and good and evil, right and wrong, truth and falsehood, beauty, and joy, and human nature, and even God—are not opaque and hopeless holes of darkness but are meaningful and discoverable.

Third, that our lives here on earth are therefore meaningful, and patterned, something other than "vanity of vanities" or "a tale told by an idiot, full of sound and fury, signifying nothing" except what we arbitrarily choose to make of them.

Fourth, that ordinary life experience is a more reliable teacher of this wisdom than university professors, newspapers, movies, or the boob tube.

Such beliefs are hopelessly old-fashioned today, of course. To return to them would be to turn back the clock. And that is exactly what we must do, for the clock is keeping very bad time indeed.

Like the Psalms, Proverbs is not meant to be read straight through as if it were a narrative. The book is a toolbench, a library: it is meant to be sampled, browsed through, picked at. It is a collection, assembled bit by bit and meant to be disassembled and used bit by bit. In our age of short attention spans, impatience, and only tiny slices of leisure time, it is an ideal book to dip into for a minute over your morning cup of coffee—much more useful than the morning paper. As Henry David Thoreau, who despised newspapers, used to say, "Read not the *Times;* read the eternities." These are the eternities.

Most of these proverbs were written by Solomon. Then a number of other writers, having learned from his example, added their own, sometimes anonymously. According to First Kings 4:32, Solomon wrote three thousand proverbs; this book includes some eight hundred of them. Solomon probably wrote them in his middle years, when he had progressed beyond youth enough to have acquired much wisdom from experience, but had not yet begun his decline into idolatry, folly, and immorality, which characterized his later years and which precipitated the catastrophic decline of the kingdom.

The reign of Solomon represented the one brief shining moment of political Judaism. A proverb lies hidden in this historical situation—in fact, two: that the folly of one man can lead a whole people astray, and that the knowledge of three thousand proverbs is not enough to insure a good life: they must be practiced, not just preached (see Mt 7:21–29).

According to Jewish tradition, Solomon wrote Song of Songs in his youth, Proverbs in his middle age, and Ecclesiastes in his old age. Most scholars doubt the Solomonic authorship of the other two books, but it is at least a fitting sequence symbolically. He journeys from youthful idealism and beauty through the wisdom of maturity to the world-weariness and despair of an old man who had lost his spiritual youth. If he had only practiced his own proverbs, his old age would have been even more spiritually successful and blessed than his middle years.

The Literary Form and the Kinds of Wisdom Found in Proverbs

Most of the proverbs have a literary form similar to that of the Psalms: parallelism through couplets. A short, pithy saying is first stated, then reinforced or (more often) contrasted with its opposite. The reason for this form is in the content, in the central teaching of the "two ways" road map. The Proverbs are meant to be a guide to choosing the right way in a world full of sales pitches for the wrong way, a guide to living a good life in an evil world. Nostalgia buffs may long for the "good old days", but realists know that ever since Eden there are only the "bad old days". Every age is an evil age, that is why the warnings of the Proverbs are perennial.

Three different levels or kinds of wisdom can be distinguished in this book. First, some of the advice is purely practical and utilitarian: ways of prospering by the use of diligence, cleverness, prudence, and common sense. These are moral virtues too, but more obviously they are pragmatic virtues—means to the end of success. Second, there is the properly moral, ethical level, the extolling of righteousness and justice, charity and chastity, not only because they "pay off" but because they are right in themselves. Finally, the Proverbs also rise to the third and highest dimension of morality, where wisdom is seen as coming from God, streaming from God as sunbeams from the sun, made of the very stuff God is made of, a divine attribute, thus a way of being Godlike.

The first of these three levels is universal: every culture and every individual knows and lives by proverbs of pragmatic wisdom like "look before you leap." The second level is widespread but not universal. A small number of great ethical teachers like Plato rise to this level, and teach that "virtue is its own reward." But no one rose to the third level in the ancient world as well as the Hebrews, because the third level is the level of a moral relationship to God. The Hebrews had a special knowledge of and intimacy with God by a unique divine revelation. On this level, wisdom is more than practical prudence and more even than moral maturity and rightness of conduct in relating to others; it is "the fear of the Lord" (1:7; 3:5–6).

This "fear of the Lord" that is the beginning of wisdom is not, of course, a crude, cruel, or craven thing. It is high and holy and happy. It is the awe of adoration, the wonder of worship. Perhaps the main reason why the wisdom of the Proverbs is missing from the modern world is that its source, the fear of the Lord, is missing.

Even when we pay proper respect to God, we do not usually share or even sympathize with the "fear and trembling" that the ancients knew. Indeed, many of our modern "experts" in religious psychology, who write most of the textbooks, are convinced that their primary task is to wipe out that very thing. They regard as primitive and reactionary what divine revelation regards as the indispensable beginning of wisdom.

We are free to choose which "expert" to follow in the matter of roads to God. But by the standards of even the lowest common denominator of prudential, practical wisdom, it would seem reasonable to let God tell us how to know God.

Probably the greatest and deepest passage in Proverbs is 8:22–31. The whole book merits endless rereading, but this passage especially rewards it. Here, wisdom, as a divine attribute, is personified (treated as a person). Usually personification is a mere literary device, a fiction. But in this case, it is not fiction but fact. For the wisdom of God *is* a Person. He is the second Person of the Blessed Trinity, who became a man in Jesus Christ. Even Proverbs is Christocentric. For it is Christ who "is the key that opens all the hidden treasures of God's wisdom", according to Colossians 2:3.

And just as Proverbs declares wisdom to be freely available to all (8:1–6, 32–35), so Christ is available to all. The clear and bold promise of the New Testament to any Christian is "If any of you lacks wisdom, let him ask God, who gives to all men generously and without reproaching, and it will be given to him" (Jas 1:5). For we have already been given wisdom in having been given Christ. Wisdom is there. In fact, wisdom is not just *in* Him; He *is* Wisdom. "God has brought you into union with Christ Jesus, and God has made Christ to be our wisdom" (1 Cor 1:30, TEV).

SIXTEEN

The Question the Rest
of the Bible Answers:
Ecclesiastes

This book is unique among all the books of the Bible. It is the Bible's only book of philosophy. Philosophy is the wisdom of human reason alone, without any appeal to divine revelation. In this book God is silent. In the rest of the Bible, God speaks. The method the author uses is the scientific method: sense observation of the visible appearances of life "under the sun", plus human reasoning about it.

In Job, for instance, we have a similar book, about a similar philosophical problem, the problem of an apparently meaningless and empty life. But in Job, God speaks to Job. In Ecclesiastes, only Ecclesiastes speaks, and not to God but only *about* God, like Job's three friends.

This book is the question to which the rest of the Bible is the answer. Whatever rabbis originally decided to include it in the canon of sacred Scripture were wise and courageous, for the question it poses is a deep and challenging one. Only great confidence in the even deeper answer they found in the rest of the Bible must have prompted them to canonize this question, which haunts us with its deep, dangerous doubt. It is dangerous because if there is no adequate answer to it, we are left with the world's worst bad news without the good news, without a gospel. For the thing we need most of all, meaning and purpose and hope, "a reason to live and a reason to die", is precisely the thing questioned in this book.

The last six verses (12:9–14) were probably added by a second author, who answered the first one by summarizing the answer of Judaism and the rest of the Old Testament: "The end of the matter; all has been heard. Fear God, and keep his commandments; for this is the whole duty of man." This positive answer contrasts sharply with the negative lack of answer to the question of life's meaning that the rest of the book begins and ends with: "Vanity of vanities, all is vanity."

No one knows who authored the book. He called himself "the Preacher [Ecclesiastes], the son of David (Solomon), king in Jerusalem" (1:1), but this was a common literary device for authors of "wisdom literature" for many centuries after Solomon. It is as if a philosopher today were to use the pen name "Socrates", meaning "a disciple of Socrates".

The Central Message of Ecclesiastes

The main point of the book is so obvious that it is stated five times at the beginning (1:2), then three more times at the end (12:8). It is "vanity". "Vanity" means, of course, not the absence of humility, as in a "vanity mirror", but the absence of meaning and purpose, as in a "vain search". The book's structure mirrors its content: it is circular, it goes nowhere, it ends on precisely the same note it began with: "Vanity of vanities, all is vanity."

The author tells how he tried at least five different life-styles, five candidates for the position of life's meaning, five keys to fit the strange hollow spaces in the lock of the door of life, and how he found each one of them inadequate. He tried wisdom (1:12–18); pleasure (2:1–11); wealth and power (2:8); honor, prestige, or working for posterity (2:18–19); and a conventional, legalistic, external religion (7:16–18). Each one failed because it was only a this-worldly key, and life has an other-worldly door. It was only a finite peg, and the human heart has an infinite hole. It was only a little answer, and he was asking a very big question. Even his God is not an adequate answer because his God is a mere object, like the moon. He is *there*, but He is not *here*. He makes no difference. He is an ingredient in the cosmos, part of the setting in life's play, not the main character, not the Lover and Savior that He really is.

Along the way of ultimate despair, little hopes and little wisdoms emerge from the darkness. There is a lot of good practical advice scattered throughout this book, like oases in a desert. But the main thrust is the desert, the emptiness, the vanity.

Ecclesiastes lays bare the God-sized hole in the human heart that all God-substitutes fail to fill—the emptiness left by the removal of God to a position of remoteness and irrelevance. This is the very emptiness that modern men and women have covered up by a thousand diversions, here in this most diverse and diverting civilization in history. Ecclesiastes blows our cover. Infinitely superior to the bland blandishments of pop psychology with its shallow "feel-good" ideals, Ecclesiastes' tough-minded honesty rises to the dignity of despair.

The Five Reasons for Vanity

The five lifestyles or values that Ecclesiastes tries are precisely the five tried in all ages and cultures, from ancient

Hinduism's "Four Wants of Man" through Augustine's *Confessions* to modern existentialist novels like Sartre's *La Nausée* and Hesse's *Siddhartha*.

Ecclesiastes finds that no matter which way he turns, all of his life is surrounded by five features that make for vanity, five reasons for his ultimate conclusion. First, a blind fate seems to rule life, so that nothing makes any difference. Neither wisdom nor foolishness, neither good nor evil really matter in the end (2:13–17; 9:2–3).

Second, it all goes down the drain in death anyway, it seems, and he sees nothing beyond death (3:19–21; 9:4–6). Clear revelation of a life after death did not come until quite late in the history of God's revelation.

Third, life is full of evil and injustice (3:16; 4:1–3; 10:1).

Fourth, time seems to be a cycle that goes nowhere, a merry-go-round without the "merry". Everything returns again. There is no ultimate progress, no hope, no gain, "nothing new under the sun" (1:4–11; 3:1–9). If you take your philosophy of time from the cycles of nature rather than from the growth of the soul, then that is indeed what time looks like.

Finally, even God seems to be part of the problem rather than part of the solution, for without faith and divine revelation, mere human experience and reason cannot understand God and His ways. His purposes remain hidden and unknowable (7:13; 8:17; 11:5).

The Relevance of Ecclesiastes Today

It is impossible to overemphasize the importance of the question, the challenge, posed by Ecclesiastes, especially for our age. The book is quintessentially modern in at least five ways. (1) It asks the modern *question:* Does life have any ultimate meaning? (2) It assumes the same modern, secular *context*, in which religion is reduced to observed behavior and conventional observance. (3) It uses the modern scientific *method* of sense observation, taking accurate pictures of life with the available light of reason, but no faith flashbulb added to the camera. (4) It comes to the modern *conclusion* of vanity, nothingness, and "the existential vacuum". (5) It even concludes with the modern *practical advice* of hedonism, "seize the day", "eat, drink, and be merry, for tomorrow we die." But there is always the grinning skull lurking behind the parties (9:7–10).

It is absolutely essential that we answer Ecclesiastes' challenge. If we do not, we have no reason, ultimately, to do anything else, anything at all. The author's argument can be summarized in a single logical syllogism:

All of life ("toil") takes place in the world "under the sun".
And everything in this world is ultimately "vanity".
Therefore all of life is ultimately vanity.

There are only three ways to answer any argument: to find a term the argument has used ambiguously; or to find a logical mistake or fallacy in the argument; or to find a false premise or assumption. We cannot do the first or second things here, but we can do the third. In fact, in light of the rest of the Bible, *both* premises are false.

First, there is a "toil" that is not "under the sun", a human work that is not confined to this world: the building of the Kingdom of Heaven. "Only one life, 'twill soon be past; only what's done for Christ will last." What we are doing here is not just filling our stomachs and our bank accounts, but building the Mystical Body of Christ, the kingdom of loving souls. If our souls are redeemed, then our bodies and even our world will also be redeemed in the Resurrection.

Death is not a hole, but a door; not the end, but the beginning.

The second premise is also false, for there is one thing here "under the sun" that escapes "vanity". There is a sixth key that Ecclesiastes never tried, but the author of the next book in the Bible (the Song of Songs) tried—and succeeded in opening life's door. It is love. Love is the meaning of life because love is the very nature of the God who designed life. In other words, Ecclesiastes' fifth key, conventional religion, is a counterfeit. True religion is the love of God and neighbor. Try that; you'll like it.

Even though we have argued against Ecclesiastes and answered his challenge, this book is tremendously valuable for us, even though it begins and ends in despair. For it exposes the deepest need of the human heart with ruthless honesty. It shows us the truth of Saint Augustine's great saying: "Thou hast made us for thyself, and [therefore] our hearts are restless until they rest in thee."

Ecclesiastes did not realize the first half of Augustine's saying, but he certainly realized the second half. Like modern man, he tried to quiet his restless heart without knowing God. That is like trying to fill the Grand Canyon with marbles. Nothing is big enough to fill the emptiness, nothing is stronger than death and evil—except one thing. That one "thing" is a Person.

Christ came to conquer death and evil. Ecclesiastes highlights the problem; Christ is the answer. All of the Bible points to Him in one way or another.

SEVENTEEN

The Great Love Story between God and the Soul: Song of Songs

This book has been the favorite of great saints, yet it is the only book of the Bible that never once mentions the name of God. Why? Because God is everywhere in this book, symbolically. The bridegroom, Solomon, stands for God; and his lady fair, his chosen bride, stands for the soul or the Church, the "people of God". The book has traditionally been interpreted on two levels: literally, as a celebration of married love, and symbolically, as a celebration of the joys of our spiritual marriage to God.

The symbolic interpretation is consistent with the rest of Scripture, which sees Israel, both the old and the new, as God's Bride: Isaiah 54:5–6; Jeremiah 2:2; Ezekiel 16:8–14; Hosea 2:16–20; 2 Corinthians 11:2; Ephesians 5:23–25; Revelation 19:7–9; 21:9–10. The symbolic interpretation does not replace the literal. God designed sexual love and marriage to be among life's greatest joys, and to reflect the one-in-many-ness of God (Gen 1:27–28; 2:24). It is fitting that this most complete and intimate human relationship is used as God's chosen symbol for the even more intimate marriage between God and the loving soul.

Love is the very nature of God (1 Jn 3:8). Therefore it is the ultimate reason for everything God does, everything in the story of our lives, the story He designs. Life is a love story, behind the appearances of a tragedy, a war story, a detective story, or a mishmash. This book implicitly answers the great question: What is the ultimate meaning of life? What kind of a story are we in? What is the answer to Ecclesiastes' "vanity of vanities"? The answer to all three questions is love. This book lifts the curtain and lets us see behind it into the mind of the Author and Director backstage.

All four loves are present here: *eros* or desire (8:5); *storge* or affection (4:9); *philia* or friendship (5:16); and *agape* or charity (2:16). This is because married love is the most complete of loves. Husband and wife give their whole selves to each other (2:16). That is why the Church opposes contraception: something is held back. *Life* is held back.

Song of Songs is a dramatic series of love poems. It is a dialogue—like life itself, which is a dialogue between God and the soul, mediated by everything in the universe. Poems do not preach, but they show. Here are some of the things this poem shows about love, both human and divine.

Nineteen Things Love Is

1. Love is a song, according to the title. Music is the natural language of love, more profound than words. We do not speak of love *speeches*, but of love *songs*. Song is not ornamented speech; speech is song made prosaic. God sang creation into being because God is love.

2. Love is the greatest song, the "song of songs" in Hebrew idiom, the song that includes all songs. All events that ever happened are notes in this song. It is also greatest in value (8:7); nothing can buy love.

3.   Love is a perpetual motion machine. The more the groom loves the bride, the more the bride loves the groom, and vice versa, without end. This is why Heaven will never be boring or static. Each singer "caps" the other's line (1: 15–17; 2:2–3).

4.   Love is not sweetly swoony and sleepy, but bright and energetic, like the images of sun, moon, morning, and a bannered army (6:10). Love is news, good news, gospel, ever-young, hopeful, and promising (2:10–13).

5.   Love is also work (3:1–4), hard work. Sheldon Vanauken, author of the magnificent, moving autobiographical love story *A Severe Mercy*, says the most frequent question he is asked is how he and his wife managed to have such a real love story that everyone else envies and almost no one else attains. His simple answer: we worked at it.

6.   Love is perfected by suffering. In turn, it perfects suffering. At first, the consummation of their love is only yearned for (1:2; 2:6). But after the bride suffers in the wilderness (1:5–6; 8:5), then there is trust: "Who is that coming up from the wilderness leaning upon her beloved?" Before that, he had to cajole her out from hiding: "O my dove, in the clefts of the rock, in the covert of the cliff, let me see your face, let me hear your voice, for your voice is sweet, and your face is comely" (2:14). God purifies the soul by suffering and hollows out a place for Himself. In suffering we hear the whispers of divine love. In turn, love consecrates suffering and turns it into a spiritual marriage bed (8:5).

7.   Love is free and cannot be compelled, even by omnipotence. The bride asks the groom to "*draw* me after you" (1:4), not to pull, push, or carry her. The one thing even God cannot do is force us to love Him. How much less can we force each other. God will seduce our souls, but He will not rape them. Love and force are contradictories. Thus the

groom repeatedly cautions us, "I adjure you, O daughters of Jerusalem [audience], that you stir not up nor awaken love until it please" (2:7; 8:4).

8.   Love is not blind. Love is the most perfect accuracy. How could love be blind?—God is love. Is God blind? "Rightly do they love you" (1:4). Only the eyes of love perceive the truth of the beloved's lovableness. Who knows you better, your simple friend who cares deeply about you, or your brilliant acquaintance who knows more *about* you but loves you less?

Yet the symbolic interpretation of the poem is severely tested since the groom (God) says such amazing things about the bride (our sinful souls) that He seems blind indeed: "You are all fair, my love; there is no flaw in you" (4:7). How can this be? It can be because God speaks from eternity, from Heaven, where we will indeed be flawless. It is prophecy. It is destiny. It is the biologist knowing the caterpillar and seeing therein the butterfly. Dante apparently shared something of this heavenly vision of Beatrice, and he insisted that the vision was objectively true and accurate. For what God sees cannot be inaccurate. If God tells you, as He does here, that you are so beautiful that He can hardly bear to look at you (4:9; 6:5), you'd better rethink your self-image, for you are made in the image of King God, not King Kong.

9.   Love is as simple and perfect as the poetry that expresses it (see 1:15–17). Nothing fancy is needed: no additions, subtractions, distractions, or complications. Love is simple because God is simple. (It is also infinitely mysterious.)

10.   Love is individual. "As a lily among brambles, so is my love among maidens" (2:2–3; 5:9–10; 6:8–9). The object of true, divine love is not "humanity" (if preachers tell you that, they're preaching a different gospel from Jesus' gospel) but "neighbor", the concrete, unique individual. You can

only ever love individuals, because only individuals ever exist. Classes and collections are abstract objects of thought, not concretely real things. We group people into groups, but real people are concrete individuals.

11.   Love is all-conquering (2:8). *Amor vincit omnia*, "Love conquers all." Obstacles are flattened: "Every mountain and hill shall be made low." Love leaps over obstacles like a gazelle. Nothing stops love.

12.   Not even death can conquer love. Love is "strong as death" (8:6). Its fire cannot be drowned by death's waters (8:7). For God is love, and God conquered death for us. When your beloved's body dies, the love between you does not die, because love is between immortal souls.

13.   Love is surprising (2:8–9; 5:2), not planned. It is like God: He never comes in the expected time or way. He is bigger than our expectations. Therefore the only way to control and master our lives is to keep love out. Love's wind reshuffles our house of cards over and over again.

14.   Love casts out fear (2:14; cf. 1 Jn 4:18). That is why Jesus is always saying, "Fear not." We all have fear, especially those who scorn it most. And nothing but love, no bluff, no substitute, will cast it out.

15.   Love somehow mysteriously exchanges selves (2:16). I am not mine but yours; you are not yours but mine. And this is the only way for me to be truly me and you you. The gift given in love is more than feelings, deeds, time, or even life: it is the very self. The givers become their own gift.

16.   Love is glorious, triumphalistic, a twenty-one-gun salute, a fireworks display (3:7–11). Thus the military imagery—the loud, colorful, shouting style of Scripture. How different from the "nice", wimpy, weepy, weary, and weak worldly loves that our "sharing and caring" gurus patronize us with!

17. Love is natural. Therefore it uses countless nature images. Everything in nature is an analogy or a symbol for this supreme point of all creation (see 4:1–5; 5:11–15; 7:2–9). Love fulfills nature as well as humanity.

18. Love is faithful and monogamous (4:12; 8:6). Love is already free, so it does not long to be free but to be bound forever. That is not its servitude, but its joy and fulfillment.

19. Love is ready, like Mary's *fiat*. In the poem, the bride is not ready for the groom (in 5:2–8) and suffers terribly because of it. When God's love calls, we must respond immediately. (The word "immediately" is constantly used of Jesus' actions in Mark's Gospel.)

There is much more in the poem than these few suggestions, and even more in the greater poem that is life itself lived in love with God and each other. But these should suffice to "prime the pump". The way to read a poem like this is with the unconscious, intuitive mind freely imagining and associating. This greatest of love poems has been a bottomless well of wisdom and joy to saints like Bernard, John of the Cross, and Thomas Aquinas. If it nourished their great souls, it can certainly nourish our little ones. There is one "trick", however: only a lover can understand it. The way to comprehend it is to do it. "If your will were to do the will of my Father, you would understand my teaching" (Jn 7:17).

EIGHTEEN

God's Big Mouths:
The Prophets

Why didn't Israel have an excess prophets tax? Are there still prophets today? How can we tell a true prophet from a false one? Why did Saint Paul call prophecy the most important of all spiritual gifts? How can we read the prophetic books of the Old Testament without getting bogged down? These chapters on the biblical prophets will try to answer such questions.

To begin at the beginning, just what *is* a prophet? The word in Hebrew means literally "mouth". A prophet is God's mouthpiece. It is an Old Testament foreshadowing of the New Testament idea that we are organs in the Body of Christ, God's hands and feet on earth. Prophets are the Body's mouth. A great prophet is a big mouth.

Big mouths are what the prophets were, and they all got in trouble for it. A prophet tells too much truth to be socially approved. A "popular prophet" is a contradiction in terms. Just being unpopular doesn't make you a prophet, but just being a prophet does make you unpopular. The greatest prophet of all (who was more, but not less, than a prophet) said this to His disciples: "Woe to you, when all men speak well of you, for so their fathers did to the false prophets" (Lk 6:26).

Being a prophet means sharing in the holy unpopularity of the Lord of all the prophets: "A servant is not greater than his master. If they persecuted me, they will persecute you" (Jn 15:20). The job description for prophet has few perks. Indeed, the only one of all the Old Testament prophets who volunteered was Isaiah (6:8). All the rest were drafted, dragooned.

But though there's no earthly profit in being a prophet, there is an earthly need. If the prophet's intended audience already knew or liked the prophet's message, the prophet would be superfluous. Prophets must tell us what we do *not* know or want to know.

The Essential Function of a Prophet

Prophets are the spiritual fax machines God uses to get His message through. Prophets are like miracles that way: signs of the supernatural. The Greek word for "miracle" means literally "sign".

Try to imagine how God could get His infallible truth through to our fallible minds without supernatural intervention—miracles and prophets. How could we know which of our human ideas had the divine approval without prophets as touchstones? The liberal or modernist interpretation of prophets, which subtracts the miraculous or supernatural, subtracts precisely the essential function of the prophet, the function of touchstone.

We need not be fundamentalists (literalists) to be orthodox, but we must be supernaturalists. We need not think God dictated to the prophets word for word, but we must believe the prophets' words are divinely, not just humanly, inspired.

But, the modernist might counter, *many* people claim divine inspiration and say, "Thus says the Lord!" If there are true,

God-given prophets, how could we tell them from false, merely human ones?

The Bible gives two very simple answers to that question. One comes from Jesus: "By their fruits you shall know them" (Mt 7:16). The other comes from Moses, the greatest Old Testament prophet, who spoke with God face-to-face. When Moses was about to die and the Jews were about to enter the promised land, Moses knew there would be false prophets as well as true ones, and that the Jews needed a rule for discernment. The rule is simply: wait. The word of the true prophet will always come true.

It is not the only function of a prophet to foretell. He is more a forthteller than a foreteller, but he is a foreteller too. All merely human foretellers will err. Only God is eternal and knows our future as His present. God's mouth never errs. God's mouthpieces will have a batting average of 1.000; false prophets will always bat under 1.000 and over .000. (A prophet whose predictions were always false would be as infallible and as useful as one whose predictions were always true. There are bound to be some good guesses among the Nostrodamuses.)

God's promises are true because they *come* true in time, in history. To see the truth, we need only patience and the long view of things—like the classicist who waits for time to reveal a true classic.

It's worth waiting for. Saint Paul ranks prophecy first among all the spiritual gifts (1 Cor 12:31; 14:1). Why? Because it "edifies", it builds the Church. The Word of God, and the will of God expressed in the Word of God, is the very food of the Church. No body can grow, can be built up, without food. To know God's mind and to do God's will is our real food (Jn 4:34; 6:55).

The Prophet Tells Us God's Mind

There are three essential steps in the process of "edification": knowing God's mind, doing God's will, and sharing God's life. The prophet starts the process by telling us God's mind, especially when ours has run off the track. We can't attain our ultimate destiny, sharing God's life, without doing God's will. But we can't do it unless we know it.

That is why prophets are so important: they are a lifeline to God. It's not just a matter of information or curiosity, but a matter of life or death to know "Thus says the Lord".

In Old Testament Judaism there were three crucial tasks, and three kinds of leaders: prophets, priests, and kings. (Jesus culminated and fulfilled all three.) Every society needs some form of these three, as a ship needs a navigator (who is like a prophet or a seer), a first mate (who is like a priest, interceding between the captain and the crew), and a captain (who is like a king).

Most great works of literature have three characters for these three functions. *The Lord of the Rings* has Gandalf, Frodo, and Aragorn. *The Brothers Karamazov* has Ivan, Alyosha, and Dmitri. *Star Trek* has Mr. Spock, Dr. McCoy, and Captain Kirk. Even Jesus' disciples had an "inner circle" of John, James, and Peter.

The reason can be seen in the very structure of the human soul. Plato first formulated this three-part structure as intellect, desires, and "the spirited part". Freud called them the super-ego, id, and ego. Common sense calls them mind, feelings, and will. These are our interior prophet, priest, and king.

Understanding and Reading the Prophets

The books of prophecy in the Old Testament contain the writings of only the later Hebrew prophets. The earlier prophets wrote either historical books (Moses, Samuel) or no books (Elijah, Elisha). There are 16 prophetic books, divided into four "major prophets" (Isaiah, Jeremiah, Ezekiel, and Daniel) and twelve "minor" ones. The four "major" prophets wrote longer, more profound, more exalted, and more wide-ranging books.

There is a "trick" to reading these books. We can't expect just to plow through them as we would plow through a story. We should know the background stories, the historical settings, and problems in which the prophets worked. So the books of the prophets should be read in conjunction with the historical books.

Also, we must not try to read their poetry as prose. This is more than just a question of interpreting correctly, a question of symbolic vs. literal meaning. Sometimes poetry can be very literal. Rather, it is a question of attitude. When we read poetry we must take a different attitude toward words. In prose, words are our instruments, our servants. In poetry, they are our masters. To under-stand poetry we must stand under it. Its words are not tools, but jewels; we must hoist them, dangle them, admire them, and let the light play with them.

The right way to interpret prophetic poetry is *midrash*, the traditional Jewish method that is itself poetic, personal, intuitive, and even mystical, rather than scientific and scholarly. *Midrash* reads with the heart as well as the mind; in awe, not curiosity. For this is *God* who speaks! To hear God, we need more than the functions of ear and mind, we need the prefunctional root, the heart. Solomon says, "Keep your heart with all vigilance, for from it flow the springs of life" (Prov 4:23). Only one whose heart is open to God's heart will understand God's prophets (see Jn 7:17).

The prophets' verbal gems, like diamonds, were hammered out under great pressure. Prophets appear during times of crisis, spiritual emergency, sin, and decay. Times like ours.

But are there prophets today? Indeed there are, though not canonical ones, for the canon is closed, the "deposit of faith" completed. Today prophets water the trees God planted in Scripture. The gift of prophecy, confined to a small number in Old Testament times, is spread to the whole Church.

Who are today's prophets? Individual popes and saints to be sure, but above all the Church herself, which Christ left as a permanent prophet and "sign" for the whole world. One mark of her true character as prophet is her unpopularity. Like her Lord she draws down the wrath of the world and its media upon herself when she dares to speak the whole truth entrusted to her instead of editing or abbreviating it. G. K. Chesterton said, "I don't want a church that tells me when I'm right; I want a church that tells me when I'm wrong." But not many are as wise as Chesterton. Why should the world love the Church? Does a cavity love a dentist?

But true prophets were never merely negative. The one-word summary of their message—"repent"—has two sides. *Repent* means "turn", and there is both a turning-from and a turning-to. The first is only there for the second.

All the prophets show us two ways: the way of life and the way of death (see Ps 1). Thus "a prophet of doom" is a contradiction in terms, for all prophets are prophets not of doom but of free choice. Moses sums up all subsequent prophets' message this way: "I call heaven and earth to witness against you this day, that I have set before you life and death, blessing and curse; therefore choose life, that you and your descendants may live, loving the LORD your God, obeying his voice, and cleaving to him; for that means life to you" (Deut 30:19–20).

There are always two ways; and they end in two places just as real, and as different, as the ends of two physical roads. The prophets give us road maps, well marked with signs. We must do the choosing and the traveling.

Most important of all, the true way the prophets point us to is not an abstract "lifestyle", but the Person who said, "I AM the Way, the Truth, and the Life."

NINETEEN

The Shakespeare of Prophecy Thunders with the Message of Salvation: Isaiah

Hebrew names are more than labels. They tell the identity, the significance, the sign-value of the person who bears them.

The name *Isaiah* means "God is salvation". That's the bottom line of Isaiah's prophecies. His book has been called "the Gospel according to Isaiah", for his prophecies of the Savior are more numerous, beautiful, and famous than those of any other prophet.

Isaiah has been called "the Shakespeare of the prophets", for his poetry is the strongest and most exalted among them. Only Job and Psalms rival Isaiah in the whole Bible, perhaps in the whole of human literature, for poetic grandeur.

At least ten passages of Isaiah have become unforgettable to all English-speaking peoples because of Handel's use of them in the world's favorite oratorio, *The Messiah*: 11:1–5; 7:14; 40:9; 60:2–3; 9:2; 9:6; 35:5–6; 40:11; 53:3–6; 53:8.

Whenever we hear these verses read, we hear Handel's music. It doesn't take an effort to join these texts and the music; it takes an effort to separate them now. I expect to hear them in Heaven.

Before reading the rest of Isaiah, you should begin with chapter 6, the story of God's call to Isaiah to be His prophet: "And I heard the voice of the Lord saying, 'Whom shall I send, and who will go for us?' Then I said, 'Here am I! Send me/And He said, 'Go . . .' "

The awesome simplicity of the language reflects the awesome simplicity of the experience, which in turn reflects the awesome simplicity of God.

If anyone thinks that linguistic style is a mere dispensable ornament added to the "message", and that therefore a business-report-style translation is as good as a poetic one, let him read the following passage from Isaiah 6 in its old, rich, poetic, *and literal* translation (Revised Standard Version, an excellent literal translation) and then compare a prosaic modernization:

> In the year that King Uzziah died I saw the Lord sitting upon a throne, high and lifted up; and his train filled the temple. Above him stood the seraphim; each had six wings: with two he covered his face, and with two he covered his feet, and with two he flew. And one called to another and said: "Holy, holy, holy is the LORD of hosts; the whole earth is full of his glory." And the foundations of the thresholds shook at the voice of him who called, and the house was filled with smoke. And I said: "Woe is me! For I am lost; for I am a man of unclean lips, and I dwell in the midst of a people of unclean lips; for my eyes have seen the King, the LORD of hosts!"

(Hardly a passage likely to be selected by one of those modern religious educators who's been taught that the beginning of wisdom is to eradicate that horrible, crude thing called "the fear of the Lord"—which the Lord's own Word calls the beginning of wisdom: Job 28:28; Prov 9:10.)

Now compare a modern translation: "Each creature covered its face with two wings, and its body with two, and used the other two for flying. They were calling out to each other: 'Holy, holy, holy! The Lord Almighty is holy. His glory fills the world.' ... I said, 'There is no hope for me!'"

Make the same comparisons with the ten passages from Handel's *Messiah* listed above.

I used to think the old, poetic versions of the Bible must be "jazzed up" and that the newer versions were more literal. Then I found that it was exactly the opposite: the new translations take out the high poetic style that is in the original, while the old translations were literal and left it in. Imagine my surprise, my joy (about the real, literal translators) and my anger (at the robber-translators).

Isaiah: A Summary of the Old and New Testaments

The Book of Isaiah is like a diptych, a two-panel altarpiece. The first panel paints a picture of God's justice and judgment; the second panel, of God's mercy and forgiveness. By a neat little trick of divine providence, the first panel consists of thirty-nine chapters, the same as the number of books in the first canon of the Old Testament (not counting the Deuterocanonical Books); and the second panel consists of twenty-seven chapters, the same as the number of books in the New Testament.

The first panel is a summary of the Old Testament's message—judgment, justice, and the need for repentance—and the second is a summary of the New Testament's message of salvation, mercy, and the need for faith and hope. These two truths have always been the two central truths of every orthodox Christian theology, from Saint Paul's Epistle to the Romans through Augustine's *Confessions* to Pascal's *Pensées:* the Bad News and the Good News, problem and solution. These are the two things we most need to know, the two words that summarize Jesus' preaching: repent and believe. Isaiah is the whole gospel in theological miniature and poetic magnification.

Like the Savior he foretold, Isaiah was tortured and murdered, according to Jewish tradition. In fact, he was sawn in half. Most modern Bible scholars saw his book in half too. That is to say, they speak of "First Isaiah" and "Second Isaiah" as two distinct persons. No one knows for sure. There are some good literary reasons for thinking that we do have two different authors here. But the three major arguments used to prove a double Isaiah are quite weak, it seems to me, without some qualification.

The first argument points to a difference in style and vocabulary between the two parts of the book. This is a strong clue, but it can prove there were two authors only if one author cannot write in two different styles.

A second argument points to a difference in the content between the emphasis on judgment in First Isaiah and the emphasis on forgiveness and hope in Second Isaiah. This argument is theologically weak if it assumes that justice and mercy are opposed, not met together with a kiss (Ps 85:10). As Aquinas points out, each of the divine attributes presupposes the others. For example, God's mercy in dealing with us presupposes the justice that it surpasses.

It must be admitted, though, that the difference in content between judgment in First Isaiah and forgiveness in Second Isaiah is a strong argument *if* this difference (not contradiction) corresponds to two different historical situations. In this view, First Isaiah warns complacent, evildoing Israel of impending disaster and exile if they do not repent. On the other hand, Second Isaiah encourages people who have already suffered (probably suffered the exile) to hope for the future restoration of their land. Both these promises came true, but two hundred years apart.

A third argument for two Isaiahs is that the prophecies in the second part of the book couldn't have been written by First Isaiah, who lived long before the events described by Second Isaiah, because these events are described so specifically that the descriptions must be written by a contemporary. The key instance pointed to is the *naming* of King Cyrus of Persia as the one who would free the Jews from captivity in Babylon and allow them to return to Jerusalem.

Once again, this argument may be either weak or strong. It is weak if it assumes prophecy never really predicts the future, as it claims to, but only *pretends* to describe the future while really only describing the past or present. In other words, there's no such thing as predictive prophecy. Not only is this theologically heretical, it's also illogical, for it assumes the thing it's trying to prove. It begs the question.

But it is a strong argument for the two Isaiahs that the second part would not make sense to Israelites before the exile. No one would know who Cyrus was two hundred years before he was born. No other biblical prophecy *names* future individuals in this way. The two-Isaiahs theory does not necessarily deny that both Isaiahs miraculously prophesied the future. It just places Second Isaiah two hundred years closer to his prophecies' fulfillment.

In fact, the Book of Isaiah itself refutes the assumption that there's no predictive prophecy. For both Isaiahs, if there were two, lived long before Christ, yet the detailed prophecies of the life of Christ that we find in Isaiah are far more numerous and far more specific than the prophecies about anything else in the Bible. At least seventeen of them were fulfilled in remarkable detail.

Take the time to look up the following seventeen passages. These seventeen are only part of the more than three hundred different prophecies in the Old Testament that are fulfilled by Christ. Even though the New Testament writers (especially Matthew) deliberately used the style and language of Old Testament prophecies to describe events in the life of Christ—as a modern preacher might use King James English to describe current events—the statistical odds that one man could fulfill all of these prophecies so completely is not much better than the odds that a monkey could type out Isaiah by randomly throwing marbles at a typewriter keyboard. Compare

1. Isaiah 7:14 with Matthew 1:22–23;
2. Isaiah 9:1–2 with Matthew 4:12–16;
3. Isaiah 9:6 with Luke 2:11 (see also Eph 2:14–18);
4. Isaiah 11:1 with Luke 3:23, 32 and Acts 13:22–23;
5. Isaiah 11:2 with Luke 3:22;
6. Isaiah 28:16 with 1 Peter 2:4–6;
7. Isaiah 40:3–5 with Matthew 3:1–3;
8. Isaiah 42:1–4 with Matthew 12:15–21;
9. Isaiah 42:6 with Luke 2:29–32;
10. Isaiah 50:6 with Matthew 26:26, 30, 67;
11. Isaiah 52:14 with Philippians 2:7–11;
12. Isaiah 53:3 with Luke 23:18 and John 1:11; 7:5;
13. Isaiah 53:4 with Romans 5:6, 8;
14. Isaiah 53:7 with Matthew 27:12–14, John 1:29 and 1 Peter 1:18–19;

15. Isaiah 53:9 with Matthew 27:57–60;
16. Isaiah 53:12 with Mark 15:28; and
17. Isaiah 61:1–2 with Luke 4:17–21.

Francis Bacon said, "Some books are to be tasted, others to be swallowed, and others to be chewed and digested." Isaiah is to be chewed, pondered, relished, and plunged into time after time after time. Like a smooth stone or an antique, it gets better, not worse, with wear.

TWENTY

The Only Alternative to Disaster: Jeremiah and Lamentations

Jeremiah is called "the weeping prophet". Expressions of woe and doom are called "jeremiads" because they are named after him.

But Jeremiah was just the opposite of our stereotype of the doomsayer: someone stern, severe, and sour, tight of jaw, bitter of bile, and hard of heart. Jeremiah was a sensitive, gentle, kindhearted man; but God called him to deliver a harsh, hard message. God often calls us to necessities that we think our natural personalities are not fit for—perhaps so that it is clear that the deed is from Him, not from us (see 1 Cor 1:18–29).

The "bottom line" of Jeremiah's message is so old and well known that it is easily overlooked, like most profound platitudes. It is the truth that the only alternative to disaster is to "trust and obey", to surrender our will to God. Jeremiah had learned and lived this message—that's why God trusted him to deliver it—but Judah had not. And they were about to be destroyed by Babylon. They were like an overripe fruit about to fall off the tree when the winds came.

Jeremiah is a fine example of the rare but necessary combination of a soft heart and a hard will. He "set [his] face like flint" (Is 50:7) to deliver God's message intact. But the task made his heart break into tears, for the message was judgment on the people both he and God loved dearly.

How do we know how God feels? Because the one who alone perfectly reveals the heart of God, the one in whom "all the fullness of God was pleased to dwell" (Col 1:19), showed us God's heart when He delivered the same message as Jeremiah's six centuries later and forty years before another destruction of Jerusalem and of the second temple, by the Romans in A.D. 70, which was to be followed by an even longer exile and dispersion of the Jews, until 1948. Here is Jesus' jeremiad: "O Jerusalem, Jerusalem, killing the prophets and stoning those who are sent to you! How often would I have gathered your children together as a hen gathers her brood under her wings, and you would not! Behold, your house is forsaken and desolate. For I tell you, you will not see me again, until you say, 'Blessed is he who comes in the name of the Lord!'" (Mt 23:37–39).

No Old Testament poetry is more heartfelt and feeling-full than Jeremiah's, except some of the Psalms. A few of his expressions have become famous, such as, "Is there no balm in Gilead?" (8:22) and his personification of death as a grim reaper (9:21–22).

A Man of Suffering and Seeming Failure

He suffered in his own person as well as in sympathy for his people. He was homesick for his native countryside, but had to live and prophesy in the city. (He describes nature in great detail, especially animals.) He suffered throughout his long career for the dangerous habit of speaking the truth. He was rejected by his hometown, unjustly tried and convicted, publicly humiliated, put into the stocks, threatened by false prophets, and forced to flee for his life from the king. He spent seven years as a fugitive and was thrown into a cold, wet well for his prison cell. Jeremiah was a political failure. It seemed that he was a spiritual failure as well, for his people did not heed his message.

But he was *not* a spiritual failure. For he remained obedient to God's command to "preach the word, be urgent in season and out of season" (2 Tim 4:2). This "failure" verifies Mother Teresa's saying, "God did not put me on this earth to be successful, but to be faithful." This prisoner verifies C. S. Lewis' saying, "I was not born to be free, but to adore and to obey."

Jeremiah's unpopular message was not merely that the people were sinners—nothing new or startling there—but that they were *unrepentant* sinners, in fact smug and arrogant: "No man repents of his wickedness, saying, 'What have I done?' Every one turns to his own course, like a horse plunging headlong into battle" (8:6). As for the false prophets, "from prophet to priest every one deals falsely. They have healed the wound of my people lightly, saying, 'Peace, peace' when there is no peace. Were they ashamed when they had committed abomination? No, they were not at all ashamed; they did not know how to blush" (8:10–12).

If God allowed reincarnation, I think Jeremiah would be the prophet he would bring back today. For the besetting sin of our society too is not so much any one particular sin— lust and greed and sloth and luxuriousness are hardly our invention—but the loss of the *consciousness* of sin. Our ancestors may have been more cruel than we, but at least they repented. They had no pop psychologists to whisper, "I'm okay, you're okay", and no pop religionists to whisper, "Peace, peace", when there was no peace.

Or perhaps they did. And in Jeremiah's time they listened to those popular false prophets. And the next step was as predictable as an equation in algebra. Divine justice is no more avoidable than mathematical justice.

Jeremiah reminds us of this equation, between sowing the wind and reaping the whirlwind (30:23; Hos 8:7). God is patient, but His patience is coming to an end. He is not a wimp or a fool; He is not made in our image. Judah's disease was so far advanced that it could be dealt with only by radical surgery, the "severe mercy", the shock treatment, of the Babylonian exile. One cannot help wondering how Jeremiah would diagnose our civilization's advanced state.

Yet even the coming exile is mercy, for it (and it alone) would turn Judah's heart to seek God again, to listen and repent. As in the second chapter of Hosea, God has to bring His people into the wilderness (suffering) to remove their worldly distractions and pride so that in the silence of suffering and the shock of failure they can hear His voice again whispering the forgotten secret: that God is love, and this love must be jealous and demanding because our divine Lover is our only possible source of joy and life and liberation. God Himself cannot change this fact: God is God and idols are idols. It's as ultimate as X is X and Y is Y.

There is always hope because God is always ready to be found. His love and mercy are as unchangeable as His justice and truth. Here is one of the most hopeful verses in Scripture: "You will seek me and find me, when you seek me with all your heart" (29:13; compare Mt 7:8).

That, incidentally, is why God seems to hide from us, why it is so hard to know or feel His presence and guidance, why "holy places are dark places", as C. S. Lewis put it. The source of light is the heart, and we do not "turn on [our] heart-light". That's why a simple, unintellectual saint like Mother Teresa sees and says things of blinding clarity, while "intellectuals" and "experts" are often the blindest of the blind and the blandest of the bland. Light and fire come from the heart that bows to God, while darkness and ashes come from a god that bows to the demands of the human heart.

Jeremiah's hope is clearly messianic. God will fulfill the wonderful promises in chapter 31 only when the Messiah brings in the New Covenant, written not on Moses' stone tablets or in a book, but in the blood of the Sacred Heart:

> Behold, the days are coming, says the LORD, when I will make a new covenant with the house of Israel and the house of Judah, not like the covenant which I made with their fathers when I took them by the hand to bring them out of the land of Egypt, my covenant which they broke, though I was their husband, says the LORD. But this is the covenant which I will make with the house of Israel after those days, says the LORD: I will put my law within them, and I will write it upon their hearts (31:31–33).

The Messiah *has* come, yet Jeremiah's messianic prophecy still applies to us, for He is also still to come, and we are still to look forward, not backward. His first coming is to be completed by His Second Coming, and our baptism is to be completed by our sanctification. All growth in the Christian life begins at the place pointed out by Jeremiah's prophecy: in our admitting the Lord into more and more inner chambers of our heart (and therefore, inevitably, of our lives).

Lamentations: Jerusalem's Funeral Oration

Immediately following Jeremiah is a series of poems lamenting the destruction of Jerusalem and the temple. Imagine the Nazis had totally destroyed Rome, the Vatican, and all sacred shrines. Worse, imagine the Eucharist disappeared from the face of the earth. This is how the Jews felt as Jeremiah composed Jerusalem's funeral oration in Lamentations.

Though the book does not name its author, the earliest Jewish and Christian traditions ascribe it to Jeremiah. The same tender heart is here. Instead of gloating, "I told you so" when his unheeded prophecies were fulfilled, he only weeps with his people.

The poems are acrostics: each verse begins with a different letter of the Hebrew alphabet in order. The author literally weeps from A to Z.

Hope arises not just *after* the tears but *out of* the tears. We see here the great Jewish and Christian mystery of the redemptive power of suffering. And we see that Judah's hope comes from the very same source as her judgment: from God. Her holocaust did not happen by chance, but by the justice of the same God who is the source of her mercy and hope. Because it was not the Babylonians but God in control of her destruction, she has hope. For God, unlike Babylon, is also the source of her restoration. The same hope—the only one—is available to every sinner and sufferer and dying person today. The powers of darkness are ultimately controlled by the power of God. The solution to "the problem of evil" is to wait. God will bring good even out of evil, if only we turn to Him:

> Remember my affliction and my bitterness,
>   the wormwood and the gall!
> My soul continually thinks of it
>   and is bowed down with me.
> But this I call to mind,
>   and therefore do I hope:
> The steadfast love of the LORD never ceases,
>   his mercies never come to an end;
> they are new every morning;
>   great is thy faithfulness.
> "The LORD is my portion," says my soul (3:19–24).

TWENTY-ONE

Two Supernatural Visionaries:
Ezekiel and Daniel

The name *Ezekiel* means "God strengthens". Ezekiel's style lives up to his name: it is both strong and supernatural. It reminds me of a Norse epic: high, remote, awesome, and wonderful. It is the Old Testament's closest equivalent to the dazzling otherworldly imagery of the Apocalypse.

Ezekiel was both a priest and a prophet. Yet he transcended the frequent conflict between these two groups of leaders in Israel. For he seems to write from a point of view higher than both. It is neither the priestly and liturgical nor the prophetic and moral, but his writings seem to echo from Heaven itself, to which both liturgy and morality point.

He lived during the dark days of the Babylonian captivity and prophesied in Babylon to his fellow Jewish exiles. When he spoke his first prophecies of the destruction of Jerusalem and of Solomon's temple, Jerusalem had not yet been destroyed, though the Jews had already been taken captive to Babylon. When the Jews in Babylon heard the news of this destruction, they began to take Ezekiel seriously. He must have seemed like a madman to them before.

It was during this second stage of his prophetic career that Ezekiel spoke to the people expressly of hope, of a future return to the promised land, and of reconciliation with God. Like every true prophet of God, Ezekiel said two things, the bad news and the good news, sin and salvation. Whenever you hear either half of this message without the other, you know the messenger is not a true prophet.

Ezekiel: God's Power and Glory Displayed

The "sin" part of his message is both aweful and awful. Like all the prophets, he knows God as more than a comfortable chum. God is holy and unchangeably just. He cannot endure sin or compromise with it. Sin and God are like darkness and light; they cannot coexist. Therefore Ezekiel describes the visible cloud of God's glory, the *Shekinah*, leaving the temple, where it had been present since Solomon built it, and disappearing into the east, because the people's sins had driven it away. The name *Ichabod* comes from this event; it means "the glory has departed."

The *Shekinah* may have been present in Eden, permeating the bodies of Adam and Eve in visible divine light, until they sinned. That may be why they covered their now-naked, unlit bodies with clothes in shame. Ever since then, every sin is a little Ichabod, a darkening of our divine glory, our sending away the light of God.

Ezekiel's imagery is arresting, bizarre, terrifying, and supernatural. For instance, chapter one contains two visions of angels. Neither comes from Hallmark; their hallmark is their heavenly origin. One is a vision of flying, four-faced, four-winged creatures in a storm of fire and lightning. The other vision is of wheels within wheels covered with eyes! Chapter 32 contains a vision of the world of the dead. And chapter 37 is a vision of a valley full of skeletons standing up and coming to life. Any Bible illustrator, cartoonist, or moviemaker who wants to fascinate small children should not ignore Ezekiel. The images burn themselves into our memory and touch something indefinable in our unconscious. They certainly banish boredom, one of the devil's most effective inventions.

Ezekiel's actions are as bizarre as his words, for both come from a supernatural source. God commands him to eat a scroll and to lie on the ground tied tightly with ropes, unable to talk (chap. 3); to lie on his left side in public for three hundred ninety days (chap. 4); and to burn his hair (chap. 5).

Ezekiel knew (or rather the God who inspired him knew) that "a picture is worth a thousand words"—that vivid symbols are unforgettable. Ezekiel's vision of the glory of God at the beginning (chaps. 1–3) must have awed and overwhelmed him so deeply that this awe stuck to all that he said. It has an otherworldly but not imaginary feel, because it has an otherworldly but not imaginary origin. When I read Ezekiel I always think of Byzantine or Coptic liturgies, certainly not our modern Western warm fuzzies. Ezekiel would never use terminology like "building community" or "affirming values". He has seen something greater: the glory of God Himself.

Though the power of Ezekiel is "primitive", the content of his message is quite "advanced" and sophisticated. He announces more clearly than any prophet before him the principle that each individual is responsible for and is justly punished for his own sins, not those of parents, ancestors, or the community (chap. 18). One wonders whether we are regressing to a pre-Ezekiel stage of moral wisdom in emphasizing the sinfulness of social structures more than the "little" sins of individuals today.

Ezekiel lived in a century (the sixth century B.C.) that has been called "the axial period in human history", because during this century God seems to have been sending a similar message to humanity throughout the world. Dramatists, philosophers, and poets like Aeschylus in Greece, mystics like Buddha in India, sages like Confucius and Lao-tzu in China, and prophets like Zoroaster in Persia were all turning their hearers inward to a new sense of self-consciousness. The external and social was becoming interiorized and individualized. One wonders whether the next century will be the next "axial period in human history" when the turn reverses itself.

Like that of all the prophets, Ezekiel's "bottom line" is not doom but hope: hope for salvation, for new life, for a resurrection. The basis of this hope is not the human mind and wishful thinking, but the mind of God and divine revelation. The most memorable of the prophetic promises in Ezekiel is chapter 37, the famous vision of the dry bones coming to life.

This prophecy was fulfilled at Pentecost. It continues to be fulfilled as Pentecost occurs in the lives of individuals, in the life of the Church, and potentially even in the whole world. Our world's slide down toward darkness can be reversed; the dead can live; the wind of the Spirit still blows from the four corners of the earth.

For this is the Spirit that brings to life dead Israel, dead churches, dead legalism, dead liturgy, dead Christians, and a dead world: the same Spirit who raised the dead body of Christ (Rom 8:11). It is Christ who fulfilled Ezekiel 37: see Luke 4:18 and John 7:37–39.

Other messianic prophecies in Ezekiel include the righteous king (21:26–27), the good shepherd (34:11–31), and the branch who grows into a tree (17:22–24; compare Is 11: 1; Jer 23:5 and 33:15; and Zech 3:8 and 6:12). All prophecies are fingers pointing ultimately to Christ. All the words of all the prophets come down to a single Word, "the Word of God". In prophets like Ezekiel this Word was made into images, but in Christ the Word was made into flesh.

Daniel: The Sweep of History from God's Perspective

The name *Daniel* means "God is my judge". He prophesied in Babylon to both Jews and Gentiles during the Babylonian captivity.

Some of the most famous and arresting stories in the Bible are found in this book, including the three young men in Nebuchadnezzar's fiery furnace (chap. 3), the "handwriting on the wall" written by a disembodied hand, prophesying the sudden doom at King Belshazzar's feast (chap. 5), and, of course, Daniel in the lions' den (chap. 6).

Most of the book is made up of visions of the future. These visions have a greater historical sweep than any others in the Old Testament and predict four great world empires: the Babylonian, the Medo-Persian, the Greek, and the Roman.

There is a philosophy of history implied in Daniel's visions. It is that history is "His story" (God's). God is the Lord of history, planning and directing it as He plans and directs each life (even, we are told later, the fall of each sparrow and the numbering of each hair).

King Nebuchadnezzar had to go mad and live like an animal to learn this truth: "You shall be driven from among men, and your dwelling shall be with the beasts of the field; you shall be made to eat grass like an ox, and you shall be wet with the dew of heaven, and seven times shall pass over you, till you know that the Most High rules the kingdom of men, and gives it to whom he will" (4:25). "He changes times and seasons; he removes kings and sets up kings" (2:21).

The Messiah is prophesied in Daniel as a great stone who will crush all the kingdoms of the world, become a great mountain, and fill the whole earth (2:34–35). "And in the days of those kings [the Romans] the God of heaven will set up a kingdom [the Church] which shall never be destroyed, nor shall its sovereignty be left to another people. It shall break in pieces all these kingdoms and bring them to an end, and it shall stand for ever" (2:44). The four kingdoms recur in chapter 7, and so does the Messiah. Here, He is the "Son of Man" who receives from "the Ancient of Days" the Kingdom "which shall not pass away" (7:13–14). Even the death of the "Anointed One" is prophesied in Daniel 9:26, and perhaps even the exact time of this Messiah's coming, in the vision of "seventy weeks"— symbolically, 490 years—in Daniel 9:25 (though the state of the text is problematic here and shows signs of later revisions).

TWENTY-TWO

More Mouths of God: The Rest of the Prophets

Hosea: The Suffering of Love Rejected

Of all the prophets, Hosea has perhaps the most tenderness and the most tragedy, both in his message and in his life. For Hosea exemplifies what is probably the greatest possible suffering, the suffering that hurt Christ more than any other: the suffering of love rejected.

God taught Israel the lesson of suffering love through Hosea, not only in words but also in deeds. He commanded Hosea to marry Gomer, an unfaithful woman, to show Israel their own unfaithfulness to God, and perhaps also something of what God felt in being spiritually betrayed by His chosen Bride. "When the LORD first spoke through Hosea, the LORD said to Hosea, 'Go, take to yourself a wife of harlotry and have children of harlotry, for the land commits great harlotry by forsaking the LORD'" (1:2).

Love multiplies suffering by the factor of the quantity of that love. God's love is infinite. Therefore God can suffer infinitely. Christ's agony in the garden and on the Cross was not just physical agony, it was the infinite agony of infinite love rejected, failed, unsuccessful. Those who object to the dogma of Hell on the grounds that it would mean that man would suffer more than God, do not understand that God "descended into Hell" on the Cross and in the Garden of Gethsemane more deeply than any man could. The vision in the garden that so terrified Christ that He sweated bloody tears and asked His Father whether it was possible to avoid this "cup" was probably a vision of Hell—a vision of all the human souls suffering eternal torment after having rejected Christ's love. Hosea is a dim foreshadowing of that.

After Hosea's personal suffering over his unfaithful wife taught him something of God's grief for His unfaithful people, and after this object lesson hopefully taught Israel the same truth, Hosea then forgave his wife and took her back— just as God forgives His people and takes them back time after time. When Jesus replied to Peter's question, "How often shall my brother sin against me and I forgive him? As many as seven times?" by answering, "I do not say unto you seven times, but seventy times seven," He was only preaching what He was practicing, throughout history. This too is foreshadowed in Hosea: "The LORD said to me, 'Go again, love a woman who is beloved of a paramour and is an adulteress; even as the LORD loves the people of Israel, though they turn to other gods'" (3:1). Love never gives up (1 Cor 13:8).

But forgiveness is compatible with punishment. God both forgives and punishes, for both are expressions of love (an essential lesson for parents). All God's punishments against Israel are out of love and for love, for the purpose of restoring and consummating the love between them, to bring her back to Him and to joy. That is also what all punishments and all sufferings are for. (Not that the two are identical: Job shows they are not.) In fact all the events in our lives are providentially designed for this end: to hedge us, prod us, inveigle us into God's marriage chamber. The whole story of the Bible, the whole story of human history according to the perspective of the Bible, is a love story.

It seems that it is not. Chapter 2 of Hosea is particularly profound in penetrating beneath the terrible appearance to the wonderful reality of life. It seems at first that Israel's (and our) sufferings are punishments from an angry God, a wronged husband. The language is harsh: "Upon her children also I will have no pity, because they are the children of harlotry" (2:4).

But the harsh treatment is really gentleness and compassion: "Therefore I will hedge up her way with thorns; and I will build a wall against her, so that she cannot find her paths. She shall pursue her lovers, but not overtake them" (2:6–7). The reason for God's inflicting suffering and failure on Israel, as on us, is to bring us to the point where we repent, turn, and return. The decision must be free, for love is by its nature free. But the sufferings and failures on the road of false, idolatrous loves that bring us to the point of freely turning, are not freely chosen but inflicted against our will (but not against our eventual joy).

The point of the sufferings is explained in the next verse: "Then she shall say, I will go and return to my first husband, for it was better with me then than now.' And she did not know that it was I who gave her the grain, the wine, and the oil, and who lavished upon her silver and gold which they used for Baal. Therefore [to teach her this truth that she needs for her joy] I will take back my grain in its time, and my wine in its season" (2:7–9).

The arresting word that more than any other explains human suffering from the divine perspective of God wooing and winning His faithless human beloved, is the word "allure" in Hosea 2:14. Sufferings are part of God's allurements, God's courtship! "Therefore, behold, I will allure her and bring her into the wilderness, and speak tenderly to her." Only in the wilderness of suffering and silence can we hear the voice of God as it really is, quiet and tender and sweet and gentle. If God truly loves us, He *must* destroy the idols and the noise that we set up to block out the still, small voice of His love. For God *is* love (*agape*), and love, remember, never gives up (1 Cor 13:8).

Thus the most frequently heard reason for not believing in God—"If God loves us, why does He let us suffer?"—turns out to be one of God's supremely loving tricks. It is precisely because of God's love that we suffer, just as it is because of the dentist's charity that he drills the decay out of our teeth.

Hosea's name means "salvation". The word *Hosea* is closely related to the word *Joshua* and *Jesus*. Hosea is a Christ-figure. The name is also closely related to the name of Israel's last king, Hoshea. The name is the message. Hosea saved and redeemed (bought back) his wife from the slave market (3:2) as God was to redeem His people from the slave market of sin, at the price of His own blood.

The story of Calvary has been repeated many times before and since. The whole Bible tells the same three-stage story: first, sin, which is spiritual adultery (chap. 1); then the consequent suffering (chap. 2); then God's response of redemption (chap. 3). After the three-stage personal story is acted out on the stage of Hosea's life, the prophecy turns to its application to Israel and moves through the same three stages: chapters 4 to 7 show Israel's spiritual adultery, chapters 8 to 10 prophesy her coming captivity, and chapters 11 to 14 promise a future restoration to her land and to her relationship of fidelity and marriage to God. "Crime and punishment" make up only the first two-thirds of the story. And crime and punishment fit into, are part of, and are framed and explained by the ultimate point of the whole story—of Hosea, of Israel, of the Bible, of history, of life, of my life and yours: God's clever, tender, indefatigable courtship of our souls.

Joel: Judgment or Repentance—Our Choice

Beginning with an account of a terrible plague of locusts that suddenly appeared in Judah like a storm cloud and destroyed every green plant in a single day, Joel announces God's judgment on sin. The locusts are only a warning, a mild version of the unthinkably terrible Last Judgment on the "Day of the Lord", which will fall on all who are not repentant and right with God.

But disaster and threat are only half the truth. Famine, locusts, fire, invading armies, and the sun and moon blotted out are symbols of "the day of the Lord" for His enemies: "For the day of the LORD is great and very terrible; who can endure it?" (2:11). Yet the other half follows: "'Yet even now,' says the LORD, 'return to me with all your heart'" (2:12). "He is gracious and merciful" (2:13).

Joel's message is the same twofold point about God— justice and mercy, sin and salvation—found in all the prophets, in fact in all of Scripture. If readers find it tedious to have the same point repeated, they should remember: first, that it is poetry, not prose; song, not statistics. Poetry and song work by repetition or variations on the same theme. Second, we keep forgetting this simple lesson over and over, and need reminding over and over.

The most famous and important passage in Joel is his prophecy of Pentecost in chapter 2:28–32, which is quoted by Saint Peter in Acts 2:16–21, when the prophecy is fulfilled. It was Christ who sent His Holy Spirit as He had promised (Jn 16:7–15; Acts 1:8), so this prophecy of Joel's was a messianic prophecy. It is also a worldwide, and not just a national, Jewish prophecy—a prophecy of the time when the God who had revealed Himself to one "chosen people" would spread that knowledge, through the Church, throughout the world, and "all who call upon the name of the LORD shall be delivered" (2:32). Joel stresses the authority of God over all nations and all nature (that God sent the plague of locusts, for example), both to judge and to save.

Amos: The Prophet with a Modern Burden

Perhaps more than any other prophet, Amos seems to fit the picture of the "prophet of doom". Yet beneath his "doomsday" exterior, we can find many precious tidbits of positive wisdom. In these nine short chapters is contained an amazing amount of spiritual wealth and literary brilliance. One could easily write a whole book about Amos without being boring or repetitive.

His name means "burden", or "burden-bearer". For a prophet, as a holy man, loves the people to whom he must announce dooms, and this is the heaviest burden in the world, a burden only love can know.

Amos' burden is that beneath the appearances of prosperity, national optimism, contentment, and military power, Israel's soul was desperately sick, rotting from within. What the X-ray eyes of God see beneath the shine and shimmer is the last few swirls of garbage as Israel is about to go down the drain. The contemporary applications to America and to Western civilization, both in general and in detail, are terrifyingly appropriate. The sins Amos labels—lust, greed, religious infidelity and hypocrisy, arrogance, individual and social injustice, materialism, and smugness—sound like today's newspaper.

Amos was like John the Baptist: a rough, rude, unsophisticated country boy fearlessly "telling it like it is" to fashionable, sophisticated degenerates. He had not come from a line of clergy or professional prophets, but was a shepherd, farmer, and tree surgeon (7:14–15). But God took him by the hair of his soul and stood him up as a prophet. This divine call is the essential mark of the true prophet as distinct from the false or self-appointed prophet.

No prophet ever used stronger, bolder, sharper language than Amos. He had hard things to say, so he had to be a hard man to say them. Although God is compassionate, He is also hard, as unyielding as the moral law itself. Jesus manifests this hardness as well as tenderness—an extremely tricky and rare combination for most of us to live or even to like. Remember the hard things He said to the Pharisees or the money-changers in the temple. They don't nail a "nice guy" up to a cross and say he was a devil.

A religion that is a non-prophet organization is always less burdensome and more tempting. It seems more "spiritual". The real truth, and the real God, is always threatening and iconoclastic to the expectations and desires of fallen, sinful, self-indulgent human nature. Thus the society, in the person of the king and his private false prophet Amaziah, try to silence Amos (7:10–13), just as the media try to silence the Church today. Not everyone who is controversial and hated is a prophet, but every prophet is controversial and hated. It is not true that to be misunderstood is to be great, but it is true that "to be great is to be misunderstood", as even Henry David Thoreau knew.

Amos used images from nature, just as Jesus did (He was a country boy too), such as the basket of rotten, overripe fruit (8:1–2) and fattened cows (4:1). Imagine calling a congregation *cows*—he obviously hasn't read *How to Win Friends and*

Influence People. All his imagery is calculated to stir, to surprise, to shock.

I was once fired from a "homily service" (writing "model homilies" for lazy priests) because I lacked the proper "tone": namely, always upbeat, quiet, and dignified. Amos never would have taken that job in the first place.

Amos characterizes God as a roaring lion (1:2)—just as C. S. Lewis did with Aslan in his *Chronicles of Narnia.* We know God's tender side pretty well today, but we've forgotten His tough side. As Rabbi Abraham Heschel says, "God is not nice. God is not an uncle. God is an earthquake." Or, as Amos says, "Lo, he who forms the mountains and creates the wind, and declares to man what is his thought; who makes the morning darkness, and treads on the heights of the earth—the Lord, the God of hosts, is his name!" (4:13). The name is not Wimpy.

Prophets announce divine punishments. They also announce God's goodness. Only in modern times did anyone feel a tension, even a contradiction, between these two divine attributes. A God who tolerates evil, who does not punish, would not be good at all. True love and compassion are not tolerant of oppression and bullying (cf. 4:1, 6:5, 8:4–6). There are no "victimless crimes". And God loves the victim and hates the crime. Yes, God, the God who is love, hates (5:21). If you love your friend's body, you will hate the cancer that is killing it. And if God loves our souls, He must hate the sin that kills souls. Not to know this is not to know sin, not to know the soul, and above all not to know God.

God is more than just, but not less. His punishments are just and fit the crime and the degree of knowledge and responsibility. In the long catalog of crimes and punishments of the Gentile nations (chaps. 1–2), they are held responsible for sins against the natural moral law known by all men by conscience. But Israel is held more responsible—responsible for sins against her special knowledge of God, her divine revelation (2:4–16).

One of the sins Amos denounces more vociferously than most moderns do is liturgical abuses (5:21–27). For liturgy is worship, obedience to the first and greatest commandment, according to both Mosaic and Christian reckoning (Ex 20:3; Mt 22:35–37). Liturgy is important because it is love—the love of God in action—and life—spiritual life, living communication between the divine and human lovers.

Amos also denounces sexual sins in the same breath as he denounces social and economic sins, as well as liturgical abuses (2:7–8). He is unlike most modern "prophets" of both Left and Right who confine themselves to a specialized and selective morality. Like the Church centuries later, Amos speaks about all three areas. Sanctity is not a specialization. There's something in Amos, as in most of Scripture, to bother all of us. The saints always "comfort the afflicted and afflict the comfortable", as Dorothy Day put it.

Amos reserves his most severe and sarcastic jibes for the comfortable: "Woe to those who are at ease in Zion" (6:1). "Woe to those who lie upon beds of ivory . . . who drink wine in bowls, and anoint themselves with the finest oils, but are not grieved over the ruin of Joseph!" (6:4–6). The most horrible state of all is a dead conscience. See Matthew 5:4 and Luke 6:25 on this.

Israel, God's chosen ones, will be punished more severely because they know God more: "You only have I known of all the families of the earth; therefore I will punish you for all your iniquities" (3:2). In this light, the claim to be God's "chosen people" is just the opposite of arrogant and triumphalistic. The same principle, of course, applies to the Church, the New Israel.

Amos, like all the prophets, announces God's philosophy of history: the social parallel to the "two ways" of Psalm 1 leading inevitably to two different goals. Spiritual roads are just as objective as physical roads. You can't find blessing through sin or failure any more than you can find the Atlantic by going west from Chicago, or the Pacific by going east. This simple but constantly forgotten principle of history is borne out in the history of nations; not only Israel but also Babylon, Assyria, Greece, Rome, Germany, France, America.

And it works not just by divine intervention, miraculously, but by divinely instituted natural law, inevitably. Injustice is always terribly expensive, economically crippling. Sexual "freedom" destroys families and creates criminals. Oppression creates resentment and new oppressors. It's really amazing how stupid we are. God has to remind us again and again that nobody ever gets away with anything.

Amos pictures God as holding a plumb line (7:7–8). God is "straight". Goodness itself isn't a little bad; light itself doesn't have even a tiny shadow in it. The God of the Bible has a character, a nature. This is the basis for morality: reflecting that character. "You shall be holy; for I the LORD your God am holy" (Lev 19:2). God's infinity does not mean He has no definite character, like a blob (that's pantheism, the Blob God). It means that each of His sharp and definite attributes is infinite: He is infinitely good, loving, just, powerful, holy, wise, and so on.

Thus morality is never arbitrary, for it is based not only on God's law and word and will, but, in turn, on His nature, which is eternal and unchangeable. The popular misunderstanding of the message of the prophets is far too anthropomorphic and childish: that God wants to be the boss, and when He sees people disobeying Him, He gets upset and takes it out on them. This is how a spoiled child perceives a parent's loving discipline. Some of us never grow up.

The appropriate and inevitable punishment for refusing to heed God's Word is to become incapable of hearing it: "I will send a famine on the land; not a famine of bread, nor a thirst for water, but of hearing the words of the LORD" (8:11). When a muscle is not exercised, it atrophies. The same is true of the spiritual ear.

Yet God will never abandon Israel, and Israel will never die (9:8). There are only two institutions in history that we know will still be around when history ends, even though they had definite beginnings in time: two exceptions to Buddha's supposedly universal principle that "whatever is an arising thing, that is also a ceasing thing." One is the Church founded on the Rock of Peter. The other is Israel (see Rom 11).

Obadiah: The Message of Crime and Punishment

The name *Obadiah*, which means "servant of God", is quite common in the Old Testament. In fact, there are thirteen Obadiahs, and no one knows whether the writer of this book is the same as any one of the other twelve or not.

He prophesied to Edom, the nation that began with Esau, Jacob's brother. Esau's story can be found in Genesis 25–35. (*Esau* means "red", because Esau was red-haired.) The struggle between Jacob and Esau began before they were born, in their mother's womb (Gen 25:22–26), and continued with their descendants, the nations of Israel and Edom. (God changed Jacob's name to "Israel". The Bible calls all his descendants "the children of Israel".)

Edom refused to help Israel when they were in the wilderness (Num 20:14–21) and also when they were conquering the promised land. Edom would not allow Israel to pass through its land. Many centuries later, one of Esau's descendants was King Herod. In Herod's attempt to murder Jesus (Mt 2) the warfare between Edom and Israel continued.

Obadiah's prophecy of doom and total destruction for Edom (vv. 10, 18) came true in A.D. 70, when the Romans destroyed Jerusalem. The Edomites who fought them were not only defeated, but utterly lost to history. Obadiah's message is short and simple (his book is the shortest in the Old Testament: one chapter of 21 verses): "crime and punishment". Nations, like individuals, will reap what they sow. "The wages of sin is death."

Jonah: The Reluctant Prophet Who Discovered the Scandal of God's Mercy

No one knows who wrote this book. (The book does not *say* that Jonah wrote it.) If the book is fact (history), Jonah is the obvious candidate. If it is fiction (parable), we have no clue to the author.

Like Job or the Cain and Abel story, Jonah is a borderline case between those books and passages in the Bible that clearly claim to be historical by their very style (for example, Kings or the four Gospels) and those passages that clearly have the form of moral parable rather than history, like the parables of Jesus.

A scholar who interprets Jonah as fiction is not necessarily a modernist or a demythologizer. It depends on his reason. There are two possible reasons: one weak and one strong. If his reason is that the story centers on a miracle (Jonah alive in the belly of the "great fish"), then he is a modernist, for his hidden premise is that miracles can't happen in real history. This premise is (1) heretical, (2) irrational, and often even (3) dishonest. It is heretical because the *essence* of Christianity is miraculous (creation, Incarnation, Resurrection). It is irrational because a God great enough to create the universe out of nothing is certainly great enough to preserve a man alive in a fish. And it is often dishonest because the real reason for interpreting a passage non-historically is seldom spelled out by the modernist theologian, but simply softly assumed, slipped in like a magician slipping a card up his sleeve.

A Fundamentalist has been defined as "one who believes in the credibility of Scripture and the edibility of Jonah". Perhaps the Fundamentalists are wrong in insisting on a literal interpretation of Jonah. But if they are, that is not because of the "great fish", but because of the literary form of the book. This is the better reason for interpreting Jonah as fable. Most Scripture scholars who are not Fundamentalists see it as a very strong argument.

"Form criticism" tells us to interpret each book within the framework of the literary form or genre that it exemplifies. If we are properly to use "form criticism", we will probably conclude that this book means to be parable, not history. In any case, we must not interpret this book, or any other, "in light of our own sincere beliefs". That is *eisegesis* or "reading-into": reading *our* beliefs into the book. All good interpretation is *exegesis* or "reading-out-of": reading the *author's* beliefs and intentions out of his book.

The strongest argument for interpreting Jonah as a fable or parable is that it has the literary form of the "tall tale", full of satire, irony, humor, and "larger-than-life" exaggeration. (For instance, it describes Nineveh as a city so large that it takes three days to walk across it!) Also there are no other references to Jonah or Nineveh's conversion in any ancient literature, either Jewish or Gentile.

These are *good* reasons for thinking Jonah to be fable, similar to the reasons for thinking Job is fable. But many times *bad* literary reasons are given to support this position.

Some argue that Jonah is a parable because it teaches three moral lessons: (1) that you can't run away from God, as Jonah tried to do; (2) that even wicked people like the Ninevites can repent; and (3) that God's mercy is for Gentiles (the Ninevites) as well as for Jews. But this argument surely does not prove Jonah to be mere parable, for God can teach moral lessons through real history as well as through invented parables. A moralist teaches moral lessons in the words he makes, but God teaches them also in the real events He providentially oversees.

Believing scholars who interpret Jonah as fable rather than history for literary reasons are *not* denying that miracles happen—or that God could provide a nearly-miraculous "coincidence", like a great fish to swallow Jonah (survival in a whale may be biologically possible). After all, Exodus says that the parting of the Red Sea (Reed Sea) was not caused simply by miracle but by a wind that God providentially arranged. The perfect timing is as much a sign of God's presence and power as a supernatural miracle would be. The point of a miracle (the word means literally "sign") is precisely that anyway: to signify, to point beyond itself to God.

By the way, "three days and three nights" is a conventional Jewish phrase for *parts of* three days. It does not mean three times twenty-four hours, but could be as little as twenty-six hours (one hour of the first day, twenty-four of the second, one of the third). Jesus was dead from three in the afternoon on Friday to early Sunday morning, but this was reckoned "three days and three nights" even though it was only about thirty-nine hours, not seventy-two.

In the story, Jonah is called by God to preach to Nineveh, the greatest and most wicked city in the world, the capital of the world empire of Assyria. Assyria had brutally and tyrannically held the civilized world in terror for three hundred years. (And we think *we* have it hard preaching repentance to the modern pagan world? We have it easy compared to Jonah.)

God gives Jonah a one-word message: "Repent." God is a great economizer with words. Remember how incredibly brief Jesus was. Often, "more is less."

But Jonah hates the Ninevites and doesn't *want* to see them repenting and being forgiven and blessed by God. God's mercy is as scandalous to Jonah as God's justice is to many of us moderns.

So he runs away—or tries to. Instead of going east to Nineveh, he goes west to Tarshish (ancient Spain) by ship. He apparently doesn't know God well enough to know Psalm 139:9–10: "If I take the wings of the morning and dwell in the uttermost parts of the sea, even there thy hand shall lead me, and thy right hand shall hold me."

Of course no one can hide from God. Nothing in God's world can hide from God, any more than a character in *Hamlet* can hide from Shakespeare.

Ironically, every person and thing in the story obeys God except Jonah. The sailors fear God. The lots they cast tell the truth. The storm arises at God's will. The fish swallows Jonah when God calls it. The Ninevites repent when Jonah delivers God's Word. The plant grows up over Jonah when God commands it. The worm eats the plant when God brings it. Everything from large fish to worms obey God—everything except God's own prophet! This book is high and holy humor.

Jesus interpreted Jonah in the whale as a symbol of His own death and Resurrection: "For as Jonah was three days and three nights in the belly of the whale, so will the Son of man be three days and three nights in the heart of the earth" (Mt 12:40).

Once Jonah obeys God and goes to Nineveh preaching repentance, the whole city obeys and repents! Which miracle is more startling and unbelievable—that a man finds physical life in the humble, dark place of a whale's belly, or that a whole nation finds spiritual life in the humble, dark place of repentance? Which miracle is more wonderful? The physical miracle, like all physical miracles, is not in itself important; its importance is that it points to the greater, spiritual miracle.

The lesson for prophets today is radically optimistic: despite ever-increasing signs of spiritual decadence in our world, repentance can come. Let us give our pagans a chance. Don't count them out. Tell them the unpopular truth that you feel sure they won't respect, believe, or obey, just as Jonah did. Then leave the results to God. Remember Mother Teresa's job description for a prophet: "not to be successful, but to be faithful."

Neither Jonah nor the Ninevites had the last word. God did, as usual. God writes the script. No matter how hard and hopeless our hearers' hearts seem, no matter how hard and hopeless our own hearts may be (like Jonah's), it is God who gives the grace. "With men it is impossible. But with God all things are possible."

When Nineveh repents, Jonah sulks. So God teaches him something about His own divine nature, full of love and compassion—by a plant, a worm, and a wind. (Children need simple, concrete lessons.)

Please don't miss the almost slapstick humor in this book. The whole tone is misinterpreted if you miss this, as so many miss the irony and satire in many of the sayings of

Jesus. Jonah needs a *fish* to bring him to where God commands! Just picture the comic scene of this reluctant prophet vomited up from a fish, his skin white and blotched from its belly, dripping with vomit, stalking through the wicked city reluctantly mumbling his one-word message, which he hopes will fail, and which succeeds! The reluctant prophet is the most instantaneously successful preacher in the Bible. His one word converts the greatest and wickedest city in the world.

The irony continues in the last chapter when God shows Jonah, through sending the worm to eat the plant that sheltered him from the sun, that Jonah has more compassion on a plant than on a city—a city that God describes as full of people "who do not know their right hand from their left" (4:11). Then the last line: ". . . as well as many animals". Even animals seem to share in human sin and repentance somehow. God cares about them too. In fact, God loves animals more than Jonah loves people!

The serious lesson in the humor (humor is often profoundly serious) is that God can and does use anything and everything: a worm, a wind, a whale, even a Jonah. He's not proud. How dare we be?

Micah: His Message Is "Who Is Like God?"

His name is an abbreviation for "Who is like God?" His message is his name: "Who is a God like thee?" (7:18).

Micah has three messages from God. First, he tells of the sins of Judah and Israel. Second, he predicts their punishment. And third, he announces hope for the future, a restoration of the people to their homeland and a reconciliation with God. These are essentially the three messages of all the prophets.

The most famous verse in Micah summarizes God's demands, the reasonable demands that were being ignored: "He has showed you, O man, what is good; and what does the LORD require of you but to do justice, and to love kindness, and to walk humbly with your God?" (6:8).

In chapters 6 and 7, Micah imagines God and His people debating in court and God calling them to account, setting forth His case. The whole universe, nature itself, is the jury. The verdict is guilty—guilty of violating the two great commandments, love of God with all one's heart and love of neighbor as one's self. The first has been replaced with false, empty, external, and hypocritical worship. The second has been replaced with injustice: oppression, exploitation, greed, cheating, pride, violence, and bribery of judges, priests, and prophets.

The third message, the hope for true peace, justice, and happiness, depends on the coming of the Messiah. Micah 5:2 is one of the clearest and most specific of the Old Testament prophecies. It pinpoints the birthplace of the Messiah as Bethlehem. This was written about seven hundred years before Jesus was born. The scribes quoted it in Matthew 2:5–6 to try to prove that Jesus wasn't the Messiah, because they thought He had been born in Nazareth, not Bethlehem. They didn't know Jesus, but they knew their Old Testament.

Nahum: The Destruction of Nineveh

Nahum prophesied the doom of Nineveh a century after Jonah preached to it. Its repentance did not last. Total destruction is prophesied, and fulfilled: not a trace of the city remained after the next great world empire, Babylon, destroyed it.

Nineveh seemed like the *Titanic*: unsinkable. It was the mightiest city on earth, with walls one hundred feet high and wide enough for three chariots side by side. Towers on the walls rose up two hundred feet, and there was a moat around the wall sixty feet deep and one hundred fifty feet across. It seemed to the world absolutely invincible. But as Nahum predicted, "a great rushing flood" destroyed the city, flattening its wall. And the Babylonians entered to burn and plunder it. The site of the city was so thoroughly destroyed that it was not found until A.D. 1842, 2,454 years later.

The destruction of Nineveh was not only Babylon's doing, but God's doing. God used the Babylonians, but it was His hand that defeated Nineveh, because Nineveh had made itself God's enemy by making itself the enemy of God's people. It was God's kindness to His people that was the reason for His destruction of their enemies.

Habakkuk: God Writes Straight with Crooked Lines

This man with the unusual name writes an unusual book about a common topic, the great question of evil. Just as with Hosea, we find here a startling turn-around of our ordinary ways of looking at evil, and we see God, the totally good and totally loving one, using evil and suffering to abolish evil and suffering. Hosea and Habakkuk form a dramatic two-part answer to the "problem of evil".

In Hosea the emphasis is on love, on how the God of pure love uses punishment and suffering to further his love-plan. In Habbakuk the focus is on justice, on how the God of pure justice allows the injustice of "the bad guys" defeating "the good guys", in order best to effect ultimate justice in history. Hosea looks at evil and good, betrayal and fidelity, suffering and joy, in the lives of individuals as well as nations, in terms of ultimate love. Habakkuk looks at evil and good, injustice and justice, in the lives of nations, on the stage of world history.

The book takes the form of a dialogue with God and begins with the poignant cry: "O LORD, how long shall I cry for help, and thou wilt not hear? Or cry to thee 'Violence!' and thou wilt not save? Why dost thou make me see wrongs and look upon trouble? Destruction and violence are before me; strife and contention arise. So the law is slacked and justice never goes forth. For the wicked surround the righteous, so justice goes forth perverted" (1:2–4).

God's reply is startling: "Look among the nations, and see; wonder and be astounded. For I am doing a work in your days that you would not believe if told. For lo, I am rousing the Chaldeans, that bitter and hasty nation" (1:5–6). God is using evil to defeat evil, using the cruel Babylonians (Chaldeans) to punish Israel for her crimes, washing Israel clean from her dirt by the very dirty work of the Babylonians.

This scandalizes Habbakuk even more: "Thou who art of purer eyes than to behold evil and canst not look on wrong, why dost thou look on faithless men, and art silent when the wicked swallows up the man more righteous than he?" (1:13). Granted, Israel is wicked, but Babylon is more wicked still. Why let the bad guys win?

Habakkuk gets an answer because he combines two essential means to hear and discern God's will and word: a strong will and a silent mind. He says, "I will take my stand to watch, and station myself on the tower, and look forth to see what he will say to me" (2:1). He knows the essential preliminary to wisdom: worship. And he knows the necessary preliminary to worship: silence. "The LORD is in his holy temple; let all the earth keep silence before him" (2:20). The older Anglican Book of Common Prayer wisely began its liturgy with this verse and this attitude.

God's answer is, in a word, "Wait."

And the Lord answered me:
"Write the vision,
   make it plain upon tablets,
   so that he may run who reads it.
For still the vision awaits its time;
   it hastens to the end—it will not lie.
If it seem slow, wait for it;
   it will surely come, it will not delay" (2:2–3).

As Saint Augustine says, in answering the "problem of evil", "Since God is the highest good, he would not allow any evil to exist in his works unless his omnipotence and goodness were such as to bring good even out of evil" (*Enchiridion* 11). We're in a fairy tale, and we're only at the place where Snow White has eaten the poisoned apple, not yet at the point where she wakes and marries the prince. God is writing a perfect script, but "God writes straight with crooked lines."

What will come in the end out of injustice is justice: "Behold, he whose soul is not upright in him shall fail, but the righteous shall live by his faith" (2:4). What is promised here is nothing less than the gospel. The gospel of eternal life through faith is more than justice, but not less.

The other side of salvation by faith is damnation by faithlessness. This is the second part of the vision God shows Habakkuk. No one gets away with anything. Babylon will reap the fruit she sowed: greed (2:5–11), cruelty and violence (2:12–17), and idolatry (2:18–20)—three very modern sins. When Habakkuk hears that God will punish His enemies, he pleads for mercy, not justice: "Thy work, O Lord, do I fear. . . . in wrath remember mercy" (3:2).

Habakkuk began by questioning God and asking for justice; he ends by adoring God and pleading for mercy. At the

end we find the prophet who had loudly complained about
God's silence and delay "quietly [waiting] for the day of trouble" (3:16) and "[rejoicing] in the LORD . . . joy in the God
of my salvation" (3:18). For God has taken Habakkuk to a
high place to see a high vision of divine wisdom in human
history. He has taken him to a mountaintop: "God, the Lord,
is my strength; he makes my feet like hinds' feet, he makes
me tread upon my high places" (3:19). It is a foreshadowing
of the vision of life's meaning that the saints have now by
faith and the blessed will have in heaven by sight. It is meant
to inspire us plodders in the muddle and the muck, "so that
he may run who reads it" (2:2).

Zephaniah: The Day of Wrath

Zephaniah means "one whom God has hidden". He was the
great-great-grandson of King Hezekiah—a prince as well as
a prophet—and was hidden from the evil king Manasseh.
After Manasseh, Judah was blessed with a good king, Josiah,
whose reforms were probably urged on him by the prophet
Zephaniah.

Zephaniah prophesied just before the Babylonian captivity. Despite Josiah's reforms, the people's hearts were still corrupt, and needed purgation and punishment. God is kind
but severe. Zephaniah, like all the writers of Scripture, sees
both aspects of God. Though most of his prophecy is dark,
grim, and gray, yet a light dawns when he looks beyond the
time of punishment to a time of joy when God will "deal
with all [his] oppressors" (3:19), a time to "rejoice and exult
with all your heart" (3:14).

A prophecy can have more than one meaning. The "day
of the Lord" prophesied by many Old Testament writers can
refer to: (1) an event in Old Testament times, such as the

Babylonian captivity or the return from it; (2) the great event of New Testament times, the coming of the Messiah; or (3) the Second Coming of the Messiah at the end of the world. Sometimes it can mean all three. The passage in Zephaniah 3:9–10 is a good example.

Zephaniah's central message is the same as that of all the prophets: "Seek the LORD [or "repent" in other translations], all you humble of the land, who do his commands; seek righteousness, seek humility; perhaps you may be hidden [*be hidden* = Zephaniah's own name] on the day of the LORD" (2:3).

The writer of the famous medieval hymn "Dies Irae" ("Day of Wrath") based his description of the Day of Judgment on Zephaniah's prophecy.

Haggai: Call to Rebuild the Temple

Haggai speaks plainly and directly, with no rhetoric or oratory, to the Jews who had returned from exile in Babylon to Jerusalem. They had not rebuilt the great temple for sixteen years. They had put their own business ahead of God's. Haggai encourages them to build God's temple by telling them God's promise to be with them and reminding them of God's sovereign power over nations and history.

The message was needed because the Jews who returned to Jerusalem from Babylon were discouraged. Their land was desolate. Crops failed. Work was hard. And the Samaritans, their neighbors on the north, hindered their work. So they stopped building. (The background story to Haggai is found in Ezra 4–6.) Haggai and Zechariah both urged them to finish—and succeeded. Haggai is one of the few prophets who lived to see his dream fulfilled.

However, the new temple was inferior to the old because it did not contain the ark of the covenant or the *shekinah* (the cloud of glory that showed God's presence). But the temple had to be built because the Messiah was due to come to it. Malachi 3:1 prophesied that. That is why Haggai said "the latter splendor of this house shall be greater than the former" (2:9). It was filled with the glory of God Himself in the flesh when Christ came to Jerusalem and taught in the temple.

Haggai 2:6–7 is famous because Handel included it in his *Messiah*. It probably refers to both the first and the Second Coming of Christ: "I will shake the heavens and the earth and the sea and the dry land; and I will shake all nations, so that the treasures of all nations shall come in, and I will fill this house with splendor, says the LORD of hosts."

Zechariah: Symbols, Visions, and Messianic Prophecies

The time and setting for Zechariah is the same as that for Haggai. Zechariah prophesied to the exiles returning to Jerusalem from Babylon. His name is one of the most popular in the Old Testament (there are twenty-nine different Zechariahs) and means "God remembers". His theme is that God remembers His covenant promises to bless Israel. Zechariah was murdered in the temple (Mt 23:35) just as another Zechariah had been (2 Chron 24:20–21). (Prophets would have found it hard to get life insurance.)

Zechariah's language is in sharp contrast to Haggai's plain and simple style. It is full of symbols and visions: riders on red, white, and dappled horses among myrtle trees (1:7–17); four ox horns and workmen with hammers (1:18–21); a man with a measuring line (2:1–13); the high priest standing before an angel (3:1–10); a golden lampstand (4:1–14); the flying scroll (5:1–4); a woman in a basket (5:5–11); and the four chariots (6:1–8). Zechariah also speaks more about angels than any other Old Testament writer.

Chapters 9 to 14 look far into the future, foretelling that Israel's neighbors would be conquered (by Alexander the Great), but that Israel would be spared for the coming of the Messiah (9:9–10), her King and Shepherd whom she would reject (11:4–17). Chapters 12 to 14 refer to Christ's Second Coming and the end of the world. Zechariah is full of messianic prophecies (3:1–2; 3:8–9; 6:12–13; 9:9–10; 10:4; 11:4–13; 13:1; 13:7), some of them extremely specific, such as the Messiah's being sold for 30 pieces of silver (11:13) and His triumphal entry into Jerusalem (on Palm Sunday) on a donkey (9:9).

Malachi: God Has Been Neglected, and Evildoers Will Not Go Unpunished

His name means "my messenger" or "messenger of God". His book prophesies the coming of "my messenger to prepare the way for me, and the Lord whom you seek will suddenly come to his temple" (3:1). This "messenger" was John the Baptist (see Is 40:3), who prepared the way for Christ. John would not appear for over four hundred years. Malachi is apparently the last Old Testament prophet—unless Daniel was written much later than the rabbinic tradition has believed. He is followed by four hundred years of silence from God. The silence was broken by John the Baptist's voice quoting Isaiah 40:3 (Mt 3:3). Jesus called John the greatest of the prophets (Mt 11:11). Malachi may have been the closest to him in time. He is at least the closest to him in the pages of the Bible.

The problem Malachi addressed in his own time was smugness and a false sense of security. Even many of the priests were corrupt, and many people questioned whether it paid to obey God, since the wicked seemed to prosper. Their attitude was not simple and clear rebellion against God, but coldness of heart, legalism, and materialistic dullness and dryness and dimness of spirit. This was just the type of attitude that, according to Matthew's Gospel, the Pharisees and Sadducees showed in Jesus' day and that Jesus condemned as harshly as the prophets did.

Malachi addresses this problem in a question-and-answer form, as a dialogue with God. His answer to the great problem of evil (if God is just, why do the wicked prosper and the righteous suffer?) is first of all that the people have neglected God, God has not neglected them. Second, their evil will not go unpunished, as the history of Edom shows. As with Habakkuk, the answer to the problem of evil is "wait." The "day of the Lord" will come, and then it will be clear that it is not "vain to serve God" (3:14).

Malachi (and the whole Old Testament) ends by mentioning Moses (4:4) and Elijah (4:5), who appeared with Christ on the Mountain of Transfiguration (Mt 17:3). The promise to send an Elijah (4:5) was fulfilled by John the Baptist (Mt 17:10–13), who prepares for "the great and terrible day of the Lord", the coming of Christ. The whole Old Testament has been like an arrow, and here is its tip, pointing to the center of the target, the center of all things (Col 1:17), Christ.

TWENTY-THREE

History, Wisdom, and Apocalyptic Visions: The Deuterocanonical Books and the Apocrypha

The following books and parts of books are listed separately because they are "Deuterocanonical". That means they are the "second canon (list of sacred writings)." They were added later to the canon of the Old Testament, both by the Jews (in Greek Alexandria) and the early Christian Church.

The Deuterocanonical Books were written only in Greek and not in Hebrew. This is one reason why most Protestants and the Jews of Palestine do not include them in their Bible. But the same Catholic Church that defined the first canon also declared the second to be inspired at the Council of Trent. The Orthodox churches of the East also accept them as canonical, with the exception of Baruch.

Tobit: God's Providential Care

Delightful, charming, enchanting in its simplicity—these are some of the characteristics critics find in the story of Tobit. Like most storytellers of the past, its writer set his tale in days gone by, in Nineveh, the capital city of the Assyrian empire. There, in exile from his native Israel, lived Tobit, a good Jew (his name means "the good"), who goes blind because of a very peculiar accident. The story centers on the journey of his son Tobias into faraway Media to reclaim a fortune Tobit had left there, with the help of a disguised angel Raphael and even a faithful little dog who makes the whole journey with them. In Media there lives the beautiful but unfortunate Sara, whose seven husbands all died on their wedding night, slaughtered by the demon Asmodeus. But the angel Raphael knows how to deal with demons and tells Tobias how to defeat Asmodeus with a fish's liver!

In addition to these supernatural elements, there are many realistic details, like Tobit's wife's irritation at her husband's scrupulous honesty, her anxiety for his blindness, which forces her to take in sewing to support the family, her constant watching the road for her son's return, and old Tobit counting the days.

Is the story meant as fiction or fact? We cannot decide it is fiction simply by pointing to the supernatural elements, for the whole of the Jewish and Christian religions are based on a supernatural and miracle-working God. But the literary style of the story is very different from the historical books, and it is probably meant to be taken as a "tall tale". Whether history or parable, biography or fiction, its lessons are true, for they are those of the rest of God's Word: faith and trust in God's providential "tender loving care" always pays off in the end.

Judith: A Courageous Woman Delivers Her People

The name *Judith* comes from the Hebrew *Jehudith* and means "Jewess". She is the heroine of a story whose historical background is hard to place accurately, since names, places, and dates seem out of historical order and treated very freely and loosely. But its point is not history but character.

Judith is a widow. Her husband has died of sunstroke three years before the story begins, and she is still in mourning. The Jewish nation is in danger of being destroyed by an enemy army. Her city Bethulia is under siege, and the evil king Nebuchadnezzar's general-in-chief Holofernes has cut off its water supply. The despairing citizens beg their rulers to surrender, but Judith has a better plan. Her courage and strong faith in God contrast with their cowardice.

She takes off her mourning clothes and makes herself so beautiful that she is sure to "entice the eyes of all men who might see her" (10:4). Then she brings gifts to the camp of Holofernes, wins his confidence, and eventually wins his head, which she cuts off and brings home in a food bag. The drunken braggart and bully is defeated by the charm and wit of a woman, and the mighty army of Holofernes is defeated in a rout. Thus King Nebuchadnezzar's plans are frustrated. His ambition was to conquer the whole world and destroy all religions that did not worship him. Some commentators see Judith in her beheading of the evil Holofernes as a foreshadowing of Mary as the new Eve crushing the head of the serpent, or Satan, the one who does indeed desire to conquer the world and destroy all true religion. Judith is the Jewish Joan of Arc. Too bad she was not around to deal with Hitler.

Esther (Greek Version): The Religious Interpretation

This is the same story as the Hebrew Book of Esther (see page 90), but with some additions. The religious lesson here is not left implicit in the events as it was in the Hebrew version, but made explicit in the Greek author's comments.

In Esther, as in the Genesis story of Joseph, God makes no outward or miraculous manifestations of His power. Rather He directs events by natural causes, yet brings good out of evil in the end, justice out of injustice, and shows that "in everything God works for good with those who love him" (Rom 8:28). The lesson that success comes from trusting in God's providence and plan is like the bones of the original Esther story (see Esther 14:14), and the Greek additions are like an X-ray that makes the bones prominent, makes the religious structure and meaning of the events clear.

The Wisdom of Solomon: The God behind the Law

This book was written not by King Solomon, but by an anonymous Jewish author a century or two before Christ who seems to have lived in the Greek city of Alexandria, Egypt, the world's center of Greek learning at the time. The title was not meant to deceive anyone, but to express the author's admiration for Solomon and to claim to be his disciple and imitator of his wisdom.

The book is a synthesis of ideas from Jewish religion and Greek philosophy and literature. Its main lesson is the same as that of the rest of the Old Testament: justice and fidelity, God rewarding those who are faithful to His law. This fidelity is the heart of wisdom. The book clearly affirms God to be all-just, all-knowing, all-good, and the origin only of good: "God did not make death, and he does not delight in the death of the living" (1:13)—a theme already taught in Genesis 3, where man's death is the result of sin, not of God.

In Wisdom, the perfections of God reach a new high point of theological development, and the author reflects on the lessons that the history of God's people have taught about the nature of God and the nature of wisdom. The understanding of God's character and intentions grows throughout Jewish history, just as a plant, an animal, a human body, or a human mind grows. For instance, the later prophets of Israel emphasized the need for personal virtue and not just external observance of the law. They place more responsibility on the individual since increased knowledge brings increased responsibility.

"Wisdom" here means not merely the practical ability to succeed well in life, or even the art of behaving ethically, but spiritual vision, understanding of God and His activity in our lives and history. This wisdom had been deepening among God's people for two thousand years, all leading up to one point: the time when the complete and perfect understanding of God would once for all become available to the whole world in Christ, God's Wisdom incarnate. The best wisdom of all the ages was a series of pointing fingers or signs to Him. "Wise men still seek him."

Ecclesiasticus: The Teachings of a Great Sage

This fifty-one-chapter book is the longest among the Deuterocanonical Books. Its author, Jesus (or Joshua) ben (son of) Sirach, was a teacher, scholar, and poet in Jerusalem about one hundred eighty years before Joshua ben Joseph, Jesus the Messiah. This book is probably a series of lectures Jesus ben Sirach gave in the school that he ran in that city.

His writing seems to indicate that he had traveled and studied widely about other countries and observed life carefully in order to build up his own philosophy of life. Most of the book resembles Proverbs in being realistic and practical. Its most beautiful chapters are the most poetic ones: 1, 24, 38, and 43.

The basic theme is a defense of wisdom and the claim that "all wisdom comes from the Lord" (1:1). This claim, repeatedly made by Jewish writers in the Old Testament, does not mean "listen to me because I'm as wise as God", but rather "whatever wisdom I have, give God the credit for it, not me." It is like the claim to be God's chosen people: a claim that seems arrogant, but is really the most humble interpretation of the fact that the Jews *are* really different. It ascribes their achievements to God, not themselves, and turns our attention from them to Him: "To fear the Lord is the first step to wisdom" (1:14).

In chapter 24 wisdom is personified, much as in Proverbs (see chapter on Proverbs). These words of Jesus son of Sirach could well be seen as applying to another Jesus, whom "God made our wisdom" (1 Cor 1:30).

Baruch: Speeches Given to the Exiles in Babylon

Baruch was Jeremiah's scribe or secretary. This book contains four short speeches by Baruch given to the Jewish exiles in Babylon. Their effect on the people was moving: "Everyone cried, fasted, and prayed to the Lord. Then everyone gave as much money as he could and the collection was sent to Jerusalem" (1:5–7). When you read it, imagine *you* are a poor, defeated, powerless Jewish exile in Babylon and that you believe this is the long-awaited message from God to give new hope to you and your defeated nation. Note especially the inspiring poetry at the end (4:36–5:9).

The Letter of Jeremiah: The Failure of Idolatry

The first verse explains the source of this book: Jeremiah the prophet sends a letter to the people of Jerusalem who are about to be captured and taken into exile in Babylon. The

prophet foretells this and interprets it as God's necessary punishment on the people's foolish idolatry. It was foolish both
for knowledge (confusing the living God with a dead idol—
but idols include to dollar bills just as much as stone statues)
and for practice (for since the idols have no power to save,
those who trust in them will not be saved). The result of
idolatry in practice is always failure, like leaning on a broken
crutch.

The Prayer of Azariah and The Song of the Three Young Men

This addition to the Book of Daniel is found in the later,
Greek version of Daniel. The "song" is a cosmic canticle of
praise that the three young men sing from the middle of the
fiery furnace into which the evil king Nebuchadnezzar had
thrown them when they refused to worship him (Dan 3). In
the song, all of creation praises God, from snow to snails.
"Inanimate" matter and "dumb" animals are living works of
art that loudly praise their Divine Artist, just as a good song
praises its composer or a great play praises its playwright.

This canticle was for a long time well known and loved in
the Church's public liturgy and is still loved and used by many
in private prayer. It brings prayer into the realm of the concrete world when we call on specific things like whales and stars
and heat to praise God. Saint Francis' "Canticle of the Sun" is
a miniaturization of it. It is an application of Psalm 150, which
commands *everything* to praise God. All goodness is God's goodness, all truth is God's truth, and all beauty is God's beauty.

Susanna: An Innocent Woman Is Vindicated

This is a short story of the same kind as Tobit and Judith:
simple, full of surprises, and enchanting. A beautiful woman,

Susanna, is falsely accused by two jealous, evil judges and saved by the young judge Daniel, who shows Solomon-like wisdom. It is one of the earliest forerunners of the modern detective story. Though only one chapter long, it contains many memorable details, such as the two trees that are silent witnesses for Susanna. Once you start the story, you cannot put it down until the end.

Like Tobit, this story seems to have the literary form of fable rather than history. I think one should not be too dogmatic either way. But the literary style is like that of Tobit and Bel and the Dragon, rather than straightforward historical narrative like Maccabees.

Bel and the Dragon: Three Detective Stories

These are three stories that the later Greek version of the Hebrew Scriptures added to the Book of Daniel. All three are exciting detective stories, or "thrillers". The first two center on Daniel and his wisdom in overcoming an idol set up by the Babylonians, who had destroyed Jerusalem and taken the Jews into captivity in Babylon. In the first story, Daniel exposes a clever technological trick by a trick of his own and proves that the idol Bel did not magically eat the food offered to it, as it seemed. In the second story, Daniel destroys a large, live dragon (perhaps a giant crocodile), which the Babylonians worshipped, without using any weapons. The point of both stories is not primarily Daniel's cleverness, but the foolishness of worshipping idols of any kind, anything in the world except the one true God.

The third story is an addition to the story of Daniel in the lion's den. It tells of the prophet Habakkuk, an interrupted stew, and an angelic air transportation by the hair from Israel to Babylon to feed Habakkuk's stew to Daniel as the lions watched, hungrily, waiting until Daniel's enemies were thrown into their den. Then they had their just desserts.

First Maccabees: Resistance against Tyranny

This is a historical book that tells of the Jewish struggle for religious and political freedom from the Greek empire of the Seleucid kings who had inherited the world from Alexander the Great. The Maccabees are a Jewish family chosen by God to stand up against the tyrant Antiochus Epiphanes ("that wicked root"), who persecuted the Jews and blasphemously desecrated the temple. This tyrant stole its holy treasures and set up altars to heathen gods, tore and burned the sacred books of the law, and mistreated any Jewish women who had their baby boys circumcised in obedience to Jewish law.

The first two chapters of the book set up the two sides of the war as irreconcilable enemies. On the one hand, the Greek rulers insisted not only on political conquest of Israel and the removal of political freedom, but also religious persecution and instituting practices the Jews considered blasphemous, especially in the temple. Many Jews compromised with the Greek conquerors and even helped them. On the other hand, those Jews who remained faithful to God, His law, and His temple worship resisted Antiochus Epiphanes both by force and by martyrdom.

The rest of the book is the story of three resistance movements, one for each of the sons of Mattathias: Judas Maccabeus, "The Hammerer", and his brothers Jonathan and Simon, who each led the resistance in turn and were killed in turn. It is a story of war, intrigue, and murder—full of detailed descriptions of ancient warfare, including mounted engines to throw fire and rocks, and elephants with towers of wood. The battle scenes remind us of *The Lord of the Rings*. Yet even in this bloody time God's hand is seen, testing His people, punishing them with national suffering only in order to bring them back to Himself, and aiding those who were loyal to Him. The Maccabees, like the Jews of older times, succeed only by God's help and fail only when they turn away from God.

God's providence over history was keeping the nation of Israel alive, against all ordinary odds, because they were His chosen people, carriers to the whole world of His revelation, the true knowledge of who God really is. They were the people from whom His promised Messiah was to come. These years, full of wars and violence, without a prophet from God for over four hundred years between Malachi and John the Baptist, were the dark before the dawn.

Second Maccabees: Praise for Martyrs of the Faith

This book covers part of the same period covered by First Maccabees. It is the story of the Jewish fight for Jerusalem and the temple, for political and religious independence. There is some overlapping, and many of the same events are told from another point of view. The style here is more like a sermon than a history. The author's purpose is to teach loyalty to God's law and to praise the martyrs who died for their faith.

Second Maccabees also contains the Old Testament's only clear passage that teaches us to pray for our beloved dead because of the resurrection.

Highlights include the stirring story of the mother and seven sons who were tortured and slaughtered for their faith (chapter 7), and the teaching on the resurrection of the dead (6:26; 7:9; 12:41–46; 14:46) and on the intercessory prayers of the saints in Heaven (15:12–16) where Jeremiah the prophet is seen praying in Heaven for Judas Maccabeus on earth. The Church Militant on earth and the Church Triumphant in Heaven are one. In prayer they have real contact with each other. Death no more destroys or even separates God's people, the Church, the New Israel, than it could destroy or separate ancient Israel. "Therefore, since we are surrounded by so great a cloud of witnesses, let us also lay aside every weight and sin which clings so closely, and let us run with perseverance the race that is set before us" (Heb 12:1).

Apocrypha

The First and Second Books of Esdras and the Prayer of Manasseh are *not* part of the seventy-two books the Catholic Church accepts as the canon or list of books of Scripture (that is, divinely inspired, authoritative, and infallible). But they are wise and useful reading. The reason they are included as part of the Apocrypha in many Catholic and Protestant Bibles is that the Jews in Alexandria, Egypt, who made the Septuagint Greek translation of the Old Testament did include them; some Protestants (mainly Anglicans and Episcopalians) include them as part of their Apocrypha; and they were used by Christians for the first few centuries. In fact, some non-Chalcedonian Orthodox churches, which have no closed second canon of Scripture, hold that First and Second Esdras are "inspired".

First Esdras: Second Chronicles 35–36, Ezra, and Nehemiah 6–8 Retold

The events told in the First Book of Esdras are also told in 2 Chronicles 35–36, Ezra, and Nehemiah 6–8. But First Esdras adds the interesting philosophical debate of the bodyguards before the emperor (chap. 3–4).

Second Esdras: Apocalyptic Visions

Most of this book consists of seven apocalyptic visions, that is, visions of the end of the world and the crises that are to come before the end. It offers answers to some of the greatest philosophical questions asked in any time: questions about the problem of evil and suffering and about the meaning and end of history. The style is more philosophical than that of the canonical books of Scripture, and more typical of the Greek mind than the Hebrew mind.

What are we to make of prophecies and visions like these that are not in the canon of Scripture but seem to be wise and edifying? On the one hand, they are not infallible. We cannot be certain that they are true. On the other hand, when they dovetail nicely with Scripture, when they explain Scripture and when Scripture explains them, we should give them a respectful hearing and expect to get from them great wisdom and inspiration.

The Prayer of Manasseh: A Prayer of Repentance

The story of Manasseh, who was a very evil king of Judah, is told in 2 Chronicles 33. This short prayer is a prayer of repentance for sin. Whether Manasseh actually composed it or not, it is a beautiful prayer to use. It begins and ends with praise, which is the main theme of prayer in the Bible, and it encloses repentance in that context.

PART TWO

THE NEW TESTAMENT

ONE

The Good News of Jesus Christ: Introduction to the Gospels

Any *one* of the four Gospels is inexhaustible. Libraries of books have been written about them, and saints and scholars alike have devoted lifetimes to reading, praying, and studying them. Even if the whole human race meditated on one of the Gospels for a thousand years, they could not exhaust its riches.

The word *gospel* is a modernization of the Old English *gospell* (or *God-spell*), meaning "good news". The original Greek word is *eu-angellos* (Latin, *evangelium*), meaning "good-message". The words *angel* (messenger) and *evangelism* (preaching this news) both come from *eu-angellos*.

Two unique facts about Christianity emerge from this word.

First, Christianity is *news*: concrete facts, specific miraculous events that really happened and were seen in this space-time world of ours. All other religions (except Judaism) are essentially universal truths, philosophies, moralities, laws, mysticisms, psychologies, rituals, or social systems—something abstract rather than concrete *events*.

Second, it's *good* news. J. R. R. Tolkien says, "There is no tale ever told that men more wish were true." Rightly understood, it is "tidings of great joy". But in the modern world

177

it's often *not* rightly understood and is seen as *bad* news: as repressive, pessimistic, negative, dehumanizing, and threatening. That fact says nothing about Christianity, but a lot about the modern mind.

The "gospel" does not mean first of all the four *books* we know as the Gospels, but the news they report, the real events in which God's plan of salvation was fulfilled. This "gospel" was preached, believed, and lived for years before these books were written. This simple fact refutes the claim that Christianity *essentially* rests on the Bible. Our unbroken link to Christ is indeed the gospel (that is, the good news about Christ); but this unbroken link was first forged in the living Church, shaped in her prayer life, meditation, practice, and preaching *prior* to any of the written texts we now possess. The Gospels are four of the books that the Church—our divinely appointed teacher—wrote and uses to teach us. We must never separate our textbook from our teacher.

The Gospels are placed in the order we have them because tradition has always claimed they were composed in that order. Many modern scholars think Mark came first, Matthew using most of Mark and adding to it. But there is good evidence that Matthew was written first, and in Hebrew. The grammatical idioms, word structures, and word play in Matthew make much more sense if they were translations into Greek of a Hebrew original.

What is the significance of the fact that there are *four* Gospels? First, it fulfills the prophecy in Ezekiel 1. The Church has always interpreted the four "living creatures" full of eyes in Ezekiel's vision as symbolic of the angels of the four evangelists. They also reappear in Revelation 4.

Second, the number four shows completeness. For example, "the four winds" blow from the "four corners" of the whole earth. These four Gospels were written to all four possible audiences in the ancient world, thus encompassing the whole world. Matthew was written mainly for Jews, Mark for Romans, Luke for Greeks, and John for everyone. This same universality was symbolized by the sign on the Cross: the charge against Jesus was written in Hebrew, Latin, and Greek, thus showing the whole world's guilt and the whole world's salvation.

Third, the fact that there are four accounts and not just one means that we can do cross-checking, like triangulation. This makes a very strong case for the historical reliability of the story. If the Gospels did not contain miraculous events, historians would accept them as accurate and factual just as they accept ancient secular documents. We have more copies and earlier copies of them than of any other ancient history.

But aren't there contradictions among them?

No substantive ones. The minor discrepancies they contain are exactly what you would expect from four independent, honest eyewitnesses to any events. If they told *exactly* the same story, we would suspect copying and collusion.

What are the minor discrepancies?

1.   Some concern numbers. For example, were there two angels at Christ's tomb (Luke) or one (Matthew and Mark)? The Bible is more concerned with quality than quantity.

2.   The *order* of events is often inverted. Only Luke claims to be an orderly account (Lk 1:3).

3.   Events are sometimes compressed. For example, sayings Jesus uttered on various occasions in the other Gospels are put in a single sermon in Matthew (the "Sermon on the Mount," Mt 5–7).

4.   Quotations are not always word for word. Parallel passages in different Gospels usually differ slightly, but the substance is always the same.

5.   The borderline between where Christ's words end and the evangelist's interpretation of them begins is not always clear, especially in John (for example, see Jn 3), since the ancients used no quotation marks.

Thus Fundamentalists have a hard time justifying the *literal* infallibility of every detail. Yet the Gospels hold up very well when scrutinized by modern, scientific, open-mindedly sceptical historical-textual investigators (as distinct from some Scripture scholars with pet theories to defend).

One such sceptical investigator, Frank Morrison, tried to disprove Christ's Resurrection by a scientific, historical study of the texts, and ended up converting. Morrison concluded that the only explanation for all the data is a real Resurrection. His book, *Who Moved the Stone?*, written in the 1920s, is still in print.

All four Gospels share common features in their structure:

- They center totally on Christ.
- They present Him as both human (Son of Man) and divine (Son of God).
- They present His work as both words (teachings) and deeds (miracles).
- They present His most important work as dying and rising from the dead.
- They present Him as "Jesus", that is, the Savior from sin, and "Christ" or Messiah ("promised one").
- They begin no later than John the Baptist and end no earlier than the Resurrection.
- They are written by eyewitnesses (Matthew, John) or those who interviewed eyewitnesses (Mark, Luke).

The Gospels can be used in at least three different ways. First, they are the data for enquiring sceptics, providing historical evidence for the faith.

Second, they are our primary devotional, meditational reading to deepen our faith as Christians. They are the place where we meet Christ. Saint Teresa of Avila said she never found anything as powerful as the Gospels for growing in holiness, even the deepest writings of the greatest saints and mystics.

Third, they are literary masterpieces. They take their rightful place among the classics of world literature. They need to be read with imagination and human sympathy and wonder as well as faith.

All three ways are legitimate, but not to be confused with each other.

Each of the following four chapters, on the four Gospels, is quite short, while the chapters on Acts and Revelation are fairly long. That does not reflect the relative importance of those books—if so, the chapters on the Gospels would have to be larger than the universe and longer than time—but their relative familiarity and clarity. The Gospels are not puzzles for theologians but lights for lost travelers. They need no additions to make them clear.

TWO

The Gospel of the Kingdom:
Matthew's Gospel

Matthew's Gospel is the first book of the New Testament, not because it was written first—some of Paul's epistles take that honor—but because it is the bridge between the Old and New Testaments.

Matthew's main point and purpose in writing, the conclusion of his whole twenty-eight-chapter argument, the verdict that all 1,071 verses of evidence point to, is this: to prove to his fellow Jews that Jesus is the One to whom all the Jewish prophets point: the Messiah, the Christ, the King of the Jews, the founder of the Kingdom of God. Matthew's Gospel is written by a Jew to Jews about the Jew who was crucified for claiming to be the King of the Jews.

Because Matthew was concerned about convincing the Jews, he uses far more Old Testament quotations and references than any other Gospel writer: forty direct quotations from the Old Testament and sixty other references to Jewish prophecies. Often these have the connecting phrase, "As it is written in the prophet ...", or, "This was done to fulfill what was spoken by the prophets ..."

That's also why Matthew refers nine times to Jesus as the "son of David". The Messiah was to be the literal descendent of David.

That's also why Matthew begins with Jesus' genealogy, tracing Him back to David and then to Abraham, the first Jew, through His foster-father Joseph rather than through His only biological parent, Mary. In accordance with the rules of Jewish genealogy, it was the father's lineage, not the mother's, that counted legally for royalty.

That's also why Matthew introduces Jesus' public ministry with John the Baptist, who pointed to Jesus, thus fulfilling the essential task of all the prophets. John is the last and greatest prophet of the old kingdom, the Old Covenant. Yet the least member of the new Kingdom is to be greater than John, the greatest of the old; of that we are assured by the King Himself (Mt 11:11).

John was the first prophet Scripture mentions in more than four centuries. The Word prepared His public ministry with silence—not just thirty years of silence, but over four centuries of it. Then He broke the silence and spoke the Word—Himself.

John sums up the teaching of all the prophets in two words: "repent" and "believe". Jesus repeats this two-word message many times. They are the two things we need to do to be saved, to enter God's Kingdom, to be justified and accepted by God, to go to Heaven, to be freed from sin, to live God's own life on earth, to be born again, to have the Holy Spirit live in us, to be in the state of grace, to become members of Christ's Mystical Body. All ten of these expressions refer to the same thing, the *unum necessarium*, the "one thing needful" (Lk 10:42).

Matthew had been a tax collector for the Roman rulers. To approximate the way the Jews felt about tax collectors (publicans), imagine all the nasty lawyer jokes you have ever heard. Then add the way people feel about IRS auditors, politicians, dentists, umpires, and Mafia hit men. Tax collectors could set their own rates over and above what their Roman masters required. Most of them lined their own pockets with extra money extorted from their own people. Thus they were regarded as both thieves and traitors. No one could have been a more unlikely convert, certainly no one a more unlikely saint. Yet when Jesus called Matthew to follow Him, he immediately left his office and his job (Mt 9:9). He had probably already heard Jesus' preaching and been moved by it. Jesus' timing was perfect, as usual. So was His choice of men. Many of the greatest saints were made out of the greatest sinners.

The fact that Matthew was one of the inner circle of twelve apostles means that Matthew's Gospel was written by a direct eyewitness to the events it describes (except for the narratives of Jesus' birth).

Matthew's Gospel has been called "the Gospel of the Kingdom". He emphasizes the kingly aspects of Jesus, as Luke emphasizes His priestly ministry and John His prophetic wisdom. The term *Kingdom* appears fifty times, and *Kingdom of heaven* thirty-two times. What is this Kingdom?

It is His Church, the new Israel, where God is known and worshipped, where sins are not only forgiven but removed, where eternal life is poured out for all her citizens. This is not a political kingdom, but a spiritual one. But Matthew also clearly presents Jesus as establishing a visible institution, headed by visible men. Though the Church is spiritual, not political, she is also visible—just as you are spiritual (you have a soul), yet visible.

Christ made Peter the "Rock", the foundation and ruler of His Church on earth (Mt 16:13–19) after Peter confessed the reality the Church has always most centrally confessed and taught: "You are the Christ, the Son of the living God." Jesus replied, "Flesh and blood has not revealed this to you, but my Father who is in heaven." For nearly twenty centuries the Church has always claimed that her message is from God, not from man, and therefore has divine authority. This claim is the fundamental scandal in the eyes of the world—the rock-hard offense that cannot be compromised. There is nothing she can do about it, for she is not the author of her message and has no author-ity to change it, only to deliver it, to announce it, to proclaim the good news, the "deposit of faith". She *interprets* this data, but she does not edit it.

Jesus then changed Simon's name to Peter ("Rock," or "Rocky"). In Judaism, only God can change your name, for only God designed your identity and your name in the first place. (Your name is not just a label but signifies your real identity.) Thus God changed Abram's name to Abraham and Jacob's name to Israel. But if an Orthodox Jew legally changed his own name, he would be excommunicated. Jesus' giving Simon a new name, then, was a claim to divinity.

After singling out Peter as the rock on which He would build His Church, He gave an incredible authority to this Church: "I will give you the keys of the kingdom of heaven, and whatever you bind (prohibit) on earth will be bound in heaven, and whatever you loose (permit) on earth will be loosed in heaven." The actions of "binding" and "loosing" in Heaven are verbs in the perfect tense, meaning that when Peter binds or looses, it will already have been accomplished in Heaven—that is, Peter follows the will of God in Heaven and not the reverse.

Jesus' last words in Matthew's Gospel also speak of this kingly authority. It is called the "great commission": "*All* authority in heaven and on earth has been given to me. Go therefore and make disciples of *all* the nations, baptizing them in the name of the Father and of the Son and of the Holy Spirit, teaching them to observe *all* things that I have commanded you; and lo, I am with you *always*, even to the end of the age" (Mt 28:18–19 *NKJV*, emphasis mine). Please note the four "alls".

Matthew shows Jesus' authority over *death* by His Resurrection.

Matthew shows Jesus' authority over *sin* by His forgiving sins. Those who heard Him claim this authority immediately perceived it as a claim to divinity. They protested, "Who can forgive sins but God alone?" (Mk 2:7).

Matthew shows Jesus' authority over *nature* by His miracles, especially the series of ten miracles he includes in chapters 8 and 9. These show His power over not only nature but disease and death as well, and even their ultimate source, the devil.

Chapter 12 is the turning point in Christ's ministry. There the Pharisees reject Jesus as Messiah and even claim His power comes from the devil. After this, Christ begins to teach in parables, which His enemies do not understand; He begins to teach more to His own disciples and less in public; and He begins to emphasize His impending death.

Matthew interrupts his fast-moving narrative five times by long discourses, each ending with the set phrase "Jesus finished" (7:28; 11:1; 13:53; 19:1; 26:1). These five discourses are: (1) the "Sermon on the Mount" (chaps. 5–7), (2) missionary instructions to the disciples (chap. 10), (3) parables of the Kingdom (chap. 13), (4) on the cost of discipleship (chap. 18), and (5) the Olivet discourse on the end of the world (chaps. 24–25).

This last discourse shows that the Gospel was written prior to A.D. 70 when Jerusalem was destroyed—an event Jesus *predicts* in this discourse. The event is often used by modernist Scripture scholars to "prove" that Matthew was written *after* A.D. 70. The presupposition is that miracles such as predictive prophecy are impossible. But in that case Jesus' prophecies have been faked, and Matthew is a liar. (The scholars are seldom forthright enough to say that!)

The Greatest Sermon Ever Preached

The most famous part of Matthew is surely the "Sermon on the Mount". It can be printed on a single page and read in fifteen minutes. Yet its influence on the world has been greater than that of any other sermon ever preached.

The high moral standards of this sermon have often been thought to be so impractical and impossible that it has been interpreted as a morality only for an elite circle of saints and mystics. Or it has been thought to describe how we will live in Heaven, but not on earth. Finally, some consider this teaching an "interim ethic" (Albert Schweitzer's term), which could be lived only for a short time before Christ's Second Coming. In this scenario, only if we shared Christ's belief that the end was near could we live in such a detached and unselfish way. This idea that true morality must be based on a false conception of history is self-refuting.

But what *is* the right answer? The problem is the extreme difficulty of "turning the other cheek" and "going the extra mile" and avoiding hate and lust as well as murder and adultery. There are two possible solutions.

The first solution is suggested by the incident with the rich young ruler in 19:16–22. The solution is that the law is deliberately too difficult for us. Jesus is *not* giving us a morality He thinks we *can* practice, but a morality He knows we *can't*. For morality is not salvation. The moral law is not the good news, the operation; it is the bad news, the diagnosis, the X-ray. It is law, not grace; law correctly and purely interpreted.

The Pharisees had misinterpreted obedience to the moral law as a performance, as external behavior. And they obeyed it to the letter. But Jesus says that God demands more, not less, than the strict observances of the Pharisees; He demands a pure *heart*. For God is a lover, not a machine. He wants not just behavior of a certain kind, but persons of a certain kind, persons who are "perfect, as your Father in heaven is perfect" (5:48). The law shows us what we must do *and can't do*. Then and only then are we in the market for grace and salvation.

The second answer is that although we cannot, God can accomplish this transformation in us. Matthew 5 to 7, like 1 Corinthians 13, describes the love-life that is natural to God, not to us. It is supernatural to us. But it is what starts to happen in us when Christ gets inside.

Many modern readers dislike Matthew's Gospel because of its hard sayings, its warnings against riches and worldliness, its announcement of divine justice and judgment, and its demand for good works. If we dislike this book, then this is precisely the book we need most. For we need to know the whole Gospel. It is precisely those aspects of it that we still find repellent and try to avoid that we need most—not those we already understand and love.

Perhaps the most challenging passage in the whole Bible for the Christian is one of Jesus' last sayings before His trial and death, taken from the parable of the Last Judgment (25:31–46). It ends with these thought-provoking words: "Truly, I say to you, as you did it to one of the least of these my brethren, you did it to me" (v. 40). If a thousand Christians really believed that and lived accordingly, the next century would be shaped by a thousand saints.

Just the Facts: Mark's Gospel

Mark (also called John Mark—Acts 12:25) was probably a good friend of Saint Peter's. Peter called him "my son Mark" (1 Pet 5:13). Mark probably got his information about Jesus from Peter. Ancient writers called Mark "Peter's Gospel" for that reason. So even though its author was not an apostle or an eyewitness to all the events described, it is based on an eyewitness account (Peter's). It was widely known in the early Church that Mark not only translated for Peter while in Rome, but Mark also is said to have written Peter's memoirs—which many think is the Gospel of Mark (see Eusebius' *Hist. eccl.* 3.39.15).

Mark was probably the "young man" who was "following Jesus" mentioned in 14:51–52, the naked "streaker" in the garden. It is usual for an ancient author to mention himself anonymously in this way. Compare John 21:20–24.

Mark later went on missionary journeys with Paul and Barnabas, his relative (Acts 12:25; Col 4:10). He had a falling-out with Paul (Acts 13:13; 15:37–39) and was later reconciled (2 Tim 4:11). He went to Rome, like Peter and Paul, and probably wrote his Gospel there. Tradition says he was martyred in Alexandria.

Because Mark wrote for Roman readers, he omitted the things in Matthew that would be meaningful only to Jews, such as Jesus' genealogy, references to Old Testament prophecies (which the Romans had never read), and Jewish laws and customs that Matthew expects his reader to know. Mark also interpreted for his Latin readers some words in Aramaic, the common language of the Jews in Palestine in the time of Christ.

The ancient Romans were in many ways like modern Americans. They were a practical, pragmatic people who emphasized deeds more than words, action more than theory. They got things done. In fact, they conquered the world! Since they admired people who got things done, Mark emphasizes these aspects of Jesus, especially His miracles. After all, Jesus was, among other things, the most effective man who ever lived.

But Jesus got things done differently than the Romans did: by grace, not by force. Mark presents Jesus not as conqueror but as servant (10:45). For example, He commands the forces of nature only by being obedient to His Father's will. Though His life was filled with humble service and ministry, it was for the glory of God the Father and the salvation of His brothers and sisters: exactly our practical model for the Christian life.

The distinctive word in Mark is "immediately", or "at once". It occurs forty-two times. Jesus obeys His Father's will "at once". He responds to human needs "at once". The power of His love flashed out suddenly, like sunlight. (It was Sonlight.) It was "love in action", not "love in dreams" (to quote Dorothy Day's favorite line, from Dostoyevsky). If we could learn just this one lesson, we would go very far toward deep personal sanctity and power to revolutionize our world. Mary did it by responding *at once*, "Be it done!" (Lk 1:38). Mark does not comment on the events he describes, or interpret their deeper meanings, as John does in his Gospel. He simply gives the facts, the fast-moving events of Christ's life and death. Mark is *data*.

He shows how Christ's words and deeds are one, especially in His miracles. The Greek word for *miracle* means "sign". These deeds were also words, signs, lessons. Mark includes eighteen of these "signs" in his short Gospel.

Two of the things these miraculous signs teach in Mark are: (1) Christ's identity as the Son of God, His divine power; and (2) His compassion and love in response to human needs. These two always go together in the Gospels. The Romans tended to separate them, to see power as unloving and love as unpowerful.

The let's-get-right-to-the-point style of Mark is evident from the very first verse: "This is the good news about Jesus Christ, the Son of God." This is just the book for busy Romans (and busy Americans) who want the "bottom line". In the words of Police Sergeant Joe Friday of *Dragnet*, "Just the facts, ma'am, if you please."

FOUR

The Great Physician: Luke's Gospel

Luke presents Jesus as the Great Physician, healer of bodies and souls. This emphasis was natural to him because Luke himself was a doctor.

Saint Paul called Luke "our beloved physician" (Col 4:14), and a popular novel about Luke uses that title. When I think of Luke, I think of Dr. "Bones" McCoy on *Star Trek*. He seems like your archetypical family doctor: down-to-earth, sensitive, compassionate, and thoroughly human. Matthew and his Gospel seem more kingly, like Captain Kirk. John and his Gospel seem more prophetic and philosophical and mystical, like Mr. Spock. But Luke seems more priestly and more doctorly, like "Bones" McCoy. Matthew emphasizes morality and the will. John emphasizes wisdom and the mind. Luke emphasizes compassion and the feelings. To complete the *Star Trek* analogy, Mark is the practical engineer Scotty.

Not only did Luke have a doctor's "bedside manner", he also had a doctor's careful, scientific method. Since he was not himself a firsthand eyewitness to the events of Jesus' life, as Matthew and John were, he says that he "carefully studied all these matters from their beginning" (Lk 1:3) so as to write "an orderly account" of them. None of the four Gospels means to be a complete, modern-style "scientific" biography, but Luke comes the closest. For instance, he includes the most information about Jesus' birth and infancy, a topic Mark and John omit entirely.

Luke was not an apostle or one of Jesus' disciples because he was not a Jew, but a Gentile convert, probably a Greek. He is probably the only Gentile writer in the Bible. If we compare Colossians 4:10–11 with the following verses 12–14, we see that Paul lists him with Gentile converts rather than with Jews.

Luke wrote for Gentile readers, especially Greeks. He translates all Hebrew and Aramaic terms into Greek and explains Jewish laws, customs, and geography to his readers, assuming they are not familiar with these things. He also possessed great skill in using the Greek language—so much so, in fact, that this book has been called the most beautifully written book in the world. Greek was almost certainly his native tongue, which was not the case with Matthew, Mark, and John.

Since Luke wrote to Gentiles, he traced Jesus' genealogy all the way back to Adam, the first human being. Matthew, who wrote to Jews, traced Jesus' ancestry back to Abraham, the first Jew.

Luke accompanied Paul on at least some of his missionary journeys. When Paul thought he was near death, he wrote, "Luke alone is with me" (2 Tim 4:11)—evidence of Luke's loyalty and closeness to Paul.

Luke and Acts are companion books. Comparing the two prefaces (Lk 1:1–4 and Acts 1:1–5) shows clearly that they have the same author. Their style and language are also very similar. Luke's name is not mentioned in either Luke or Acts, but all the most ancient sources call this book "the Gospel according to Luke."

Luke's Gospel and Acts were both written to Theophilus. No one knows who Theophilus was. His name means "friend of God". The title "your excellency" (Lk 1:3) indicates that he was quite powerful. He was probably also rich, for to have two books written and published was a very expensive proposition in an age when all books had to be copied by hand.

Each evangelist offers us a word picture of Jesus, the Word of God. But no two photographs of the same subject, like two reflections in a pool, are ever exactly alike due to differences in lighting, angle, speed, and composition. Each evangelist, like a photographer, highlights a different aspect of the infinite, inexhaustible, multi-faceted Christ. The aspect Luke highlights is His perfect humanity.

Thus Luke's favorite title for Jesus is "the Son of Man". His divinity is not hidden or minimized, by any means. In fact, it shines through even more clearly in the perfection of His humanity, especially His love. Luke repeatedly shows Christ's compassion for the poor, the needy, the sick, and the sorrowing, for example: the poor disciples (6:20); sinful women rejected by society (7:37), in particular, Mary Magdalene (8:2); the despised Samaritans (10:33); tax collectors (15:1); beggars (16:20–21); lepers (17:12); and the crucified, dying thief (23:43).

Luke emphasizes Jesus' sensitivity and feelings, probably because as a doctor he was himself especially sensitive to human suffering. As a doctor, Luke would also be fascinated with Jesus' miraculous healings.

The Greeks admired human perfection; they were the world's first humanists and the world's first idealists. So Luke shows Jesus as the answer to their quest, their ideal.

Luke also emphasizes grace and salvation, just as Paul does (especially in Romans and Galatians), for Luke was a close friend of Paul's and probably influenced by Paul's theological vision and emphasis. Without omitting or watering down law, justice, and judgment, Luke emphasizes God's universal grace in passages such as 2:32, 3:6 and 24:47. Compare Luke's theology of grace here with Pauline passages such as Romans 3:22–30 and Ephesians 3, and you will see the striking spiritual kinship.

To my mind, the two most distinctive and attractive features of Luke's Gospel are its emphasis on Mary and on the Holy Spirit. Both are mentioned far more often than in the other Gospels. The Holy Spirit is mentioned twenty-two times in Luke. He tells the story of Jesus' birth from Mary's point of view; Matthew tells it from Joseph's.

Mary and the Holy Spirit belong together, because they were united in spiritual marriage (see 1:35). The one who made Mary conceive Jesus was *not* Joseph, but God. As the Creed says, Jesus was "conceived by the Holy Spirit, born of the Virgin Mary". Just as an ordinary human marriage is indissoluble, so is Mary's spiritual marriage to the Holy Spirit.

Another typical emphasis in Luke is on prayer—something that necessarily flows from both the example of Mary and the presence of the Holy Spirit, because Mary is the ideal pray-er and the Holy Spirit is the source and inspiring principle of all prayer.

Luke includes three parables on prayer not found in the other Gospels: the midnight friend (11:5–8), the unjust judge (18:1–8), and the Pharisee and the publican (18:9–14). He also includes many of Christ's prayers: at His baptism (3:21), in the wilderness (5:16), before choosing His disciples (6: 12), at the transfiguration (9:29), before giving us the Lord's Prayer (11:1), for Peter (22:32), in the Garden of Gethsemane (22:44), and on the Cross (23:46).

Luke states Jesus' basic purpose in 19:10: "The Son of Man came to seek and to save the lost." The three parables in chapter 15 illustrate this basic point: the lost sheep, the lost coin, and the lost son (the "Prodigal Son").

The story of God's search for us, His lost children, has a beginning but no end. It continues in Acts, in all of history, and in the present life of the Church—that is, *our* lives. This is what the Church is: God's eyes and hands searching for His lost children. Even after He has found us, God is still searching for us in more aspects of our lives. We respond to this search every time we pray, "Thy kingdom come."

The fundamental drama of Luke's story of this search, his "story line", is created by human free will making its fundamental choice: Will we accept God in Christ, or will we reject Him? Though Luke is "upbeat", he is also realistic and honest and chronicles the hard-hearted human rejection of this soft-hearted, compassionate God. As Christ reveals Himself and His claims more clearly and publicly, He is rejected all the more.

The turning point in this drama comes in chapter 11, when the Pharisees conclude that Jesus has (or is) a demon. Jesus now knows that they are beyond hope since they have committed the "unpardonable sin" (Lk 12:10)—the sin against the Holy Spirit, the sin of deliberate, hard-hearted, impenitent refusal of the light of truth.

Then comes the last, fatal journey to Jerusalem to die, prefaced by the ironic "triumphal entry" on Palm Sunday.

Before He is captured and killed, Jesus gives His disciples long instructions (which Matthew and John also recount). The topics that Luke emphasizes in these private instructions are: prayer, fidelity, gratitude, repentance, humility, discipleship, service, forgiveness, evangelism, and readiness for His Second Coming. The common theme to all these topics is that this is the business His Church is to be in. This is the Church's business card. We would do well as members of the Church to read these instructions prayerfully and then act on them.

The story does not end with His death, or even with His Resurrection or ascension. A new phase in the story begins with the coming of the Holy Spirit in Acts. For this is "the never-ending story". It is "the greatest story ever told". And we are in this very same story still.

FIVE

The I AM Reveals Himself: John's Gospel

Long-standing tradition has identified John the author of the fourth Gospel with John "the disciple Jesus loved" (13:23; 19:26; 20:2; 21:7, 20). He was the one to whom Jesus entrusted His mother when He was dying on the Cross (19:26–27). He was the youngest of the apostles and lived the longest—until the time of the emperor Trajan (A.D. 98–117). We know this from Irenaeus, who was a disciple of Polycarp, who was, in turn, a disciple of John. He was one of the "inner circle" of Peter, James, and John. Most importantly, he was an eyewitness to the events he describes in his Gospel (1:14; 19:35; 21:24–25; see 1 Jn 1:1–3).

It has been a virtual touchstone of ideological acceptability in modernist theological circles to date this Gospel after John's death in the second century and to hold that not John but "the Johannine community" wrote it. But this position is not based on any conclusive evidence in the text itself or on any evidence at all from history and the earliest tradition. It is rather based on a theological prejudice against John's "high Christology", that is, his strong emphasis on Christ's divinity. The belief that this Gospel is not historically accurate because it was not written by an eyewitness (John the apostle), and that Jesus never really said the uncomfortable things this Gospel says He said—this is simply assumed and asserted as "the accepted results of modern scholarship". In my opinion, this is what students call "a snow job".

The case *for* John the apostle as author is very strong. First, the author's knowledge of Jewish customs and geography indicates that he was a Jew.

Second, his attention to numbers (2:6; 6:13; 6:19; 21:8; 21:11) and names (1:45; 3:1; 11:1; 18:10) indicates that he was a contemporary and an eyewitness, as he claims to be (1:14; 19:35; 21:24–25).

Third, he refers to himself as "the disciple Jesus loved". The other three Gospels all name Peter, James, and John as the inner circle. Peter cannot be the author because he is referred to as another person than "the disciple Jesus loved", and James cannot be the author because he was martyred too early (Acts 12:1–2). This leaves only John.

Fourth, a papyrus was discovered in Egypt (the Rylands Papyrus 52) containing parts of John 18, which has been dated to A.D. 135. This suggests a first-century date for the original Gospel, for the papyrus would have required considerable time to be copied and circulated.

Finally, all the early Church Fathers ascribe this Gospel to John, including Irenaeus, Clement of Alexandria, Theophilus of Antioch, and Origen.

The Gospel is arranged topically, not strictly chronologically. The central topic is the identity of Jesus. He is the great mystery man. People ask of others, "*Who* is He?" but of Jesus, "*What* is He?" They ask where He is *from*—not His hometown but His home world. His startling answer is that He is from Heaven, from God. He is the most incredible thing that has ever happened: the eternal God has stepped into the world of time He created.

The identification of the man Jesus with the eternal Logos, or Divine Mind, is first asserted in the magnificent, mystical prologue in chapter 1. Then it is gradually unfolded both by Jesus' *words*, which more and more clearly claim divinity, and by His *deeds*, especially His miracles.

John arranges Jesus' words around seven "I AM" statements:

1. "I AM the bread of life" (6:35, 48);
2. "I AM the light of the world" (8:12; 9:5);
3. "I AM the door" (10:7, 9);
4. "I AM the good shepherd" (10:11, 14);
5. "I AM the resurrection and the life" (11:25);
6. "I AM the way, the truth, and the life" (14:6); and
7. "I AM the true vine" (15:1–5).

"I AM" is the divine name God revealed to Moses from the burning bush (Ex 3:14). It is the name no Jew ever even pronounces, because to speak the name "I" is to claim to bear it. Exodus 3:14 is the only time God ever revealed His own essential name, as distinct from His relations and appearances to us (for example, as Lord, Creator, Father). In Hebrew, this name is called the sacred tetragrammaton or four-consonant name, JHWH. No one knows for certain how to pronounce it because the vowels were not written down and it was not spoken. (The old guess was "Jehovah" and the new guess is "Yahweh.") However He pronounced it, when Jesus spoke this unutterable name, claiming it for Himself, He was clearly claiming divinity.

The most explicit occasion of all is in the passage 8:58: "Truly, truly I say to you, before Abraham was, I AM." The Jews' reaction to this was a clear and logical one: they tried to kill Him. For if He was not God, He was the most wicked blasphemer in history and the most worthy of death. This is one of Christianity's oldest apologetic arguments: *aut deus aut homo malus*: "either [he is] God or a bad man." The only thing Jesus couldn't possibly be is the very thing nearly everyone except orthodox Christians say He was: a good man, but only a man.

People are complex. There are many attitudes we can take toward any person who ever lived—except to Jesus. There are only two possible attitudes to Him. John shows them emerging more and more clearly as the story unfolds, like two characters coming out of hiding. Either He is God, as He claimed to be, and must be worshipped, adored, loved, believed, and obeyed; or else He is the most dangerous liar or lunatic in history. John makes every honest reader choose between these two attitudes to Jesus because Jesus Himself did exactly that.

John arranges his story of Christ's life around seven signs (miracles). Where each of the other evangelists record many miracles, John chooses only seven. But he carefully records people's reactions of belief and disbelief after each one. This culminates in the crucifixion, where unbelief seems to triumph—until Easter Sunday.

John emphasizes how Jesus was hated and rejected. He never fit people's prejudices, categories, ideologies, or set agendas. All were amazed at Him. Some were enthralled, and some were scandalized. Teachings like the one about eating His Body and drinking His Blood (6:58–69) sorted out His hearers into two camps: those who said, "This is a hard saying; who can listen to it?" (6:60) and those who said, "Lord, to whom shall we go? You have the words of eternal life" (6:68).

These are the only two camps that will ever be for all eternity. John shows us, more clearly than any other writer, the ultimate spiritual geography, the eternal map, behind the drama of belief versus unbelief. C. S. Lewis summarized the map this way: "Although there were a thousand paths by which he might walk through the world, there was not one of them that did not lead, in the end, either to the Beatific or the Miserific Vision."

The seven signs around which John organizes this drama are:

1. changing water to wine (2:1–11);
2. healing the nobleman's son (4:46–54);
3. healing the paralytic (5:1–16);
4. feeding the five thousand (6:1–13);
5. walking on the water (6:16–21);
6. healing the man born blind (9:1–7); and
7. raising Lazarus from the dead (11:1–44).

These seven miracles supply the seven basic human needs, both physically and spiritually:

1. wine symbolizes joy (see Ps 104:15);
2. physical health symbolizes spiritual health (virtue);
3. physical power and mobility symbolize spiritual power;
4. bread symbolizes "the bread of life", spiritual nourishment;
5. overcoming sea and storm symbolizes faith overcoming fear;
6. physical sight symbolizes spiritual sight (wisdom); and
7. resurrection from physical death symbolizes salvation from eternal death.

Thus Christ saves completely. Joy, virtue, power, life, faith, sight, and immortality replace thirst, disease, paralysis, hunger, fear, blindness, and death.

Jesus speaks much in this Gospel of eating and drinking and life and death. There are two words in Greek for "life": *bios* (natural life) and *zoe* (supernatural life). *Zoe* is the word John uses for what Jesus offers us. This is a life natural to God but supernatural to us. It includes divine power over nature via miracles, over selfishness via *agape* love, and over death via resurrection.

But no one can give what he doesn't have. The practical importance of the dogma of the divinity of Christ is this: Christ can give us supernatural life only if He has it Himself, by nature. The case for Jesus' divinity is also the case for our salvation.

John presents a compelling case, including many kinds of evidence, for the incredible claim that this man of flesh and blood was God incarnate.

First, most obviously, there are His miracles. These are signs (*semeia*) of His divinity, and of our own supernatural destiny. Only a supernatural being can perform supernatural acts.

A second, even clearer sign is His Resurrection. This is the final, dramatic, climactic proof of who He is. You just might come up with some natural explanation for other miracles if you were desperate to do so, but not for conquering death. Thus John goes into greater detail about Jesus' post-Resurrection appearances than the other evangelists.

A third piece of evidence is Jesus' character. It is as far as it could possibly be from that of a liar or a lunatic. He is good, wise, mature, clever, compassionate, and trustworthy. This is exactly the opposite sort of person from the madman who thinks he is God or the charlatan who dupes dumb disciples for private profit, power, and prestige, like Jim Jones or Reverend Moon.

Fourth, He forgives sins—all sins. "Who can forgive sins but God alone?"

Fifth, He changes people's lives, characters, destinies, and even their names. Your name tells your self. Only God gives you that.

Insistently, repeatedly, and step by step John builds the case for Jesus' divinity and challenges each reader with His claim to be not just *the* Savior but the *reader's* Savior. How the reader responds is literally a matter of life or death. This book is, simply, the most important book ever written. It is the book of life.

No book lays it out more plainly. John tells us explicitly why he wrote his Gospel in 20:31. (How can so many scholars *discuss* the issue, as if there were some secret code or hidden agenda only the scholars knew?) It is the Gospel in a nutshell: "[T]hese things are written that you might believe that Jesus is the Christ, the Son of God, and that believing you may have life (*zoe*) in his name."

SIX

The Gospel of the Holy Spirit: Acts

Christians in the first century were called "these men who have turned the world upside down" (Acts 17:6). How did they do it? How can we do it again?

The Acts of the Apostles is like a mystery and adventure novel. The mystery is how twelve men who were mostly peasants and fishermen changed the world more than any other group has ever done. What was their secret? The adventure moves through life-and-death situations, black magic, real miracles, murder, shipwreck, trials, torture, stoning, prison, earthquake, encounters with angels, conspiracy, and conversion. It leaves you breathless, like an Indiana Jones movie.

Two of the three main characters are Saints Peter and Paul. Peter was the first pope, the "Rock" on which Christ promised to build His Church. Paul was like a whirlwind. He was the greatest missionary of all time. No person ever did more to Christianize the world than Paul. If we need more rocks and whirlwinds in the Church today, maybe we should go back to this book for our models.

But the main character in Acts is Jesus Christ. Acts is a continuation of Luke's Gospel (read Lk 1:1–4; then Acts 1:1). Just as the Gospel is the story of Christ, Acts is the story of the Body of Christ, the Church.

This book brings us back to basics. It shows us what the Church most basically is: a conspiracy of love for a dying world, a spy mission into enemy-occupied territory ruled by the powers of evil, a prophet from God with the greatest news the world has ever heard, the most life-changing and most revolutionary institution that has ever existed on earth.

The Church is not just a human institution. It is not just an organization but an organism. Just as your body is not simply a bunch of cells, the Church is not simply a collection of human beings. Just as your soul is the life of your body, the Holy Spirit is the life of the Church.

Acts has been called "the Gospel of the Holy Spirit". That's why after Jesus' ascension it begins with Pentecost, the birth-day of the Church, the coming of the Holy Spirit. That same Spirit is the secret power that turned murderers into martyrs and sinners into saints. He planned and directed the whole plot of Acts. He empowered and inspired its human actors. The Holy Spirit is the real hero of the story. (Yes, "He", not "it". He's a person, like the Father and the Son, not a "force".)

The first part of Acts tells the story of the Church in the East, in Jerusalem and Antioch. The storyline centers on Peter, the Apostle to the Jews. The second part tells of the Church in the Roman West and centers on Paul, the Apostle to the Gentiles. Together these two great saints-martyrs-evangelists-missionaries are the joint "pillars of the Church".

Luke, the author, was Paul's companion on his missionary journeys around the Roman world. That's why he often uses "we" (for example, see Acts 16, 20, and 27). The action begins in Jerusalem and ends in Rome, the center of the ancient world, with Paul, a prisoner in the emperor's household, mak-ing converts everywhere and waiting to be martyred.

How is this story of ancient times relevant to us and our world today? Our world is just as corrupt, just as hard and proud, just as violent, just as needy, as the world was then. This book gives us the pattern for turning it upside down again.

We have the same Church, the same power source (the Holy Spirit), the same good news, and the same last orders from our Lord, "Go therefore and make disciples of all nations" (Mt 28:19). No force on earth can stop us except our own laziness and lack of faith.

We need to recapture the forward-looking optimism of the apostles in Acts. After Jesus left them and ascended to Heaven, you would think they would now look back to the past, the glorious time when He had been with them. But no, they looked to the future, for the future was to be even more glorious. Jesus Himself had told them that it would be better for them if He left and sent them the Holy Spirit (Jn 16:7).

How could this be *better*? Wouldn't it be better if we had Jesus still physically, humanly present? No. When He was here, His disciples still misunderstood Him. Only when He sent the Spirit could they begin the tremendous tasks narrated in this book.

Why? Because God the Father is *outside* us, and God the Son *beside* us, but God the Holy Spirit is *inside* us. (This is only a view of the *roles* of the three Persons of the Godhead; of course, there are not three Gods—one outside us, one inside us, and one beside us.)

Being *inside* another is maximum intimacy. Intimacy is what love aims at, and God is love. The whole Bible is the love story between God and His people, His Church. Acts begins the third and last and most intimate stage of all.

The Church is the most powerful force on earth not only because she has the highest ideal above her, but above all because she has the greatest power within her. This book shows us what that power can accomplish.

The Holy Spirit, the Church's Power Source

Acts begins with Jesus' ascension. But this is not the end of the story. It is the beginning. With a sense of mounting excitement, the reader turns, like the apostles, from the departing Jesus to the coming Holy Spirit.

The physical presence of Jesus wasn't enough. If the Holy Spirit hadn't come, Christians could never have won the world. Here is shocking evidence for that, in the form of one of the stupidest questions ever asked. After teaching His apostles for forty days the meaning of His Kingdom (1:3), Jesus gets this question: "Lord, will you at this time restore the kingdom to Israel?" (1:6). In other words, "Your kingdom *is* a political kingdom, a this-worldly kingdom, isn't it? Are we finished with all this spiritual stuff now and can we get down to the 'bottom line' of kicking out those awful Romans and liberating our nation? That's what you came for, right?"

Not until the Spirit came did they understand. Not until the Spirit came did they have the spiritual power to win hearts and minds. Jesus knew that. That's why He told them *not* to go out to all the world and preach the Gospel, not yet (1:4–5). That would have been like trying to pull a plow with a kitten, or light up a city with a flashlight. There was a power shortage.

The Spirit is as necessary as Jesus. The Spirit is like a plug, Jesus is like electricity in the wires, and the Father is like the dynamo that generates the electricity. You need to plug into the power. Having an ideal, a blueprint, without the power to live it produces only a sense of failure, frustration, and guilt. Only God the Holy Spirit can empower us to live the life that God the Son lived and God the Father commanded.

That is the secret of the Church. That is the reason for her staying power, her enduring through centuries of persecution, her saints and martyrs, her profundity of doctrine, her infallibility and consistency throughout two thousand years. Nothing but God working inside her, not just outside her or beside her, nothing less than God the Holy Spirit as the soul of the Church, could perform this miracle in history.

Thus, this book, which is a history of the early Church, begins with Pentecost, the descent of the Holy Spirit. Pentecost is the birthday of the Church. Just as God breathed His Spirit into Adam and turned mere "dust of the earth" into a man (Gen 2:7), so He again breathed His Spirit into a band of confused, weak human beings and turned them into the one and only thing on this earth that the gates of Hell themselves will never prevail against, the one thing we can be certain will last until the end of time: the Church, Christ's own new Body.

You see the change the Holy Spirit makes most strikingly in Peter. Read all the passages in the four Gospels that refer to Peter, and you will see how confused and weak he is. Then read all the passages in Acts, beginning with his Pentecost sermon, that mention Peter. You see a new man, a real Rock for the first time.

His impromptu sermon on Pentecost converted three thousand people (2:41). It was so effective that after it was over, his listeners asked not, "What should we think?" but, "What should we do?" (2:37). When the great orator Cicero made a speech before the Roman senate, all the senators said, "How well he speaks!" But they remained seated. When the great general Demosthenes addressed his Greek troops, they stood up, clashed their swords upon their shields, and shouted, "Let us march!" Peter is now like Demosthenes, not Cicero.

Peter's answer to their question, "What shall we do?" summarizes the whole Bible, all three parts of God's plan for our redemption. First, the Old Testament prophets, culminating in John the Baptist, focus on one thing: "Repent." Turn away from sin and back to God. Second, the Gospels show us the way to be incorporated into Christ and receive His forgiveness: "And be baptized, every one of you, in the name of Jesus Christ for the forgiveness of your sins." But there is a third part too: "And you shall receive the gift of the Holy Spirit" (2:38).

Then, as if he were looking over the heads of his immediate audience and down the centuries to us, he added, "For the promise [of the Holy Spirit] is to you *and to your children and to all that are far off, every one whom the Lord our God calls to him*" (2:39, emphasis mine).

A poor European family was immigrating to America. They had saved for years to buy the tickets. The only food they had with them for the journey was bread and cheese. After a few days, the little boy said to his father, "I can't stand this any more. Nothing but cheese sandwiches. Please give me some money for some real food." The father gave him his last nickel and told him to buy something in the ship's dining room. (This was 1900.) The boy came back in two hours, fat and happy. "I had soup and steak and ice cream and pie. It was great!" "What?" the father asked. "Did you buy all that with a nickel?" "Oh, no, Dad. The food's free. It comes with the ticket."

The Church today is surviving on cheese sandwiches. The Holy Spirit is steak and pie. He's part of the package deal, part of God's plan for us. He comes with the ticket. The great things the Church accomplished in Acts can be done in our day, if we only had the power. That power is available for the asking. Read and pray Luke 11:5–13.

Peter, the First Pope, and Stephen, the First Martyr

Acts tells the dramatic story of the early Church—a Church that was very poor in material wealth and power, but very rich in spiritual wealth (full of saints and martyrs) and power (miracles).

At other times in the Church's history, especially the Renaissance, it was just the reverse. The Church had amassed great worldly wealth but had gotten weak and corrupt. That contrast is the point of the story of a Renaissance pope who was proudly showing a saintly friend all the riches of his treasury. "See?" he said, "Peter can no longer say, 'I have no silver or gold.'" "No," replied the friend, "but neither can he say, 'In the name of Jesus, rise and walk!'"

The pope and his friend were referring to the story in Acts 3. Peter and John, newly filled with the power of the Holy Spirit at Pentecost, go into the temple and see a man who had been lame from birth. The man was begging for money, but instead of material wealth he found spiritual wealth in Peter, who said to him, "I have no silver or gold, but what I have, I give you: In the name of Jesus Christ of Nazareth, rise up and walk!"—and the man rose and walked.

The Renaissance pope said, "*Peter* can no longer say, 'I have no silver or gold'" because the chain of popes stretches back to Peter, whom Christ appointed when He said, "On this rock I will build my church" (Mt 16:18).

But the name *Peter* does not seem to fit him in the Gospels. It means "rock", but Peter is hardly "Rocky" before Pentecost. He is more like "Sandy". Peter is weak and vacillating, misunderstanding Christ, making mistakes (like fighting with his sword in the Garden of Gethsemane), and cowardly (denying Christ three times during His trial). Naming him "Rocky" is a joke, like naming a skinny man "Fats".

Yet in Acts Peter fulfills Jesus' prophecy about his name. He becomes a real rock. He leads the infant Church through persecutions, uncertainties, and hard times (let's not romanticize the early Church!), just as all his successors have done. (Only later were they called *popes*.)

Acts centers first on Peter. Then, beginning with chapter 9, it focuses on Paul. In both parts, we see the Church growing in the face of problems that would have destroyed any merely human institution.

Peter's boldness in Acts contrasts strikingly with his former cowardice. He dares to say straight out to the people who called for Jesus' crucifixion—and who might well have called for Peter's too—"[You] killed the Author of life" (3:15). But he adds, "I know that you acted in ignorance" (3:17). When commanded by the authorities to stop preaching the Gospel, he answered, "We must obey God rather than men" (5:29), and "we cannot but speak of what we have seen and heard" (4:20). His message is clear and uncompromising: "There is salvation in no one else, for there is no other name under heaven given among men by which we must be saved" (4:12).

Everyone wondered at Peter and the other apostles, just as they had wondered at Jesus: "Now when they saw the boldness of Peter and John, and perceived that they were uneducated, common men, they wondered, and they recognized that they had been with Jesus" (4:13). Everyone who met Jesus wondered at Him: His friends (whose wonder turned to worship), His enemies (whose wonder turned to bitter hatred), and those who just didn't know what to think. The wonder of Jesus now rubs off onto the apostles.

In chapters 6 and 7, we find the story of Stephen, the first Christian martyr. Wherever Christianity is strong, there have always been martyrs; wherever there have been Christian martyrs, Christianity has been strong. "The blood of the martyrs is the seed of the Church", said Tertullian, a prominent thinker of the early Church.

It's not that Christianity teaches that you should seek out martyrdom, but that whenever the world sees great

Christians, it fears and hates them, as the decayed tooth
hates and fears the dentist, or the cancer fears the surgeon.

Jesus promised, many times, in the Gospels, that His followers would be hated, persecuted, and martyred, just as He
was (see Jn 15:18–20; 16:33; 16:2; 17:14; Lk 6:22; Mt 10:22;
24:9).

In those parts of the world in which the Church has been
persecuted in this century, she has become stronger: China,
Russia, Poland, former East Germany, and Czechoslovakia.
But wherever being a Catholic is easy, the Church becomes
weaker: France, Holland, England, former West Germany,
America, Canada, and even Italy.

After fifty years of China welcoming Christian missionaries (1905–1956), there were only two million converts. But
after thirty years of persecution under Mao Tse Tung, there
were an estimated twenty-five million Christians in China
by 1986.

The martyr Stephen does not mince words or beg for
mercy. He sounds like an Old Testament prophet (see 7:51–
53). Yet as he dies under the stoning of the Jewish leaders in
Jerusalem, he prays, "Lord, do not hold this sin against them"
(7:60), just as Jesus prayed on the Cross, "Father, forgive them"
(Lk 23:34). This combination of toughness and love runs
throughout the Bible, for it is what God Himself is like: neither wimpy nor nasty. The apostles are like Jesus now, for
they are filled with *His* Spirit. This is the power that fueled
the Church like a rocket ship through history.

The Conversion of Paul (Acts 9)

What happened in Acts 9 is crucial for the history of the
Church and the world that it was about to convert and change.
It is the conversion of Paul, the greatest Christian missionary

of all time, the one who more than any other single individual after Christ was responsible for converting half the
world. Most of the rest of Acts is about him, and most of the
rest of the New Testament after Acts is written by him (13 or
14 epistles). This chapter tells how Saul became Paul.

God changed his name and his life. As we saw with Peter,
only God can change your name, for the ancient Jews did
not think of a name as a mere label given by parents, but as
signifying your real, true identity, which only God can give
you.

Like Abram (Abraham), Jacob (Israel), Simon (Peter), and
Saul (Paul), we all are destined to have a new name if we are
on the road to Heaven (see Rev 2:17). This is a name we do
not yet know; only God knows it. Do you think the change
that happened to Saul on earth in Acts is great? You are destined for an even greater change in Heaven.

Let's look at Saul before his conversion first, since the rest
of Acts centers on Paul after his conversion.

The first thing we learn about him is that he was present
at the stoning of Stephen, the first Christian martyr (chap. 7).
He watched the coats of the men who threw the stones.
And he consented to his death (8:1).

The next thing we hear is that he "was ravaging the church,
and entering house after house, he dragged off men and
women and committed them to prison" (8:3). The "drag-
ging" was literal. The fact that he also put women in prison
was especially cruel and unusual.

We would call this man a "religious fanatic" and "bigot"
and probably dismiss him as hopelessly wicked. But that just
shows how different our thinking is from God's. God picks
out this man to become an apostle, a missionary, and a saint.

Why? Because God always surprises us. Throughout the
Bible, He never does the expected. He often chooses what

seems foolish in the eyes of the world to shame the worldly wise (see 1 Cor 1 on this, especially v. 27). We constantly forget that God's work does not fit human expectations.

Also, no one, however hate-filled and bigoted, is hopeless. If God can convert and save a murderer, do you think your sins are too much for him to handle?

A religious fanatic at least has passion. He's moving in the wrong direction, but at least he's moving. It's easier to move a car to the right if it's already moving to the left than if it's not moving at all.

God never made a saint out of a wimp. He wants lovers because He is love. He does not want wrongly directed love, but he does want love, not laid-back, "cool", blasé, detached, uncaring laziness.

At the beginning of chapter 9, we find Saul "still breathing threats and murder against the disciples". But on his way to Damascus to search for Christians to throw into prison, he is literally knocked off his high horse: "Suddenly a light from heaven flashed about him. And he fell to the ground and heard a voice saying to him, 'Saul, Saul, why do you persecute me?' And he said, 'Who are you, Lord?' And he said, 'I am Jesus, whom you are persecuting'" (9:3–5).

Saul must have been absolutely and totally dumbfounded. He had thought he was serving God and doing God's will by persecuting Christians. He had thought Christians were the worst blasphemers in the world, because they worshipped a human being who claimed to be God. Now God—the God Saul served with misdirected passion—speaks to him and says he is persecuting *Him*!

When Saul humbly asked, "Who are you, Lord?" that may well have been the first time in his life he admitted a mistake. (Fanatics are not usually humble.) And what a mistake! He didn't even know who God was—the God he worshipped and served, the God in whose name he was persecuting Christians. Saul suddenly gets an open mind. And into that opening steps Christ.

Notice the amazing fact that Jesus said to Saul that Saul was persecuting *Him*, even though Jesus was now ascended and in Heaven. For Saul was persecuting the Church. What a dramatic way to learn the identity of Christ and His Church!

When Paul later wrote in Ephesians 5 that Christ is the "Head" and the Church is His "Body", he meant this just as truly as the thing between your ears is your head and the thing it is perched on top of is your body.

Jesus had said to His disciples, "Truly, I say to you, as you did it not to one of the least of these my brethren, you did it not to me" (Mt 25:45). "Truly, I say to you" is a formula for "I really mean this, don't water this down, it's no exaggeration." So when we snub or exploit or abort our fellow human being, we snub or exploit or abort Jesus Christ.

Paul's conversion did not take him out of the war he had been fighting, but it put him on the other side and changed the weapons from physical to spiritual ones and from hatred to love. Christ chose Paul to suffer for Him rather than inflict suffering (9:16). Shortly after he is converted, those who had commissioned him to kill Christians (9:2) try to kill him (9:23).

To be converted is to become more like Christ. Christ did not fight, but He did not avoid a fight either. He went right into the center of the fight—where good and evil cross—and suffered on that Cross. Now Paul is ready to follow Him.

Are we?

If you were brought to trial on the charge of being a Christian, would there be enough evidence to convict you?

How Big Is Christianity? Acts 10–15

We take for granted today that Christianity is universal, for everyone. Acts 10–15 shows how this was not so obvious at first to the early Christians. Most of them were Jews. Judaism had always been a special divine revelation, for Jews only. We do not realize what a great shock it was to recognize that now, for the first time in history, the knowledge of the true God was to spread throughout the whole world.

Orthodox Jews, who believe in a real Messiah to come, do not prosyletize or send out missionaries to make converts, because their Old Testament prophets said that the knowledge of God was to "cover the earth as the waters cover the sea" *only* when the Messiah comes. And they do not believe that the Messiah has come yet (Jews who are not Orthodox do not usually believe in a literal Messiah, and they do not prosyletize either, but for other reasons.)

God had to teach this surprising new truth of Christianity's worldwide destiny to the two "pillars of the Church", Peter and Paul, in dramatic ways. He knocked Paul off his horse and shone a great light from Heaven on him to show him that Christianity was not a heretical sect but the truth for everyone (chap. 9). The fact that God would now reveal Himself to everyone, Gentiles as well as Jews, through Christ, was so shocking to Paul that he called it a great "mystery" in Ephesians 1:9–10 and 3:3–6.

God had to shatter *Peter's* narrowness too. He did this by sending him a strange vision (chap. 10) of a great sheet let down from Heaven with both kosher and non-kosher animals in it, commanding him to eat them all, contrary to Jewish dietary laws. The age of the law was over; Christ had begun the age of grace.

Even though it was not easy for Peter to change his life-long habits, he was open to God's leading (10:28–29, 34–35; 11:17) because he had been filled with the Holy Spirit at Pentecost. Peter now follows where his Master leads. Ever since this first pope, the Spirit has led the popes, and through them the Church, where He wants them to go.

Catholics believe in a single, visible Church. From the beginning, the single, visible Church has had authority over all Christians. This is evident in Acts 15 with the question of whether Gentile converts had to be circumcised and made Jews before they could be baptized and made Christians (see 15:5–6, 22–30). Peter clearly assumed a leading role and was the main speaker at this first Church council. Their decision is expressed in words claiming divine, not just human author-ity: "It seemed good to the Holy Spirit and to us" (v. 28). From the beginning, there was one Church for the whole world.

Also from the beginning there were divisions and disputes within the Church. Paul and Barnabas were good men (see 11:24; 15:37–40), yet they had an angry argument and sep-arated. Internal divisions are much harder for the Church to endure than external persecutions. Yet she endures both, for even the gates of Hell will never prevail against the Church Jesus built on the rock (Mt 16:18).

In chapter 12 King Herod kills James and imprisons Peter. But God has other plans for Peter, and no human force can confine God's plans. An angel frees Peter from prison, just as Psalm 91:11 and Revelation 3:7–8 promise.

This same wicked King Herod is struck dead when he blasphemously accepts the title of "a god" (Acts 12:21–23), just as Ananias and Sapphira were struck dead in chapter 5 when they lied to God. The armies of the supernatural world, both good and evil, are encountered in these extraordinary incidents, breaking through into our world. Another example of this is Elymas the Sorcerer (13:8–11), whose spiritual blindness breaks out in physical blindness. These are not fanciful myths but real miracles, told in a matter-of-fact, eyewitness style.

Acts is the history of a spiritual warfare between supernatural good and evil, Christ and Antichrist, powers from Heaven and Hell. The spiritual war becomes physical when Christians are persecuted. For instance, Paul is stoned almost to death (14:19) and later imprisoned (chap. 16).

Does the Gospel produce such reactions today? Indeed it does—at least wherever the true Gospel is preached, instead of some mild, popular, watered-down part of it.

Almost no one hates or persecutes you if you preach those parts of the Gospel that are popular today, such as peace, justice, compassion, and social action. But you are often hated and rejected today if you dare to say such unpopular things as these:

- that Jesus is not just one among many equal religious figures, but the only true God;
- that sin, judgment, and Hell are real;
- that sexual sins, like other sins, are really sins and need to be repented of and turned away from;
- that Christianity is not a moral fable but a supernatural, miraculous fact; or
- that there is objective truth and objective values, that people can be wrong, that "true for me" isn't enough.

The methods of persecution have changed. They don't stone believers today. They ostracize them socially and censor them in the media. The media (especially the movies) nearly always portray Christians as bigoted, rigid, harsh, intolerant, narrow-minded, and stupid. These are some of the stones thrown today: word-stones. But they cannot kill the truth, just as they couldn't kill Paul. Media censorship can't imprison the truth, just as Peter (chap. 12) and Paul and Silas (chap. 16) could not be imprisoned. When God opens doors, no one can close them.

God opened Gentile doors only after He gave the Jews the first opportunity. Wherever Paul went, he preached the Gospel first to the Jews (see Rom 1:16). Acts 13 tells how he did this at Antioch, showing how Jesus fulfilled the Jewish prophets, Jewish Scriptures, and Jewish history. A Jew who accepts Jesus as the Messiah today, just as in the first century, does not become a Gentile but a completed Jew.

But Paul's hearers reacted with envy and tried to kill him. In the first century, Jews in authority sometimes tried to kill Christians. Once Christians became part of the power structure, they often tried to kill Jews. No one has a monopoly on evil.

It was ironic that most first-century Jews rejected Christ while many Gentiles accepted Him, for God had entrusted His most complete revelation to the Jews. They should have known God better than anyone else and recognized Christ, for "like Father, like Son" (see Jn 8:19; 5:39).

Acts 17: How Christianity Went West

Acts 17 tells us why we in the Western world know about Christ today, as much of the Orient does not. It tells the dramatic story of why Christianity went to Europe rather than Asia—an event that changed the next two thousand years of world history.

It also tells the story of the first meeting of Christianity and Greek philosophy. These were the two strongest and most long-lasting spiritual forces in the ancient world. They are the two forces that have influenced the Western world more than any other. And they are the two forces from the ancient world that met and married and made the next great era of history, the Middle Ages.

The Holy Spirit was directing history by directing the apostles. In Acts 13:2, Luke writes, the Holy Spirit said, "Set apart for me Barnabas and Saul (Paul) for the work to which I have called them." (Notice how real and personal the Holy Spirit is. He is not just a force but a real Divine Person, who speaks and commands specifically and concretely. If the apostles had not been open and obedient to Him, God's plan for human history would not have been fulfilled. God uses human instruments; we the Church are His hands and feet.)

In Acts 16:6, Luke writes that they had "been forbidden by the Holy Spirit to speak the word in Asia". ("Asia" here means what was called "Asia Minor", that is, modern Turkey.) If the apostles had insisted on their own plans instead of following the Holy Spirit, they would have gone East with the Gospel instead of West. If they had done that, Europe would probably have remained pagan, Asia rather than Europe and America would have become the Christian continent, and we would probably not be Christians today.

This didn't happen, because Paul obeyed a dream God sent him, the "Macedonian vision": "A vision appeared to Paul in the night: a man of Macedonia [northern Greece] was standing beseeching him and saying, 'Come over to Macedonia and help us.' And when he had seen the vision, immediately we sought to go into Macedonia, concluding that God had called us to preach the gospel to them" (16:9–10).

So Paul worked his way down through northern Greece to Athens, the capital city and the home of Greek culture and philosophy. Here now for the first time, the two great forces of Christianity and Greek philosophy meet.

Athens was full of idols, and this "provoked" Paul (chap. 16). The whole ancient world, except for the Jews and the Christians, worshipped false gods (idols) and many gods (polytheism). Yet even here, Paul is able to make a positive point of contact.

The reason this could happen and the reason the Gospel took root there was that some of the Athenians were genuinely seeking the truth. They were honest, open-minded, and "devout" people (see 17:11–12, 17).

So when the philosophers (17:18) asked Paul to preach to them (17:20), Paul began by praising them for being "very religious" (17:22). Though their theology was wrong and idolatrous, their hearts were honest and seeking the truth about God.

In contrast, when Paul wrote to the Christians in Corinth, Greece's second city after Athens, he severely criticized them for their pride and arrogance, even though their theology was much more correct than the theology of the Athenian pagans.

Like Jesus, Paul gave his different audiences what each really needed. Humble and ignorant truth-seekers like the Athenians need encouragement and knowledge. Proud know-it-alls like the Corinthians need a dose of humility and even insult (see 1 Cor 1:18–3:23).

In fact, what Paul says in 1 Corinthians 3:18 is almost exactly what the wisest, best, and most famous Greek philosopher Socrates had taught four hundred years earlier: true wisdom consists in recognizing that we are *not* wise. Some of the philosophers Paul preached to in Athens had learned that Socratic spirit of humility and were thirsting for truth. Now finally their thirst was about to be quenched.

Socrates had been a stonecutter. He may have actually cut the very words Paul referred to in Acts 17:23 on the altar:

"To an unknown god", for he believed in one single God whom he did not claim to name or define, unlike most other Greeks, who believed in many gods, like Zeus and Athena.

Here now is the point of contact, like two wires crossing. Paul says something astonishing in 17:23: "The God you worship in ignorance, I now declare to you." Paul says that these Socratic, God-seeking Greek pagans were already worshipping the true God just by seeking Him, even though they did not know Him.

Incidentally, this is a very strong reason for believing that pagans can be saved. As Christ promised, all who seek, find (Mt 7:8).

First Paul approves the Athenians' initial step: admitting they did not know God and seeking Him. Then he takes them to the second step: he tells how God made Himself known to the Jews as the one supreme, perfect Creator and Father. Finally, he tells them about God incarnate, Christ the Son. It is a natural three-stage teaching that can be used as effectively with modern post-Christian pagans as it was used with ancient pre-Christian pagans by Paul.

It works because what was said by Pascal, the great seventeenth-century Christian philosopher, is true: "There are only three kinds of people: those who have sought God and found Him and now serve Him; those who neither seek Him nor find Him; and those who are busy seeking Him but have not yet found Him. The first are reasonable and happy, the second are unreasonable and unhappy, the third are reasonable but unhappy." The Athenians were in the third class. They were reasonable and wise because they were seeking, but not yet happy because they had not yet found.

Everyone in the third class eventually gets into the first, unless Christ's promise is a lie. But no one from the second class gets into the first. Only those who seek God, want God, and love God, find Him. We are saved by our love, not our knowledge; by our hearts being open to God. The pagan Western world was seeking God. That's why it found God and was converted. The modern world can be reconverted too. All it has to do is seek, as honestly and humbly as the ancient Greeks, and the story of Acts can come alive again today.

SEVEN

The Church in Acts and the Church Today

What's the difference between the Church in Acts and the Church today?

Essentially, nothing. It's the same Church: the Church Christ founded, the Church that teaches with His authority ("He who hears you, hears me", Lk 10:16), the Church to whom He promised that the gates of Hell and the power of death would never prevail against her (Mt 16:18).

But compared with the Church in Acts, there seems to be a spiritual power shortage today. When Paul asked the Christians in Ephesus, "Did you receive the Holy Spirit when you believed?" (19:2), he must have seen something missing there. I think he would ask us the same question today.

How do we stack up? Let's detail some of the specific results of the Holy Spirit directing the Church in Acts. Keep in mind that this is supposed to be normal, not abnormal.

1.   The Spirit is heard personally, directly, and concretely as a Person (see 21:4 and 23:11). He is not just an *object* of belief. He certainly is not thought of merely as a vague idea or force. How many of us know Him personally today?

2.   Miracles are done so powerfully through Paul that even his handkerchiefs are an agency for healing (19:11–12)! The

promises Christ made in the Gospels (see Mk 16:18) are literally fulfilled. For example, in Acts 28:3–6 Paul is bitten by
a poisonous scorpion on Malta and is unharmed. How many
miracles have happened in your parish lately?

3.   Demonic activity appears (19:13–19), and exorcism is
needed, for the devil does not sit idly by when heavenly
forces march boldly into spiritual battle. How many of our
clergy are trained to be exorcists?

4.   Confession, repentance, and turning away from sin
are clear and strong (19:18–19). Today when the idea of spiritual warfare is largely forgotten among Catholics, the practice of confession is infrequent and the sense of sin is weak.

5.   The faith is so strong that unbelievers are offended.
Spiritual warfare erupts as visible troubles, even riots (chap.
21). Why? No one feels threatened by a vague, wimpy faith.
But the idol-makers in Ephesus were threatened by the
Church's uncompromising condemnation of idolatry (19:23ff).

Today, the enemies of God fear His Church only when
she speaks boldly against modern idolatries, whether of sexual immorality, or of "freedom of choice" to murder unborn
babies, or materialistic consumerism, or trusting in war to
solve international problems. The true faith in its fullness is
bound to offend unbelievers. Christ is like chemotherapy to
the world's cancer. Worldliness fears holiness (see 24:25).

6.   Worship is such a joy that long church services are
common. In Acts 20, Paul preaches so long that a young
man, Eutychus, falls asleep, falls out of a window, and dies.
(God uses Paul to bring him back to life.) When did you last
attend a two-hour Mass?

7.   Christians are ready to die as martyrs (21:13). In the
next few centuries, many *were* martyred. They were willing
to die for Christ because they had found Christ more precious than life itself (see Phil 3:8). Can we say the same?

8. The "good news" is preached as historical fact, not mere "values"; and as *present* fact, not just past. Paul's speech at Jerusalem to the Jews who wanted to kill him (chap. 22) and his speech to the pagan king Agrippa (chap. 26) both center not on theology or ethics or argument, but personal testimony. He shares how he met Jesus.

Today, Fundamentalist churches are growing many times faster than the Catholic Church, especially in Latin America, largely because of this kind of appeal. You can't argue with the facts of changed lives.

9. The faith is not politicized, as it often is today. All political factions, left and right, are threatened and conspire against Paul. All the "powers that be" hate him for he serves not one of them, but a Higher Power. The true Church is neither the "establishment" nor a political "liberation" movement.

10. The Church is bold. Paul could have saved himself if he hadn't appealed to Caesar (25:12; 26:32), but he goes right to the top, refusing no risk and no task. He has total confidence, for "If God is for us, who is against us?" (Rom 8:31). He speaks directly, powerfully, without subtle "nuancing" like modern theologians, and without worrying about being "acceptable" like modern "Catholic" politicians (see 26:24–29).

11. Prophecies abound, and the Church is open to them (see 27:10, 22, 31 and 34). Have you heard any good prophecies lately?

12. Angels interact with humans (5:19; 8:26; 10:3; 12:7–11; 27:23), just as happened in the Old Testament, as recounted by Paul (7:30, 35, 38). This is part of the "package deal". Angels are real, not myths or symbols. Did you ever meet anyone who had met an angel?

13. Though tiny, the Church is famous, even notorious, just as Jesus was (28:22). They had "turned the world upside down" (17:6). They were "countercultural" and feared no

earthly establishment, for they served God, not a human power structure (5:29).

And we today? Are we turning the world upside down? Or is it turning us upside down?

Acts is meant to be not dead, rusty history but a pattern for the Church in all times, including the present time. Just as Stephen treated Moses' life not as dead history but as God's pattern of action that was being repeated in his own day (chap. 7), so we are meant to repeat in our day the acts of Acts.

It can happen again, if only we want it. Saint Francis of Assisi said, "Tell me, who do you think is the readier: God to give grace, or we to receive it?"

Not only *can* it happen again, but I think it *will* happen again. I think it is already beginning to happen again. Part of the reason is that John Paul II is in many ways like Saint Paul.

His whole religious life centers on the person of Christ, meeting Christ, obeying Christ.

He has traveled around the world like a missionary.

He has performed exorcisms (two at the Vatican).

He speaks boldly and plainly, offending his enemies.

He is ready to die as a martyr. He lived under Nazi and Communist persecution in Poland. He was shot and nearly killed.

When he preaches, he appeals to experience, not just theory.

He has experienced prophecies and healings, and other charismatic gifts of the Spirit.

I do not know whether he has ever seen an angel. But I would not be surprised.

Let us pray that God has raised up a second Paul to help convert the world a second time. For our civilization, like ancient Rome, is dying. Nothing can carry us through the second Dark Ages, into which we are moving, except the power that carried us through the first.

EIGHT

The Church's Treasure
Trove of Wisdom:
Introduction to the Epistles

In the Acts of the Apostles we glimpsed a slice of the early history of the Church whose apostles wrote the New Testament. The natural next step would be to read the writings of those apostles: the twenty-one epistles or letters in the New Testament. Most of their authors and recipients are mentioned in Acts; Acts is *about* the apostles, the epistles are *by* the apostles.

Both the Old and New Testaments are divided into three parts: books of history, wisdom literature, and prophecy. (That's the order in the Table of Contents.) The epistles are the New Testament's "wisdom literature", corresponding to Job, Psalms, Proverbs, Ecclesiastes, and The Song of Solomon in the Old Testament. While history focuses on the past and prophecy on the future, wisdom literature deals with eternal truths for all time.

Paul, the greatest missionary apostle, wrote the most epistles: thirteen, from Romans through Philemon. He and other apostles wrote many other letters too (some are mentioned in these epistles), but they are all lost. These twenty-one are the ones God providentially chose to preserve for us.

Romans comes first because it is the longest and also the most important for two reasons: (1) it was written to Christians in Rome, the capital of the world; and (2) it is the world's first systematic, logically organized Christian theology. Ever since, every orthodox Christian theologian has elaborated the same two essential themes as Romans: sin and salvation, the "bad news" and the "good news". Chapter 8 is, I think, the very best news, the most exalted and joyful chapter ever written.

First Corinthians offers an intimate look at many specific serious problems in this local church: factions, lawsuits, incest, divorce, conduct in church, relation to pagan religious practices, and charismatic gifts like "speaking in tongues". The two most important chapters are about Christian love (1 Cor 13) and the resurrection (1 Cor 15). Chapter 13 is probably the most famous chapter in the Bible.

Second Corinthians shows that many of the problems had not been solved. (Christians were not all models of wisdom and holiness then any more than now.) This letter is very personal and very emotional—more like a father talking to his problem children than like a theology professor to his students.

Galatians, like Romans, is about salvation by faith. The Galatians so missed this central point that Paul called their heresy of self-salvation "another gospel", that is, another religion, not Christianity. They thought they were saved by the law, that the way to Heaven was obeying the Ten Commandments, rather than faith in the One who said, "I am the Way, the Truth, and the Life. No one can come to the Father but through Me." Many religiously uneducated Catholics still believe this Galatian heresy today. They desperately need to read Galatians.

After reading Galatians, they should read James to get "the rest of the story", as Paul Harvey would say. Though James

doesn't come next in the Bible, I put it here because its basic
point is that "faith without works is dead", is not real faith.
It will not save you. Faith and good works are like the root
and flower of the same plant.

Ephesians is the Bible's greatest book about the Church as
the Body of Christ. It is a deep and exalted meditation on
the mystery of God's plan to save all men through Christ.

Philippians is full of personal intimacy, love, confidence,
and joy (the word is used fourteen times in four pages). It
contains some famous, eloquent, moving, and unforgettable
passages (2:1–11, 3:4–14, and 4:8).

Colossians centers on how enormous Christ is (1:13–20)
and how enormously He transforms our lives (3:1–17).

First Thessalonians is similar to Colossians. It contains a
famous passage about Christ's Second Coming (5:1–11) that
the Thessalonians misinterpreted. They left their jobs and
sat around waiting for the end of the world! So Paul corrected their mistake in his second letter to them (2:1–17).
Both letters are pastoral, personal, and practical.

First and Second Timothy were written to Paul's spiritual
son or "junior apostle". Paul gives Timothy kindly, fatherly
advice about how to be a good apostle, bishop, pastor, and
preacher. Titus is written to another bishop about the same
practical issues: doctrinal teaching, moral living, and church
organization—the three visible aspects of religion ("words,
works, and worship"). The two letters contain basic practical principles for the Church today as well as then.

Paul wrote the Letter to Philemon to persuade him to
receive back Onesimus, a runaway slave who had fled to Paul,
"no longer as a slave but as a beloved brother". It is a little
psychological masterpiece of reconciliation.

Hebrews (author unknown) is a systematic treatise on
Christianity and Judaism, about how the New Covenant

(Testament) fulfills and surpasses the Old; about the superiority of Christ to Moses and the Jewish Levitical priesthood. Chapter 11, on the heroes of the faith, and chapter
12, on endurance in troubles, are especially eloquent.

Peter, the apostles' leader and the Church's first pope, wrote
his first letter to encourage Christians who were suffering
persecution. Like James' letter, Peter's is very practical and
ethical. His second letter warns against false and immoral
teachers. It speaks of Christ's Second Coming and the end
of the world.

First John is one of the most beautiful and "upbeat" letters ever written. It is graceful, poetic, and elegant. "Light",
"life", and "love" are its three main concepts. John's second
and third letters, each less than a page long, warn against
false teachers in the Church (again), as does the one-page
letter of Jude.

The epistles are all about issues that are still with us today.
Every one of them is utterly up-to-date. The Church's problems and God's solutions are essentially the same today as
two thousand years ago. The epistles are a major part of the
Church's treasure trove of wisdom for dealing with today's
issues. They are like letters you find written many years ago
by your mother, who is still alive and still teaching you her
wisdom. Guided by Jesus and the Spirit, the wisdom of holy
Mother Church never dies and never goes out of date.

NINE

The First Systematic Christian Theology: Romans

Samuel Taylor Coleridge called Romans "the most profound book in existence". Godet called it "the cathedral of the Christian faith". It is placed first among the epistles not only because it is the longest, but also because it is the greatest.

Romans was probably written shortly before Nero's persecution began in A.D. 64. According to Tacitus, the Roman historian, Christians were already "an immense multitude" then.

Paul had not founded the Roman church, Peter had. But Paul came to Rome to appear before the emperor and to be martyred. Acts ends with his preaching the gospel from house arrest in Rome.

Rome was, of course, the center of the entire world, the greatest city in the world in power and population, but already decadent with slavery, political corruption, and extremes of wealth and poverty. Into this cesspool, Paul drops the seed of the gospel, which was to conquer the world.

Romans is the only systematic theology in the Bible, except for Hebrews, which is not about Christianity as such but about Christianity and Judaism, like Romans 9 to 11. But Christianity is not a theory, a philosophy, but a story, "news".

The epistles interpret this "news". They teach timeless truths, but truths about time: (1) the significance of the temporal events in the Gospels, especially Christ's death, the event each Gospel lingers longest over; and (2) the outworking of these events in our lifetimes.

The main point of Romans, and of Christianity, and of life itself, is Christ. Romans presents Him as the Second Adam, the new man, and humanity's second chance. He is "the righteousness of God". This is the phrase Paul uses to identify his main theme at the beginning (1:16–17): "For I am not ashamed of the gospel; it is the power of God for salvation to every one who has faith, to the Jew first and also to the Greek. For in it the righteousness of God is revealed through faith for faith; as it is written, 'He who through faith is righteous shall live.' " This is a two-verse summary of the entire book.

Romans is the book that sparked the Protestant Reformation when Luther discovered the doctrine of justification by faith in it. The Catholic Church teaches this doctrine too, of course. The Church cannot contradict the Bible. That would be like a house contradicting its foundation. Nor is there any contradiction between Paul's doctrine of justification by faith (in Romans and Galatians) and James' teaching that faith without works is dead (Jas 2:14–26). Luther thought there was, and he called James "an epistle of straw". But even Romans includes James' point. It ends with chapters 12 to 16 about the necessity of good works.

There is no book in the Bible in which it is more necessary to look at the outline. For Romans is an extended logical argument, especially chapters 1–8. The more you read, study, and think about it, the tighter and clearer it becomes. It is much better to do the detailed outlining yourself than to let any commentator do it for you. It may sound like dull "schoolwork", but you will find it extremely rewarding and even exciting.

The unity of the argument centers around four key concepts: *righteousness, faith, law,* and *sin.* Paul uses each term over sixty times. The main outline is as follows:

Personal Introduction: 1:1–15
Main Theme: 1:16–17
I. Doctrine
  A. Christianity
    1. The problem, the bad news, sin: 1:18–3:20
    2. The solution, the good news, salvation: 3:21–8:39
  B. Judaism: 9–11
II. Practice: 12–15
Personal postscripts: 16

At each major transition point in Paul's argument, there is a key "therefore" or "but".

The major transition, from sin to salvation, in the passage of 3:20–21, is this: "For no human being will be justified in his sight by works of the law.... *But now* the righteousness of God has been manifested apart from law" (emphasis mine).

Chapter 5 draws a corollary with another "therefore": "Therefore, since we are justified by faith, we have peace with God through our Lord Jesus Christ."

Chapter 6 also begins with a "therefore": "What shall we say then [therefore]? Are we to continue in sin that grace may abound? By no means!"

Finally, chapter 8, Paul's great, triumphant conclusion, begins with the final "therefore": "There is therefore now no condemnation for those who are in Christ Jesus." Each chapter expands upon its first verse, exploring a new step in the argument.

The first step is the problem, the "bad news" that we all have a mortal disease called sin, "the Jew first and also the Greek (Gentile)". The good news is that all are offered salvation, "the Jew first and also the Greek. For all have sinned and come short of the glory of God."

Gentiles may think they have an excuse because they do not have divine revelation, so Paul first shows that Gentiles are inexcusable and responsible for their sins because they too know God, by nature and conscience. This passage (1: 18–31) lays the foundation for "natural (rational) theology".

Jews may think they need no Savior because they do have revelation and are God's chosen people. Paul replies that the Jewish law cannot save you if you disobey it, and all do (2:1–3:8).

This demolishes the answer most Catholics give to the most important question in the world: How are you going to get to Heaven? Most Catholic students I have polled think they will be saved because their obedience to some law is good enough, whether the Ten Commandments or the principles of pop psychology.

The good news makes no sense unless you believe the bad news first. A free operation is not good news if you don't think you have a mortal disease. In a more realistic age, the main obstacle to believing in Christianity was the *good* news. It seemed like a fairy tale, too good to be true. Today the main obstacle is the *bad* news: people just don't believe in sin, even though that's the only Christian doctrine that can be proven simply by reading daily newspapers. When did you last hear anyone, even your priest, use "the s-word"?

Calling a person sinful is not to deny that his *being* remains good, any more than calling the statue of Venus de Milo a damaged work of art means denying that its sculptor created a masterpiece. Humanity is a good thing gone bad, the image of God in rebellion against God, God's beloved in a state of divorce.

The transition from the bad news (1:18–3:20) to the good news (3:21ff.) is objectively Jesus' death and subjectively our faith. More exactly, Paul mentions three aspects of justification: by grace, by blood, and by faith. Its origin is grace (3:21–24), its means is Christ's death (3:25–26), and our reception of it is by faith (3:27–31).

Paul distinguishes three steps in God's plan for our salvation: (1) the Father's plan and predestination, (2) our justification by the death of the Son, and (3) our sanctification now and glorification hereafter by the Spirit. Salvation, like God, is trinitarian.

Chapter 4 proves that even Abraham was justified by faith. It incidentally demolishes the common fallacy that Judaism is only a religion of law, justice, judgment, and fear, while Christianity invented grace, mercy, forgiveness, and love.

Chapter 5 explores the *consequences* of justification by faith, including peace with God (5:1), joy in suffering (5:3–8), and hope rather than fear toward God's judgment (5:9–11).

Then comes the contrast between Adam and Christ (the Second Adam), as the historical basis for the two main points, original sin and salvation.

Chapter 6 answers the natural objection: Why not go ahead and sin if we're saved by grace, not by law? The answer is that our identity is now bound up in Christ. We are new creatures, little Christs. We hate and avoid sin now not out of fear of punishment (the former motive), nor simply out of gratitude (Luther's answer, but not Paul's here), but because of *who we are*: Christ's. The point in Romans 6:1–3 is the same as in 1 Corinthians 6:15.

If we are alive with Christ's life, we are dead to Adam, sin, and the law. Chapter 7 explores this death. God gave us the law not to save us but to reveal our sinfulness, not as our operation but as our X-ray. Not law but Spirit saves us—that is, God the Holy Spirit, really present in the believer's soul. This salvation is completed by our sanctification. Jesus is called "Savior" not because He saves us only from *punishment* for sin but because He saves us from *sin*. The three trinitarian aspects of salvation are like the root, stem, and flower of a beautiful plant. But the flower is the fairest, and the consummation. It is fitting, then, that chapter 8 is the fairest, most joyful chapter in the Bible. Our sanctification in this life (8:1–17) and our glorification in the next (8:18–39) are the point of the whole divine plot. Tolkien calls this "happy ending" the "eucatastrophe", the good catastrophe. "There is no tale ever told that men more wish to be true", he says. But unlike lesser fairy tales, this one *is!*

The next three chapters in Romans show how Christianity views Judaism: their past election by God (chap. 9), their present rejection of God (chap. 10), and their future restoration by God (chap. 11).

The concluding practical, moral chapters include the seminal passage about the Christian and politics (13:1–7), love as the fulfillment of the law (13:10), the best passage in the Bible for the aging (13:11–12), the passage that delivered Saint Augustine (13:14; see *Confessions* 8,12), and the meaning of "life or death" (14:7–8), among other gems. Romans, quite literally, shows us the way to Heaven, the way to receive God's greatest gift—eternal life with Him. Who could ask for anything more or settle for anything less?

TEN

How a Christian Is Different:
First Corinthians

Today, especially in America, Catholics, like everyone else (except Orthodox Jews and Fundamentalists), want to be "accepted". Paul's First Letter to the Corinthians is especially relevant to such people. Though it talks about dozens of separate issues, the most unifying theme is that Christians must be different.

Corinth was the largest, most cosmopolitan, and most decadent city in Greece. Two-thirds of its seven hundred thousand citizens were slaves. It was a major port and hub of commerce. Much of the commerce was in human flesh. "To act like a Corinthian" was an ancient saying meaning debauchery, especially prostitution. Men went to Corinth to take a moral holiday.

The city was also full of idolatry, which centered around Aphrodite, the goddess of sex. Her temple, atop an eighteen-hundred-foot promontory, had a thousand temple prostitutes. Paul had come here in the years A.D. 51 and 52 to evangelize. Now four or five years later, he writes this letter to address some of the problems of this new, struggling Church surrounded by an "advanced" world just like ours: a world in "advanced" stages of decay.

His main point is that Christians are called out of paganism to a radically distinctive lifestyle. For Christ is the Lord of every aspect of life. Paul is utterly Christocentric; in 1 Corinthians 1:30 he identifies four great abstract ideals (wisdom, righteousness, sanctification, and redemption) with Christ Himself. In 1 Corinthians 2:2 he says that he "decided to know nothing among you except Jesus Christ". Any addition to *Him* would be a subtraction.

America is strikingly similar to Corinth. According to polls, most Catholics consider themselves "Americans who happen to be Catholics", rather than "Catholics who happen to be Americans". Two of the words they dislike the most are "authority" (or "lordship") and "obedience". Yet these are precisely what Paul calls for.

Christ always sought out the most needy, and His Church has always followed His lead. Christianity naturally flows to the lowest places, like water. Corinth was the world's lowest place, the spiritual gutter. Yet the Corinthians thought of themselves as high, not low—like the high and airy temple of Aphrodite. For one thing, they were rich due to trade and prostitution. For another, they were well educated. Though they did not produce any philosophers, many philosophers from Athens taught there. The most prominent philosophical school at the time was probably Scepticism. The last thing any of them would believe was a man rising from the dead.

Into this atmosphere heavy with lust, greed, and pride, Paul had introduced the clear light of Jesus when he first visited (2:1–5). And he now continues the same strategy: not compromising, not pandering, not patronizing, but calling for the hard way, the distinctive way of living the life of Christ in a Christless world.

This is not a systematically ordered letter, like Romans. It moves from topic to topic. There are many minor topics, but the four major ones are (1) sectarianism, (2) faith and reason—Christianity and philosophy, (3) sex and love, and (4) the resurrection from the dead—both Christ's and ours. Other topics include incest, pagan lawyers, eating food offered to idols, prostitution, virginity, marriage, divorce, the Eucharist, order in worship, speaking in tongues, and other spiritual gifts.

The first two of these major points are treated together since simple faith unites while pride in reason divides. Paul is utterly scandalized at the growing factionalism in the Corinthian church (1:10–13). Can anyone seriously wonder which of the many "denominations" he would approve today?

Paul sees the source of division as the proud claim to possess superior "wisdom" and not submitting to Christ as God's Wisdom. The wonderful irony and paradox of God's folly being wiser than human wisdom (1:18–3:23) is the definitive passage for philosophers or theologians with "original" minds who tend to resist Christocentrism and want to "advance" in different and schismatic directions.

If all Christians had kept this passage uppermost in their minds for the last two thousand years, I believe that the tragedies of 1054 and 1517 and the hundreds of tears in the seamless garment of the Church since then could never have happened. If the Church ever becomes visibly one again, this passage will be the foundation for unity. Yet she always remains substantially and invisibly one, holy, Catholic, and apostolic.

On the number one topic in modern morality, sex and love, Paul does three things. First, he condemns sexual immorality in chapters 5 and 6, as well as the Corinthians' lax attitudes that accepted it. Instead of justifying incest, they should excommunicate the offender. Instead of justifying prostitution by the slogan "all things are lawful" (6:12), they should realize that in doing so a Christian, as a member of Christ's Body, makes *Christ* fornicate with a prostitute (6:15)!

Second, Paul gives a positive alternative picture of Christian marriage in chapter 7. Here he clearly distinguishes God's commands from his own opinion, which is to stay single. I think there is a wonderful divine humor in God revealing some deep and perennial principles of marriage through a celibate who confesses that he personally does not recommend it! I also see a wry divine humor in including in Scripture (7:6–12) a clear distinction between what is divine revelation and what is not. The distinction between divine revelation and human opinion is a matter of divine revelation, not human opinion!

Third, Paul writes the most famous passage about love ever written, chapter 13. This is the essential alternative to pagan lust for both married and unmarried. It is also a call to a clear and distinctive lifestyle and Christian witness. After all, Christ had prophesied that the world would be able to distinguish Christians from others by the special kind of love they had (Jn 13:35), not by having the same kind of love as the world had.

First Corinthians 13 is often read at weddings because it is the best definition of love ever written. This love (*agapē*) is not a feeling or desire (*eros*) but a *life*; it is as Dostoyevsky put it, "love in action" rather than "love in dreams."

The first paragraph (13:1–3) shows the infinite value of love by contrasting it with other things of great value: speaking in tongues, prophecy, knowledge, faith, and even the works of love without the soul of love.

The second paragraph distinguishes this love from all others by describing it in fifteen characteristics (vv. 4–7). Love is the skeleton key that unlocks all these doors. For instance, it is impossible to be patient with difficult people without love, but love brings patience with it.

Finally, the last paragraph shows the eternal destiny of love. Everything else, including all the things the Corinthians set their hearts and lives on, is doomed to die. Even faith and hope and earthly wisdom are not needed after death. But love is. When we love now, we plant seeds for eternity.

Chapter 13 is sandwiched between two chapters on spiritual gifts, especially the gift of tongues, and their use in worship. Paul shows moderation and wisdom in avoiding both the extremes of naïve enthusiasm and suspicion, and in subordinating everything, even supernatural gifts, to love. He himself speaks in tongues and wants everyone to (14:5, 18), but the issue is much less important for Paul than most charismatics *and* their critics think.

Next to chapter 13, chapter 15 is the most famous and most important. It is the primary text in Scripture on the resurrection of the body. None of the Greek philosophers in Corinth believed in bodily resurrection, not because they did not believe in miracles, but because they did not believe the body was good and created by God. Their sexual materialism and their philosophical spiritualism went hand in hand. Paul revealed instead that the body is more real and good and important than they thought. It is a holy thing, the Spirit's temple now (6:19) and the seed of something destined to live with God eternally, not a mere animal organism seeking sexual pleasure as its greatest good.

Plato had called the body "the soul's tomb". Paul tells the Corinthians, who were probably influenced by this philosophy, that to deny or ignore Christ's bodily Resurrection is to abandon the whole faith. Without the Resurrection, "our preaching is in vain, and your faith is in vain" (15:14), "you are still in your sins" (15:17), and "if for this life only we have hoped in Christ, we are of all men most to be pitied" (15:19).

And this Resurrection is no mere symbol, no merely subjective and spiritual "resurrection of Easter faith", or some such silly subterfuge. The Greek words for "the resurrection of the body" are *anastasis nekron*, which means "the sitting-up of the corpse"! Denial of the literal Resurrection, according to the Word of God, is denial of Christ, denial of the faith.

After demonstrating its existence (15:12–34), Paul gives some hints about its nature (15:35–58) through natural analogies. This body is the seed of another one. This body is as different from the resurrection body as a planet differs from a star. Paul's contrast between a "physical body" and a "spiritual body" does not mean that the post-resurrection body will not be tangible. Christ's was and is. It means that the source of this physical body is *physis*, nature, the dust we return to, while the source of our resurrection body is the Spirit of God, who will raise us as He raised Christ.

Paul concludes the great chapter with words that sound like trumpets (indeed, that is why Handel accompanied them with a trumpet in his "Messiah"). He concludes by sticking his tongue out at death, taunting it: "O death, where is thy victory? O death, where is thy sting?" Death is now a stingless bee for us because its stinger is in the body of Christ crucified. He took the stinger of Hell out of the bee of death for us.

The central theme in each of the specific topics Paul deals with (probably from questions in a letter the Corinthians had written to him) is the theme of Christian distinctiveness. This is seen most strikingly in chapter 6, where Paul is scandalized that Christians sue other Christians before pagan lawyers and judges. No one today even blinks at that practice, for we have so radically lost that sense of distinctiveness.

But why would a cat go before a dog to adjudicate a dispute with another cat? The difference between a Christian and a non-Christian is like the difference between a cat and a dog. It is not, for Paul, merely a difference between two *beliefs*, but a difference between two *beings*, two species.

I continually ask my theology and philosophy classes the simple question, "According to the New Testament, what is a Christian?" They always answer it not according to the New Testament but according to something else. For they always say what a Christian thinks, or believes, or feels, or does, or likes, or desires, but not what a Christian *is*. Paul knew what a Christian is: a Christian is a little Christ, a member of Christ, a cell in Christ's body.

Because of this radical transformation of our very "I", everything in our lives is transformed. As he was to put it in his second letter to these Corinthians (5:17), "If any one is in Christ, he is a new creation." In our desperate, bored search for novelties and "new theologies", we can never be more radically new than to simply rest on "the Church's one foundation—Jesus Christ her Lord".

ELEVEN

A Different Christ Means
No Christ:
Second Corinthians

This is the most intensely personal, passionate, and intimate of all Paul's letters. Though there is not as much doctrinal or moral teaching content here as in his other letters, there is more emotion, personal confession, biographical revelation, and direct personal address.

Between the time Paul wrote his first letter to the Corinthians and the time of this second letter, false teachers had turned the Corinthian Christians against him. They were probably reacting against the strong principles and discipline in the first letter, just as all "dissenters" in the Church today want to minimize, not maximize; weaken, not strengthen; subtract, not add to, the fullness of the principles of the gospel.

These false teachers denied Paul's authority as an apostle (11:5) and preached "another Jesus", another religion, another gospel. Paul's response is passionate not because his authority has been challenged but because the authority of Christ has. He responds in words few would dare to use today in similar situations. For a different Christ means no Christ, no Savior, and no salvation. Only in Galatians (1:8) did Paul respond so strongly, for the same reason.

Paul had made a quick trip to Corinth to settle the controversy before he wrote this letter, but he was unsuccessful. Pained and humiliated, he wrote a troubled letter to the Corinthians between the time of the two letters we have. This is mentioned in 2:3–4 and 7:8–12. Some scholars think this letter was preserved and put into 2 Corinthians, as chapters 10–13, because the sarcasm of these chapters is in such strong contrast to the joy and tenderness of chapters 1 to 9. But this argument ignores the fact that parents and lovers are often moved by their passion and intimacy to both tenderness and despair almost simultaneously.

The content theme of 2 Corinthians is the distinctiveness of the Christian, the Christian's faith, and the Christian's life in an unbelieving world. This was the theme of 1 Corinthians also. As medieval Christendom recedes more and more and paganism returns more and more, these two letters become more and more directly relevant to our lives.

This letter contains the only account in the New Testament of a mystical experience: Paul's own (12:1–10). It is striking that he recounts this only to relegate it to a second, lower place compared to his weakness and suffering, which is a much more effective means to sanctity. It also contains the most complete and lengthy passage in the Bible about generosity or Christian giving (chaps. 8 and 9).

Other familiar, eloquent passages are 3:17, 3:18, 4:7, 4:10, 4:16–18, 5:6–7, 5:21, 6:2, 6:8–10, 8:9, and 10:5. Paul could never write a letter without writing unforgettable quotes.

In 1 Corinthians, Paul is on top of the problems of his beloved "problem children" in Corinth. In 2 Corinthians, he is wrung out and even exasperated. Like Christ, Paul experienced all natural human emotions. I think He must feel exactly the same toward us, *His* "problem children".

Back to Basics: Galatians

Galatians is the only letter of Paul's that does not contain a single word of praise. Even when Paul wrote to the Corinthians, who were having *very* serious problems, including getting drunk at the Eucharist, practicing and justifying incest and prostitution, splitting the Church into rival factions, arrogance and superiority about the gift of tongues, and proudly placing pagan philosophy above the Christian faith—even when he wrote to a church with all these shocking problems, Paul still found something to praise them for and to thank God for in them (1 Cor 1:4–7). Not so at Galatia. Instead of the customary praise, he begins with this sledgehammer paragraph:

"I am astonished that you are so quickly deserting him who called you in the grace of Christ and turning to a different gospel—not that there is another gospel, but there are some who trouble you and want to pervert the gospel of Christ. But even if we, or an angel from heaven, should preach to you a gospel contrary to that which we preached to you, let him be accursed" (1:6–8).

What elicited such Pauline heat and outrage? The mistakes of the Corinthians were mistakes of addition; the mistake of the Galatians was subtraction. The Corinthians had polluted the gospel. The Galatians had abandoned it for another religion, "a different gospel". No mistake could be more serious. Yet as we shall see, this is the single most common mistake in the Church *today*.

More evidence of how crucial the issue is lies in the fact that Paul feels he has to begin his letter by "pulling rank" and establishing his authority as an apostle, equal to the eleven and Peter (1:11–2:14). The Galatians may not listen to argument, but Paul hopes that they will at least listen to authority.

An immediate and specific issue masked the more fundamental one. The immediate issue was whether Christians had to be circumcised. The more fundamental one was how to be saved. The first issue is a total non-issue today; *no* Christians think it is necessary to be circumcised. But the second issue, alas, is still very much at issue. It was the issue that split the Church in the Protestant Reformation. And if the informal questions and formal questionnaires that I give to my college students are any indication, not a small minority but a large majority of Catholics today not only do not know the basic doctrines of Catholic theology anymore, they do not even know how to get to Heaven!

Until this unbelievable failure is remedied, it is pointless to pray to God for ecumenical peace and reunion between Christian churches. For ecumenical unity means unity among *Christians*, and it is not clear that one who does not even know how to get to Heaven can accurately be called a Christian.

I am not suggesting, as many Protestant Fundamentalists do, that most Catholics are not saved. But I am suggesting that perhaps most will be saved as good pagans, as "anonymous Christians" rather than as Catholic Christians. For when the time comes to present their entrance ticket for the heavenly plane (God has a large angel air force: see Mk 13:27), if they do not present Christ as their Savior, but only present themselves as "good people", can this be called Christianity? If the responses I hear are typical, many will rely instead on the same old "other gospel" the Galatians relied on, namely, the works of law, or more likely on the updated, "soft" revision of it, good *intentions*. "I'm a good person", "I try to do good", "I'm sincere", and "I try not to hurt people" are four of the most common counterfeit tickets I see. They all begin with the same fatal word.

What *I* say about this matters nothing. But let's see what God's apostle says about this. He says, in effect, that whatever the answer I give at the gate of Heaven it had better not begin with my favorite word, "I", but with the Word, Christ. The Word had better be my favorite word.

The connection between circumcision and salvation is this: to be circumcised, in Old Testament Judaism, was to bind yourself to the covenant, bind yourself to obey its laws, just as you do when you get married (the marriage "covenant"). Thus, being circumcised—the immediate issue in Galatia— meant relying on the law for salvation. That was the fundamental issue.

There was also a third intermediate issue *between* circumcision and salvation: Judaism. Being circumcised meant becoming a Jew. Must one become a Jew before becoming a Christian? Those in Galatia who were insisting on circumcision were making Christianity a Jewish sect, forgetting that Christ was "the stone of stumbling and the rock of offense". According to Christianity, we are saved *not* by the Jewish law, the Old Covenant, entered by circumcision. We are saved by Christ and by His New Covenant, entered by faith.

Paul points out very simply and clearly that no one can be saved by the law: "We ... know that a man is not justified [saved] by the works of the law but through faith in Jesus Christ ... because by works of the law shall no one be justified" (2:15–16; see 3:11). The simple reason why no one can be saved by obeying God's law is that no one obeys it! (See Is 64:6; Phil 3:9.)

If we were saved by obeying the law, we would save ourselves and would not need a savior. Jesus would then be reduced to a human teacher, prophet, guru, social worker, psychologist, philosopher, or moral example—as in modernist theology.

The law is like an X-ray. Sin is like cancer. Salvation is like an operation. Jesus is like the surgeon. Faith is like consent to the operation. The Galatian heresy is like thinking the X-ray will save you.

Salvation occurs by faith (though, as we shall see in the last half of Paul's letter, it is completed by good works), because faith is not just some subjective process inside our psyches, but an objective transaction: *believing* means *receiving* (Jn 1:12).

Thus Paul contrasts law and faith (2:16; 3:11; see Eph 2: 8–10) as the answers to the most important question anyone can ask: "What must I do to be saved?" (Acts 16:30). The point is so crucial—how could anything possibly be more important than eternity?—that Paul equates turning away from this doctrine with turning away from Christ (1:6). He even calls the Galatians fools under the spell of witchcraft (3:1) for abandoning it.

Paul uses five lines of argument to prove his main point.

First, this gospel "is not man's gospel. For I did not receive it from man . . . but . . . through a revelation of Jesus Christ" (1:11–12). When Paul submitted this teaching to the apostles in Jerusalem, they all acknowledged its truth and authority (2:1–10). Paul even rightly corrected Peter when he failed to apply it, when he submitted to Jewish laws only when he was with Jews (2:11–16). Paul's dispute with a pope was like that of Saint Teresa of Avila: not with the teaching but with the failure to live the teaching.

Second, Paul argues that men and women were saved by faith, not by the law, even in Old Testament times. This is shown in the case of Abraham, who received the promise *before* Moses received the law. Paul uses the same argument in Romans 4 as in Galatians 3.

Third, the purpose of the law cannot be to save because its purpose is to condemn, to specify sins (3:19–22). It is the diagnosis, not the cure; the bad news, not the good news.

Fourth, the law is essentially preparatory. It is like a custodian or child's nurse (3:23–26), who takes the child to school but does not teach him—like the school bus driver. Slaves are under law. Family heirs are under promise, and we are family heirs by adoption (4:1–7)—not servants, but sons and daughters of God.

Fifth, the law binds us while the gospel frees us (4:8–31). Thus the two are opposed, not identical. Paul illustrates this by allegorizing Abraham's two rival sons, Isaac (faith) and Ishmael (law) (4:22–31).

So far, Paul sounds like an evangelist. But in chapters 5 and 6 he sounds like a moralist. He is both, of course; for the gospel transforms morality as well as salvation.

Paul admitted that the law *defined* sins (3:19–22), but the law does not *save* us from either sin or sin's punishment. God's grace, received by faith, does both. Not only justification (being made right with God) but also sanctification (being made holy) have the Spirit, not the law, as their source and power. ("Spirit" means not man's spirit, but the Holy Spirit here.) Christians cannot be legalists because they have been freed from the law by Christ. They are now no longer under the law but under grace.

But *license* is as far from Christianity as *legalism*. In fact, these two apparent opposites are two sides of the same coin. Both rely on self, not God. Neither can say, "I have been crucified with Christ; *it is no longer I who live, but Christ who lives in me*; and the life I now live in the flesh I live by faith in the Son of God, who loved me and gave himself for me" (2:20 emphasis mine). *That* is the good news; that is the thing both opposite heresies miss; that is the link between faith and works, between justification and sanctification, between being saved and being virtuous. The life of Christ comes into the soul by faith and out by works. It is not that you get to Heaven because you live a good life. Rather, you live a good life because Heaven has gotten to you.

Legalism, license, and liberty are three totally opposite ways of life, three different religions, and three different kinds of love. Legalism is self-love and self-righteousness. License is self-love and self-indulgence. Liberty is selfless love of God and neighbor: "No longer I . . . but Christ in me."

Paul concludes Galatians by talking about virtue and good works because that is part of the Gospel too. Works as well as faith are part of salvation, just as fruit as well as roots are part of a tree. If we have no good works, we are not saved, for faith without works is dead faith, fake faith (Jas 2:14–26). Luther could not see this, and dismissed James as an "epistle of straw". That's because he didn't see the living link between faith and works. That link is the very life of Christ in the soul, which gives us a second, divine nature (2 Pet 1:4), a new birth (Jn 3:3–6).

Luther could not see this essential theological truth because bad philosophy held him back. Bad philosophy can produce bad theology. Luther was an Ockhamist, that is, a Nominalist, who did not believe there were any such things as real species or universal essences like human nature. If there is no real universal human nature, there can be no second nature or transformed nature.

Luther thus reduced salvation to a mental attitude on God's part (God *looks* at us *as if* we were His children because He looks at us covered by Christ's Blood, which hides our sins) and to a legal transaction (God *declares* us righteous even though we really aren't). This merely transfers the legalism from the human to the divine! Catholic theology more perfectly fulfills Luther's own desire to escape legalism than Lutheran theology does.

Paul ends by contrasting the two kinds of life, *bios* and *zoe*, natural and supernatural, "flesh" and "spirit". "Flesh" (*sarx*) and "spirit" (*pneuma*) do not mean body (*soma*) and soul (*psyche*) but (1) fallen human nature inherited from Adam and (2) the very life of God the Holy Spirit given by Christ. "The works of the flesh" listed in 5:19–21 include both mental and physical sins. "The fruit of the Spirit" listed in 5: 22–23 includes both corporal and spiritual virtues.

Galatians is Paul's simplest letter. Once you see its single central point, you see how everything he says is a spoke in the single wheel that is held together by that hub. Once you know that hub, you know what Christianity essentially is: Christ Himself (Col 1:27–28). Without a firm grasp of that center, heresies are bound to come, whether legalistic or licentious. "This is the true God and eternal life. Little children, keep yourselves from idols" (1 Jn 5:20–21).

THIRTEEN

We Are Christ's Mystical Body: Ephesians

Ephesians is to the epistles what John's Gospel is to the Gospels: the most mystical, profound, and universal of them all.

Paul probably wrote Ephesians, Philippians, Colossians, and Philemon from prison in Rome around A.D. 60 or 62. Ephesians seems to be an encyclical (circulating) letter for all the churches in the region (Asia Minor), for it mentions no specific problems or controversies in any local church. Its topic is universal—totally universal, in fact. We may call it Paul's treatise on "the cosmic Christ".

Although Ephesians, like life, is really only about one thing—Christ—we can distinguish at least twelve subthemes or aspects of this single point.

1. The mystery of predestination—that God "chose us in him [Christ] before the foundation of the world" (1:4) and "destined us in love to be his sons through Jesus Christ" (1:5)—implies a Christian philosophy of history in which Christ makes a *total* difference. The Christian era is the fulfillment of this divine "plan for the fulness of time, to unite all things in him [Christ]" (1:10).

2. How big is this Christ? Colossal, as Colossians will point out (Col 1:15–20; 2:3, 7), gigantic, cosmic, even more

than cosmic. For Christ is "far above all rule and authority and power and domination, and above every name that is named, not only in this age but in that which is to come . . . he has put all things under his feet" (1:21–22).

The classic passage about the "length and breadth and depth and height" of Christ is Ephesians 3:14–21. I think it is the second most exalted passage in Scripture, next to Romans 8:31–39. If you are wise, you will stop reading this chapter and read that passage right now, slowly and prayerfully.

3.   Christian wisdom means perceiving the size, the all-inclusiveness, of Christ. Paul writes this letter for that purpose: "that the God of our Lord Jesus Christ . . . may give you a spirit of wisdom and of revelation in the knowledge of him, having the eyes of your hearts enlightened, that you may know . . . what are the riches of his glorious inheritance in the saints, and what is the immeasurable greatness of his power in us who believe" (1:17–19). In the words of an old classic title by J. B. Phillips, Paul's message to the Ephesians (and to us) is that "Your god is too small."

4.   A theme that could well be called the central theme of Ephesians is the Church as Christ's Mystical Body, an invisible organism, not just a visible organization. Ephesians has been the basis of much of the Church's theology of herself ever since Pope Pius XII's great encyclical *The Mystical Body of Christ*.

Paul calls the Church "his body, the fulness of him who fills all in all" (1:23). Therefore the Church "fills all in all". As G. K. Chesterton says, the Church is not in the world, the world is in the Church, as a setting is in a play. God created the whole universe for the Church, for His Son's Body, for his Family.

And we are actually, *literally*, parts or organs of Christ's invisible Body. Paul uses the metaphor of a living building,

"Christ Jesus himself being the cornerstone, in whom the whole structure is joined together and grows into a holy temple in the Lord, in whom you also are built into it" (2:20–22). The building is only a metaphor, but the body is not.

5. In this Body, Jews and Gentiles are united (2:11–21). Gentiles, who were "separated from Christ, alienated from the commonwealth of Israel" (2:12) are now "no longer strangers and sojourners but fellow citizens with the saints" (2:19). For in Christ God planned to "create in himself one new man [the whole Christ, Head and Body] in place of the two" (2:15). This is what Paul calls "the mystery of Christ" (3:4–6): His extension through the whole Gentile world.

By way of aside, Jews do not send out missionaries, for Orthodox Jews believe that only when the Messiah comes will the Gentiles be given the knowledge of the true God. It was Christians who fulfilled this Jewish prophecy. Secular Jews, of course, like secularized Christians, have no missionaries because they have no mission.

6. "The unsearchable riches of Christ ... in whom we have boldness and confidence of access" to God (3:8, 12) are infinite. Christians are like millionaires content to draw pennies from their account. Paul lists Christians' heavenly assets throughout the first half of Ephesians. The second half draws out the radical implications for earthly living. There are no imperatives, no "oughts" in the first half—only facts. All are based on our being "in Christ"—a phrase Paul uses over thirty times in this short letter.

7. These infinite riches are pure grace, pure gift. Ephesians repeats the theme of Romans and Galatians: "For by grace you have been saved through faith; and this is not your own doing, it is the gift of God—not because of works, lest any man should boast. For we are his workmanship, created

in Christ Jesus for good works, which God prepared before-hand, that we should walk in them" (2:8–10). Works are the fruit of faith and as much a part of God's predestined plan for our salvation as faith. But the whole plan first comes as pure gift, simply received by faith.

8.   What we have received is the most radical change con-ceivable: not only a new mind but a new life. "And you he made alive when you were dead through [your] trespasses and sins" (2:1). Everything is different for a Christian, for Christianity is not just a new lifestyle, but a new life.

9.   But we must grow into this new life "until we all attain to the unity of the faith and of the knowledge of the Son of God, to mature manhood, to the measure of the stat-ure of the fulness of Christ" (4:13). "We are to grow up in every way into him who is the head, into Christ" (4:15). *That* is the definition of "maturity".

10.   In this body we are "members one of another" (4:25) because we are members of Christ. "Members" here means not "members" of a *group*, like a political party or a social club, but members of a *body*, like ears and toes. As Pascal says, "imagine a body of thinking members".

This is the Christian basis for total truth and honesty: "Let everyone speak the truth with his neighbor, *for we are mem-bers one of another*" (4:25, emphasis mine). A far more pow-erful basis for "communication" than any human psychology.

11.   In this body there are three main relationships. We find the same three relationships in all societies in the world, but in Christ they are all transformed. They are husband-wife, parent-child, and ruler-ruled (in Paul's world, that included master-slave). Each of the two parties in each of these three relationships has reciprocal but diverse duties; there is neither one-way superiority and privilege nor dull, flat, repetitive equality. Each owes a different form of the

same thing—love—to the other. In each case there are two things that the modern mind scorns: authority and obedience. But in the Church these are of a radically different kind than in the world. Ephesians 5 is really Paul's working out of the consequences of Matthew 20:25–28.

Wives, children, and slaves are liberated by Christ from inferiority. But they are told to obey, not to disobey. For their obedience is to be no longer that of the world, based on force and fear, but that of Christ, based on faith and love.

If you think it is demeaning to obey, consider who was the most obedient person in history: God incarnate. Christ obeyed His Father in all things (Jn 5:30; 6:38). If obedience is the mark of inferiority, Christ was the most inferior man who ever lived. See how far our minds are from being transformed? We still think with worldly categories if we shrink back from Christ's call for obedience to each other.

Ephesians 5:21–33 is the most profound passage in the Bible on the most fundamental institution in the world, the one whose decay is destroying our civilization: marriage. Christian marriage, says Paul, is not just a good thing, but a profound mystery that refers to Christ and the Church (5:32). There are three in every Christian marriage, not two, as Fulton Sheen put it in the title of his classic on marriage, *Three to Get Married*.

This is the key to interpreting the most hated and resented verse in Scripture today, Ephesians 5:22: "Wives, be subject to your husbands . . ." For Paul adds the phrase that transforms everything: "as to the Lord". In this Lord there is no lording it over, no chauvinism, no bossiness. Christ is not the "boss" of the Church, but its *Head*. And "the husband is the head of the wife *as Christ is the head of the Church, his body*" (5:23, emphasis mine).

Christ is the "Head" of the Church as the round thing between your shoulders is the head of your body, not as an executive is the head of his corporation. And only a neurotic head tries to enslave its own body. "Even so husbands should love their wives *as their own bodies*.... For no man ever hates his own flesh" (5:28–29, emphasis mine). What we have here is a radical alternative to both the old chauvinism and the new egalitarianism. Here we have organic unity, ontological intimacy, the "one flesh" of head and body, a great mystery (5:32).

12.   Though this new life in Christ is love and marriage, it is also war. Spiritual warfare is one of the most common themes in the lives of the saints, but it is almost totally neglected today. Ephesians 6:12–17 is Scripture's most famous passage about it.

Paul makes clear that this is *spiritual* warfare, not physical. "For we are not contending against flesh and blood, but against the principalities, against the powers, against the world rulers of this present darkness, against the spiritual hosts of wickedness in the heavenly places." We are, like it or not, wrestling against demons. Ignorance of this fact is as disastrous as an army's ignorance of an opposing army.

Since this is spiritual warfare, we have spiritual weapons, "the whole armor of God". This includes (1) the loincloth of truth, (2) the breastplate of righteousness, (3) the shoes of the gospel, (4) the shield of faith, and (5) the sword of the Spirit, the Word of God (6:13–17; see Heb 4:12). In this war, "if God is for us, who can be against us?" (Rom 8:31). Goliath doesn't stand a chance against the Son of David, *and we are the body of the Son of David.* You don't read Ephesians aright unless it makes you want to shout, "Hallelujah!"

FOURTEEN

Christ-Mindedness: Philippians

Philippians is neither a treatise on systematic theology, like Romans, nor a treatment of one point of it, like Galatians. Nor is it a practical, moral letter answering many specific questions and local problems, like 1 Corinthians. It is a pastoral, personal, intimate letter whose unifying theme is *sanctity*, or Christ-mindedness (2:5). It was written from house arrest in Rome where Paul was awaiting death.

Along this broad unifying thread, Paul strings pearls: some of the most moving, memorable, and oft-quoted passages in all of Scripture. Since the structural outline is not prominent, the best way to introduce this little gem of a letter is to point out some of these passages, like a tour guide showing stunning highlights of a small exotic island.

1.   The letter begins with a dash of confidence for parents, pastors, and those entrusted to care for souls in danger of losing the faith: "I am sure that he who began a good work in you will bring it to completion at the day of Jesus Christ" (1:6). For faith is a work of God, and God never gives up and never fails.

2.   The whole Christian life is summed up in two words in the passage of 1:9–10: love and discernment. "It is my prayer that your love may abound more and more, with

knowledge and all discernment, so that you may approve what is excellent." All you need is love, but love needs eyes. And love *makes* eyes: see John 7:17.

3.   The most perfect and simple statement ever written on the meaning of life and of death is in 1:21: "For me to live is Christ, and to die is gain." In other words, death is only more Christ. Like Christ, Paul does not describe sanctity as *imitating* Christ but as living in Christ and living out Christ: "for me to live is Christ" (compare Jn 15:4–5). Denying the real presence of Christ in the Christian is as harmful a heresy as denying the Real Presence of Christ in the Eucharist.

4.   The most famous passage in Philippians is the "kenosis" (emptying) passage (2:5–11), which demands of all Christians the same "emptying" as Christ chose in the Incarnation: "Have this mind among yourselves, which is yours in Christ Jesus, who, though he was in the form of God, did not count equality with God a thing to be grasped, but emptied himself, taking the form of a servant, being born in the likeness of men. And being found in human form he humbled himself and became obedient unto death, even death on a cross."

Like Buddhism, Christianity is mercilessly threatening to the "grasping" greed and desire in which the world finds its hope for happiness. But unlike Buddhism, Christianity has a positive alternative. It does not call for an empty mind but a taking on of the mind of Christ and the hope of glory: "Therefore God has highly exalted him and bestowed on him the name which is above every name, that at the name of Jesus every knee should bow, in heaven and on earth and under the earth, and every tongue confess that Jesus Christ is Lord, to the glory of God the Father" (2:9–11).

5.   In the life of the Christian, our free will and God's grace are one, as they were in the life of Christ. The mystery

no philosopher can explain is stated in all its paradoxical force in the passage of 2:12–13: "work out your own salvation with fear and trembling; for God is at work in you, both to will and to work for his good pleasure."

6. A perfect slogan for the Christian in a decadent and dying culture, whether ancient Rome or modern America, is 2:15: "Be blameless and innocent, children of God without blemish in the midst of a crooked and perverse generation, among whom you shine as lights in the world." Jesus told us the same thing: to be lights, to be salt, to be distinctive. God never told anyone to be popular, not even a bishop.

7. With this piece of advice goes another, namely, to "glory in Christ Jesus, and put no confidence in the flesh" (3:3). Modern American Christians lack Christ's *realism*. Aren't we shocked by John 2:23–24? We remember that human nature is precious, but we forget that it is fallen. We remember to love human beings, but we forget to put our faith and hope in God, *not* in human beings. That's why our faith falters when we hear of clerical scandals.

8. Paul practices what he preaches. He himself puts no confidence in the flesh, in any human and worldly advantages. After listing all his considerable advantages (3:4–8), he summarizes them in a shocking four-letter word that no Bible since the sixteenth century has dared to translate literally:

> If any other man thinks he has reason for confidence in the flesh, I have more: circumcised on the eighth day, of the people of Israel, of the tribe of Benjamin, a Hebrew born of Hebrews; as to the law a Pharisee, as to zeal, a persecutor of the church, as to the righteousness under the law blameless. But whatever gain I had, I counted as loss for the sake of Christ. Indeed I count everything as loss because of the surpassing worth of knowing Christ Jesus my Lord. For his sake I have suffered the loss of all things and count them as refuse.

"Refuse" (*skubala*) is a euphemism for a four-letter word that begins with an "s" in modern English.

Paul's point is not that the world is worthless, but that its very great worth is nothing compared with Christ. A trillion is nothing compared with infinity.

9. The goal of this life in Christ is summarized in unforgettable words in 3:10–11: "that I may know him and the power of his resurrection, and may share his sufferings, becoming like him in his death, that if possible I may attain the resurrection of the dead."

A constant sense of incompleteness animates the Christian life, like a race: "Not that I have already obtained this or am already perfect; but I press on to make it my own, because Christ Jesus has made me his own. Brethren, I do not consider that I have made it my own; but one thing I do, forgetting what lies behind and straining forward to what lies ahead, I press on toward the goal for the prize of the upward call of God in Christ Jesus" (3:12–14). Salvation is both complete—he said, "It is finished"—and incomplete. For while God has completely made us His own, we have not completely made Him our own.

10. Christians who pin their hopes on a political or national agenda had better read 3:20–21, a definition of Christian patriotism and the Christian *patria* (fatherland): "Our commonwealth is in heaven, and from it we await a Savior, the Lord Jesus Christ, who will change our lowly body to be like his glorious body, by the power which enables him to subject all things to himself."

11. For the listless and despondent, Paul has a command—not just an "ideal"—to "rejoice in the Lord always; again I will say, rejoice" (4:4). It's worth repeating a few hundred times a day. Try it. See the difference it makes.

12. Perhaps the most beloved of all benedictions is 4:7: "And the peace of God, which passes all understanding, will keep your hearts and your minds in Christ Jesus." The peace that comes from understanding will keep the mind, but only the peace that surpasses understanding can keep the heart, which surpasses the mind.

13. The perfect definition of Christ-mindedness comes in 4:8: "Finally, brethren, whatever is true, whatever is honorable, whatever is just, whatever is pure, whatever is lovely, whatever is gracious, if there is any excellence, if there is anything worthy of praise, think about these things."

Elsewhere (2 Cor 10:5) Paul commands us to "take every thought captive to obey Christ." For thought is the source of all life: "Sow a thought, reap an act; sow an act, reap a habit; sow a habit, reap a character; sow a character, reap a destiny" (Emerson). "Therefore let us think well. This is the principle of all morality" (Pascal).

Yet this is the area in which many demand freedom rather than obedience—as if God had a right to control my actions but not my thoughts, as if it were un-American for God to interfere with my "freedom of thought".

14. Another un-American virtue taught by Saint Paul and all the saints, is detachment from worldly ambitions. While exactly contrary to what the world thinks, this is the secret of happiness and contentment: "I have learned, in whatever state I am, to be content. I know how to be abased, and I know how to abound" (4:11–12).

The two most important lessons in any game are how to be a good loser and how to be a good winner. And worldly ambition is only a game for Christians. That does not mean that we cannot play the game with passion, but we cannot treat it as "the real thing". *Christ* is the real thing.

15.   For all "losers", for all the weak, for "little" Christians, Paul offers the amazing claim of 4:13: "I can do all things in him who strengthens me." The answer to the question: How much can we do? is the answer to the question: How much can Christ do? For we are "in Christ", branches of that one vine. "All" is no exaggeration: "with God all things are possible" (Mt 19:26).

16.   But how much will He do for us? Like Jesus, Paul makes the astoundingly unqualified promise, "My God will supply every need of yours" (4:19). This is reasonable, believe it or not. The reason is that the supply is "according to his riches in glory in Christ Jesus" (compare Rom 8:28–39).

Of course, he does not say that God will give us everything we *want*—unless what we want is identical with what we need. Christ-mindedness, the pervasive theme of Philippians, means learning to bring our wants into alignment with our needs by learning to bring our minds into alignment with the mind of Christ. Insofar as we do this, it is inevitable that we will experience more of the power and the contentment that this saint writes of so eloquently and effortlessly.

Such effortless eloquence comes only from experience. Sanctity cannot be taught, like theology—only caught, like measles. The more we expose ourselves to highly contagious words like these, the more likely it is that we will be increasingly infected. They are words to get under our skin, under our conscious minds, into our memories and our hearts.

FIFTEEN

Christ, the Fullness of God: Colossians

Colossians is simply colossal. It is about how big Christ is. How big is that? Pascal said, "Without Christ we cannot know the meaning of life, or death, or God, or ourselves." Those are the four most important questions there are.

Colossians is even more colossal than Ephesians. Ephesians is about the greatness of the Body of Christ. Colossians is about the greatness of the Head.

Paul's basic answer in Colossians to this basic question: How big is Christ? is the key passage of 1:15–20. It says that Christ is no less than the full and complete expression of God, the source and purpose of the whole universe, the Savior and center of all things in Heaven and earth.

He is the image of the invisible God, the firstborn of all creation; for in him all things were created, in heaven and on earth, visible and invisible, whether thrones or dominions, or principalities or authorities—all things were created through him and for him. He is before all things and in him all things hold together. He is the Head of the Body, the Church; He is the beginning, the firstborn from the dead, that in everything he may be preeminent. For in him all the fullness of

God was pleased to dwell, and through him to reconcile to himself all things, whether on earth or in heaven, making peace by the blood of his cross.

Like most of Paul's letters, Colossians is divided into two parts: first doctrine (chaps. 1 and 2), then practice (chaps. 3 and 4). The two are connected, as is everything, by Christ: because Christ *is* the center of everything (the fundamental doctrine), Christians must *put* Him first in everything (the fundamental practical point). Because He is the center of reality, He must be the center of our lives.

This connection can be seen in Paul's little transition words, which he puts at the beginning of the following key sentences in chapter 1. Because "*he is* the image of the invisible God" (v. 15), because "*he is* before all things" (v. 17), because "*he is* the head" (v. 18), therefore Paul concludes, "*And you*, who were once estranged ... he has now reconciled ... to present you holy" (vv. 21–22). The basic moral point of Colossians is that we must live according to this vision of ourselves in the colossal cosmic Christ.

The argument is this: (1) Christ is divine. (2) And you are in Christ. (3) Therefore, "if then you have been raised with Christ ... set your minds on the things that are above, not on things that are on earth. For you have died, and your life is hid with Christ in God" (3:1–3).

What a liberation: we are already dead! Old Adam died with Christ on the Cross and was buried with Christ in baptism. Now "it is no longer I who live, *but Christ* who lives in me" (Gal 2:20, emphasis mine).

The Church at Colossae was infected with an early form of Gnosticism, the popular Greek philosophical religion of the day that became the source of just about all the heresies in the early Church. In modern forms, it is still the source of most heresies today. At least five elements of the Gnostic heresy can be seen in Colossians:

1. It confused Christianity with the speculations of Greek philosophy (2:4–10).
2. It confused Christianity with legalism, inherited from branches of Judaism that insisted on circumcision and strict dietary laws (2:11–17).
3. It confused Christianity with mysticism, visions, and experiences (2:18).
4. It confused Christianity with occult lore, which involved the idolatrous and superstitious worship of angels as mediators or intermediaries with God (2:20).
5. It confused Christianity with ascetic views and practices that sought to flee matter, the body, and the physical world (2:21–23).

Just as the Church would do for the next two thousand years, Paul said No to these little heresies because he knew how big Christ was. Whenever the Church condemns a heresy, it is for this reason. All heresies *reduce* Christ. The Church, however, knows how big Christ is, and out of love and loyalty she will not tolerate such narrow-mindedness and reductionism.

Gnosticism displaced Christ from the center and replaced Him with five small things: speculation, legalism, mysticism, occultism, and an anti-Incarnational asceticism. So Paul first states the truth positively about who Christ is (1:15–20). Then, in that light, he condemns the Gnostic heretical theories (chap. 2). Finally, he applies this vision to daily life. After refuting Gnosticism doctrinally, he refutes it practically, showing that Christian doctrine and practice, orthodoxy and orthopraxy, are inseparable.

All heresies deny or reduce something about the complete Christ or the Christian's completeness in Christ. These are the two fundamental themes of Colossians because they are the two fundamental themes of the whole Christian life:

1. "Christ, in whom are hid all the treasures of wisdom and knowledge" (2:3), "for in him the whole fulness of deity dwells bodily" (2:9);
2. "And you have come to fulness of life in him" (2:10).

In his *Soliloquies*, Saint Augustine dialogues with his own reason and seeks to know only two things—the only two things we absolutely need to know because they are the only two things we can never, to all eternity, escape or avoid. Colossians supplies these two things:

Augustine: Behold, I have prayed to God.
Reason: What, then, do you desire to know?
Augustine: Those things for which I have prayed.
Reason: Sum them up, briefly.
Augustine: I desire to know God and my soul.
Reason: Nothing more?
Augustine: Nothing more.

You might know God without knowing yourself. You might know yourself without knowing God. But you cannot know Christ without knowing both, and you cannot know either your true self or the true God without knowing Christ.

SIXTEEN

How to Misunderstand
the Second Coming:
First and Second Thessalonians

*First Thessalonians: Living in Newness of Life as We Await
His Coming*

Thessalonica was a major city in Macedonia (northern
Greece). It was near Mount Olympus, fabled home of the
Greek gods. The city still stands today. It is called Salonica.

Because the congregation contained both Greek and
Hebrew members, Paul began his first letter to them with
his usual greeting combining the Greek "grace" (*charis*) and
the Hebrew "peace" (*shalom*). His letter is generally one of
personal encouragement. It contains just one important doctrinal passage (4:13–5:11). But this passage is one of the most
important and explicit passages in the Bible about Christ's
Second Coming at the end of the world.

> We would not have you ignorant, brethren, concerning those
> who are asleep, that you may not grieve as others do who
> have no hope. . . . For this we declare to you by the word of
> the Lord, that we who are alive, who are left until the com-
> ing of the Lord, shall not precede those who have fallen asleep.
> For the Lord himself will descend from heaven with a cry of

command, with the archangel's call, and with the sound of the trumpet of God. And the dead in Christ will rise first; then we who are alive, who are left, shall be caught up together with them in the clouds to meet the Lord in the air; and so we shall always be with the Lord. Therefore comfort one another with these words.

These words are not merely comfort, they are also *true*. Paul is not telling fairy tales to children. The issue is serious. It is a matter of life and death. For it is the meaning of death and, therefore, the meaning and end of life. The Thessalonians had apparently become distressed over the death of some of their members. Paul comforts them with the truth that all believers in Christ will be united and resurrected at the Second Coming.

In 1 Thessalonians, as in all his letters, Paul joins doctrine and practice, dogma and ethics, theology and morality (the two things the Church is entrusted to teach infallibly). His connecting point here is that since we will live again in resurrected form when Christ comes, we should live now in newness of life in readiness and preparation for that event. Life is a rehearsal (*melete*) for that great event. The play gives meaning to the rehearsal.

This means at least eight specific things, eight practical consequences in the present life as we prepare for the Second Coming:

1. hope, encouragement, and comfort (4:18);
2. alertness, open-eyed expectation (5:4);
3. firmness, "stand[ing] fast in the Lord" (3:8);
4. critical questioning (5:21: "Test everything, hold fast what is good"); and
5. sobriety, both mental and physical (5:6) (Imagine Christ coming and finding you too drunk to recognize Him!);

and the three universal responses of 5:16–18:

6. "rejoice always";
7. "pray constantly"; and
8. "give thanks in all things, for this is the will of God in Christ Jesus for you" (see Rom 8:28).

Everything in our lives should be transformed by this hope of our ultimate end. The most practical way to discern good or evil is to ask: Would I want Jesus to find me doing this when He comes again? The Second Coming is not a strange myth to be tucked away in some remote corner of our mind, but a truth to be lived daily, like everything in the Bible. God's revelation is not misty-eyed escapism but clear-eyed realism. For no event in history is as important, as spectacular, or as final as that ultimate event, "when the Lord Jesus is revealed from heaven with his mighty angels in flaming fire" (2 Thess 1:7).

Second Thessalonians: The Disastrous Effects of Misunderstanding the Second Coming

Paul's Second Letter to the Thessalonians is the second stage of the story of his trying to teach the Thessalonians the real implications of the doctrine of the Second Coming. It is essential to get this doctrine right, for it is close to center stage in the Christian gospel. It is mentioned no less than three hundred and eighteen times in the New Testament!

The Thessalonians had misunderstood Paul's teaching in two ways.

First, they seem to have thought they knew how soon Christ would come, even though Christ Himself did not (Mt 24:36) and even though Paul too had told them that the Lord would come not when expected but "like a thief in the night" (1 Thess 5:2).

Second, some had given up their jobs and were just waiting around until the end, even though Paul had explicitly warned them about this in 1 Thessalonians 4:11–12: "Aspire to live quietly, to mind your own affairs, and to work with your hands, as we charged you, so that you may command the respect of outsiders and be dependent on nobody." But Paul had to repeat his warning against idleness in his second letter (3:6) and lay down the common sense economic principle (which is no longer common sense today), "If anyone will not work, let him not eat" (3:10). (This was not universally recognized in Paul's day either; Rome was soon to grow into a swollen welfare state of "bread and circuses".)

It is enlightening to see the oneness of orthodoxy and orthopraxy, right doctrine and right life, throughout the New Testament. The Thessalonians' misunderstanding of the doctrine of the Second Coming necessarily had disastrous effects in their lives.

Even today this doctrine is more of a touchstone of orthodoxy than most of us realize. The mistake Paul corrects in 1 Thessalonians is essentially the same mistake that is made by modernism: ignoring, denying, or reducing to myth and symbolism the Second Coming. And the mistake Paul corrects in 2 Thessalonians, apparently made in misunderstanding Paul's first letter, is essentially the same mistake that is made by many modern Fundamentalists and extremist sects: a fixation and obsession with the imminence of the Second Coming.

Modernism tends to ignore the next life for this one. Fundamentalism tends to ignore this life for the next. But orthodoxy sees the two as mutually reinforcing, like life before birth and life after birth.

Paul uses the Old Testament term "the Day of the Lord" to refer to Christ's Second Coming. In the Old Testament, this is a phrase full of mystery. What is clear about it is that it will be the time when God does His greatest work in history and inaugurates a radically new era. That no one understood very well just what that work was to be is shown by the fact that *no* one understood Christ when He came, neither His enemies nor His friends, not even His apostles. Even His mother was puzzled.

The term "day" (*yom* in Hebrew) does not necessarily mean a literal twenty-four-hour day but a period of time, perhaps a very long time. The six "days" of creation in Genesis 1, for instance, took millions of years. When Paul spoke of "the day of the Lord" to the Thessalonians he meant the last times, the last era in world history. In one sense this era had come already with Christ's first coming. Yet in another sense (the one Paul emphasizes here), it had not yet come, for there are certain events that have to happen before the end, such as the appearance of "the man of lawlessness . . . the son of perdition", that is, the Antichrist (2:3).

The correct practical results of correct belief about Christ's coming "like a thief in the night" should be to motivate us to work for our salvation, for others' welfare, and above all for their salvation while there is still time. This is just the opposite of laziness and passivity. It means not leaving your job but taking on a new job. If every Christian lived out his essential missionary vocation, the world would be reconverted in two generations.

Since we do not know the day or the hour, we must be ready at any time, not by doing nothing, but by doing everything we are called to do, by knowing and doing the whole of God's will for us. As a bumper sticker on a college campus put it, "Prepare for your finals: read your Bible".

SEVENTEEN

Letters to Paul's Helpers:
First Timothy, Second Timothy,
and Titus

First Timothy: "How to Be a Bishop"

Timothy was a young convert via Paul's preaching. He became the bishop of the important city of Ephesus while still young. Paul wrote this letter to him personally for encouragement and advice on how to administer this great responsibility. The title could be "How to Be a Bishop".

There were problems in the Church at Ephesus (where aren't there?). Some members needed discipline, widows and old people were being neglected, and there was false teaching. Timothy was apparently having a difficult time dealing with these problems because he was young (4:12), sickly (5:23), and timid (2 Tim 1:7). Paul encourages him to "fight the good fight of the faith" (6:12).

The qualifications for a bishop mentioned in this letter are not worldly administrative or organizational skills, but personal piety and spiritual strength (3:1–13). The same is true also for the more practical office of deacon.

Ten notable passages are the following:

1. First Timothy 2:9–15 is perhaps the most hated passage in Scripture to feminists. Women are forbidden to have authority over men in the Church. They are commanded to be silent, submissive, and modest in dress. That seems pretty clear, however unpopular. Less clear is the assertion that woman will be "saved through bearing children" (2:15). The one thing that should be clear is that Paul exalts the uniquely feminine work rather than demeaning it. Those who interpret Paul in the latter way reveal nothing about him but much about themselves.

2. The passage of 3:4–5 makes clear that it was normal for bishops at this time to be married. That is not a matter of unchangeable *doctrine* but of changeable *discipline*, like fasting rules.

3. First Timothy 3:16 seems to be an early creed: ". . . the mystery of our religion: He was manifested in the flesh, vindicated in the Spirit, seen by angels, preached among the nations, believed on in the world, taken up in glory."

4. The passage of 4:1 speaks of the middle of the first century as already "the last days", and already full of heresies, especially Gnosticism (4:3–4), with its attack on nature, especially marriage. Radical feminism corresponds exactly to ancient Gnosticism in every way (except Gnosticism's disapproval of sexual promiscuity).

5. First Timothy 4:8 should prove an embarrassing verse to modern health fanatics.

6. The passage of 4:14 speaks of the sacrament of Holy Orders.

7. First Timothy 5:8 is a stronger version of "charity begins at home": "If anyone does not provide for his relatives and especially for his own family, he has disowned the faith and is worse than an unbeliever."

8.   The passage of 5:23 threatens the principle of teetotalling for everyone. Note, however, that Paul recommends only *a little* wine.

9.   First Timothy 6:6–8 is a famous and beloved "contentment" passage: "There is great gain in godliness with contentment; for we brought nothing into the world and we cannot take anything out of the world; but if we have food and clothing, with these we shall be content. . . . For the love of money is the root of all evils." Jesus said the same thing many times and surprised His disciples then as He surprises us now.

10.   The passage of 6:16 reveals two things about God that may be surprising. First, He alone is immortal by nature. (We are immortal not by nature, as Plato thought, but by grace, through the miracle of resurrection.) Second, He "dwells in unapproachable light, whom no man has ever seen or can see." God is *I AM*, pure Subject, not the object of our knowing. He is "the I who can never become an It" (Buber). We know Him only because He has revealed Himself (see Jn 1:18).

Second Timothy: A Letter of Encouragement

Paul wrote this second letter to Timothy from prison, awaiting execution. Christianity had become illegal in the Roman Empire since the sadistic and insane Nero had blamed the Christians for the great fire that burned half of Rome in A.D. 64—a fire he probably caused himself. The persecutions and martyrdoms had begun. Paul's enemies used this opportunity to get him arrested.

When he wrote this letter, Paul had no hope of being rescued (4:6–8, 18). He asked Timothy to visit him before he was killed (4:9–21). He complains that everyone had abandoned him, except for Luke (4:10–11).

The first time Paul had been arrested, it had been only a house arrest. He had hope of release or trial, and he was free to preach to friends who visited him (Acts 28:16–31). Now he had only death to look forward to—or rather, something much better than death, and better than this life (4:6–8).

From his prison Paul writes not complaints but encouragements to Timothy and warns him that he will have to endure hardships and persecutions too, not only from Roman authorities but also from false teachers within the Church. He encourages Timothy to overcome his timidity and youth (1: 5–9). Paul's language is very strong (as I think it would be today if he were writing to certain contemporary bishops who are over-timid and try to be popular): "I charge you in the presence of God and of Christ Jesus who is to judge the living and the dead . . . preach the word, be urgent in season and out of season" (4:1–2)—when convenient and inconvenient, when popular and unpopular. "Share in suffering as a good soldier of Christ Jesus" (2:3).

Christianity has always flourished under persecution. "The blood of the martyrs is the seed of the Church" because the Cross is the strongest force in the world. Spilt blood has more power than split atoms. The strongest churches today are still found in countries where it costs something to be a Christian.

Timothy's weapon that guarantees him success is truth, found in God's Word (see Jn 17:17). Second Timothy 3: 14–17 is Scripture's classic passage about itself.

Other memorable passages include the following:

1.   Second Timothy 1:12 is a great expression of Christian confidence and boldness: "I am not ashamed, for I know whom I have believed, and I am sure that he is able to guard until that Day what has been entrusted to me."

2.   The passage of 2:15 is the Christian teacher's job description: "Do your best to present yourself to God as one approved, a workman who has no need to be ashamed, rightly handling the word of truth."

3.   Second Timothy 3:1–7 sounds like a prophecy of modern moral and intellectual decadence.

4.   The passage of 3:12 is a universal promise of persecution: "All who desire to live a godly life in Christ Jesus will be persecuted." Therefore, if we are not being persecuted, we can deduce what logically follows from that fact.

5.   Second Timothy 4:7–8 is Paul's own self-composed epitaph: "I have fought the good fight, I have finished the race, I have kept the faith. Henceforth there is laid up for me the crown of righteousness, which the Lord, the righteous judge, will award to me on that Day, and not only to me but also to all who have loved his appearing." May every reader be able honestly to engrave that on his or her gravestone.

Titus: A Letter of Advice

Like Timothy, Titus was a young pastor with a difficult responsibility: the Church in Crete. The inhabitants of this Mediterranean island were famous for immorality; in fact, Paul quotes Epimenides the Cretan poet who had written six centuries earlier, "Cretans are always liars, evil beasts, and lazy gluttons" (1:12). "To act like a Cretan" was a saying in the ancient world that means "to be a liar".

Titus has to organize the Christian Church in Crete. Paul writes some good advice to him. First, as a bishop himself, Titus should appoint other bishops who are of strong moral character, who *practice* what they preach. Then Paul advises Titus to exercise his authority firmly (perhaps Titus, like Timothy, tended to be timid), refuting false teachers and forbidding evil deeds. For the Church, as we have seen, needs both orthodoxy (right belief) and orthopraxy (right practice), and the two are always connected.

The strong note of *authority* in Paul, here as in his other letters, should not be misunderstood. It is not sheer power or bullying, but speaking in the name of Christ, who Himself spoke "with authority" (Mt 7:29) and who commissioned His followers to preach in His name and His authority (Mt 28: 18–20). It is not *might* but *right*, "with firmness in the right". Paul's attitude to false teaching and practice is neither "burn the heretics" nor "anything goes", but "what does Jesus say?"

EIGHTEEN

A Personal and Tender Letter to a Friend: Philemon

This shortest of all Paul's letters (it could fit on a postcard) is to many readers the most personal, simple, direct, and appealing of all. There is a dramatic and poignant story behind it.

Onesimus, a slave, had run away from his master, Philemon, who was a friend and convert of Paul's. Onesimus had made his way to Rome and to Paul. There he had come to faith in Christ through Paul's influence (v. 10). Now Paul sends him back to his master with this note, telling Philemon to forgive him and accept him back not as a slave but as a brother in Christ (v. 16).

By Roman law, a runaway slave could be killed. Only because he was now a Christian would Onesimus think of voluntarily returning to his master. Only because Philemon was a Christian would he forgive and free Onesimus, as Paul suggests (vv. 16–17).

The letter is full of tact and tenderness, and also wit. Verse 11 is a pun on the name *Onesimus*, which means "useful". Onesimus had proved useless to Philemon by deserting him, but now he is "useful" to both Paul and Philemon. Paul asks Philemon to treat Onesimus as he would treat Paul himself (v. 17). He promises to repay any debt Onesimus may owe.

The parallel to Christ saving us by paying our debt to the Father is obvious, and Paul is confident that this Christlike example will win Philemon's good will.

There is deep religious significance in this little personal drama. It shows how relationships are transformed by Christ from slavery to freedom, from bondage to brotherhood. It shows how Christians who have been freed and forgiven by Christ must free and forgive others, how Christians should set aside their rights (vv. 8–9) to serve others as Christ set aside His rights to serve us, and how Christians should pay each other's debts as Christ paid our debt of sin.

Love goes far beyond justice, grace far beyond law. Like us, Onesimus is saved only by grace. Like Christ, Paul pays and forgives another's debt. Like God the Father, Philemon accepts this substitution and takes back his runaway as a member of his family. It is a perfect object lesson of theology-in-life, Christianity-in-practice.

NINETEEN

Christ as Prophet, Priest, and King: Hebrews

No one but God knows who wrote Hebrews, or to whom. The clue in 13:23 seems to point to Saint Paul. But for a variety of reasons, most scholars no longer hold to Pauline authorship of Hebrews. However, the jury is still out.

Hebrews seems to be addressed to Jewish Christians who were undergoing persecution for their new belief and were tempted to abandon their faith in Christ under this severe testing (10:32–34), though it had not yet reached the point of martyrdom (12:4). The author argues the need to hold fast to Christ as Lord and Savior—the very essence of Christianity.

As Romans is the world's first *systematic theology*, Hebrews is the first *apologetic* for the Christian faith. *Apologetic* here does not mean "excuse" but "defense"; not "I was wrong" but "I am right." Hebrews argues for the superiority of Christ in every way to pre-Christian Judaism, to prevent Jewish Christians from choosing the shadow over the substance, the promises over their fulfillment, the arrow over the bull's eye.

The author emphasizes Christ's threefold office as prophet, priest, and king—the three Old Testament offices that fore-shadowed Him. It emphasizes both His divinity (1:1–8) and

His humanity (2:9–10; 2:14–18; 4:15; 5:7–9; 12:3; 13:12). The overall theme is like that of Colossians: the all-sufficient greatness of Christ (compare Hebrews 1:3 with Colossians 1:15–20).

Along with Genesis, 1 John, and John's Gospel, Hebrews begins with one of the four great first verses in the Bible, which reveal a total sweep of history: "In many and various ways God spoke of old to our fathers by the prophets; but in these last days he has spoken to us by a Son." This beginning sets the theme for the whole book: Judaism is not *wrong* but *fulfilled and completed* in Christ and the Church, through whom God has spoken a new Word. The author constantly quotes God's (Old Testament) Word, as Matthew does, for a similar purpose (to convince and convert Jews). He has a high, holy, and practical attitude of existential urgency toward the Word. It is not just "proof texts" but the present, living speech of the present, living God. "Take care, brethren. . . . 'Today, when you hear his voice, do not harden your hearts'" (3:12, 15). This Word is described (in 4:12–13) as "living and active, sharper than any two-edged sword, piercing to the division of soul and spirit [do you know that difference?], of joints and marrow, and discerning the thoughts and intentions of the heart. And before him no creature is hidden, but all are open and laid bare to the eyes of him with whom we have to do."

The whole point of the Old Testament Word, according to Hebrews, is to point to Christ. It is incomplete in itself (11:39–40). The Old and New Covenants are strikingly contrasted in 12:18–24, as Paul contrasts law and grace in Romans. By the way, the more I compare Hebrews and Paul's letters, the more I see Paul in Hebrews—if not his authorship, at least his doctrine.

Christ is shown to be superior in every way:

1. He is superior to angels, for they worship Him (1:4–2:18).

2. He is superior to Moses and Joshua, for they are creatures, while He is the Creator (3:1–4:13).

3. He is a better priest than the human priest Aaron, for His sacrifice was once for all (8:1–10:18). His priesthood is greater than that of Levi, akin to the priesthood of Melchizedek (4:14–7:28). The Old Testament priesthood and liturgy were *symbolic* of Christ and of Heaven (8:1–5).

It needs to be pointed out here that the medieval penchant for interpreting Scripture symbolically is rooted in Scripture itself. Some modern exegetes turn it upside down and interpret symbolically not the symbol (the Old Testament) but the reality symbolized (Christ's divinity, Resurrection, atonement, and Second Coming).

4. He is superior to the Old Law, or Old Covenant, for His Blood takes away our sin (8:1–10:39). As a consequence, we have real, objective access to God, and felt, subjective confidence (10:19–20).

The most famous chapter in Hebrews is chapter 11, the great roll call of the heroes of faith, the Christian hall of fame. It begins with the famous description of faith itself (v. 1): "Now faith is the assurance of things hoped for, the conviction of things not seen." See the passage 2:8–9: "As it is, we do not yet see everything in subjection to him. But we see Jesus". Faith goes beyond the seen, but it begins there. It is not like a blind date but like a marriage.

The faith-works controversy is solved (without even being posed) by seeing faith as a thing that *works*, that acts. "*By faith* Abraham obeyed. . . . *By faith* the people crossed the Red Sea. . . . *By faith* the walls of Jericho fell down. . . . *through faith* [they] conquered kingdoms, enforced justice, received promises, stopped the mouths of lions" (11:8, 29, 30, 33, emphasis mine).

Faith and hope are virtually identified in the passages 11:1 and 11:14–16. Here "faith" includes hope. In 1 Peter 3:15, "hope" includes faith. Hope *is* faith directed to the future.

The exhortation of Chapter 12 is the practical consequence of chapter 11: "Therefore, since we are surrounded by so great a cloud of witnesses, let us also lay aside every weight and sin which clings so closely, and let us run with perseverance the race that is set before us, looking to Jesus the pioneer and perfecter of our faith, who for the joy that was set before him endured the cross, despising the shame, and is seated at the right hand of the throne of God" (12:1–2). The Greek word for "witnesses" means (1) martyrs, (2) those who testify, as in court, and (3) those who see or observe, implying that these saints are now watching us from Heaven. How would you feel if you saw thousands of eyes outside your window?

There is a weighty consequence to such a weighty theology of such a weighty Christ: "How shall we escape if we neglect such a great salvation?" (2:3). No more urgent and heart-stoppingly serious passage exists in all the world's literature than Hebrews 12:25–29. It concludes with a vision of God's essential nature as "fire", just as Moses saw Him in the burning bush, and as Pascal saw Him on the night he met Him: "God of Abraham, Isaac, and Jacob, not the God of philosophers and scholars" (*Pensées*, 913). As C. S. Lewis says of his Christ-figure Aslan, "He's not tame. But he's *good*." Goodness is not tame. The essential root of modernist theology is right there, in the *taming* of God.

Chapter 12 also contains one of the greatest exhortations on suffering and its meaning ever written (vv. 5–12). This short passage says more about life's most popular problem than most complete books on the subject.

Chapter 13 gives us one of Scripture's many classic passages on the need to be countercultural (vv. 11–14). This is as necessary today as nineteen centuries ago, for the only difference between the old, pre-Christian paganism and the new, post-Christian paganism is that the new version knows more and is more responsible.

Other not-to-be-missed gems in this diamond mine of a book include the following passages, all of them surprising points to learn something new from, not soporific reinforcements of what we all know already:

- Hebrews 2:11, on our participation in divine life (compare Jn 15:5; 2 Pet 1:4);
- the passage of 2:14–15, on how Christ destroys not only death but also the *fear* of death and the bondage this fear keeps us in (what we really fear is not death but Hell!);
- Hebrews 2:18, on how fully and thoroughly human Christ is;
- the passage of 5:8, on how even Christ had to learn obedience through suffering (George MacDonald says, "Christ suffered, not that we may be freed from suffering but that our suffering may be changed into his") ;
- Hebrews 6:5, on how we already taste "the powers of the age to come" (Heaven), like appetizers;
- the passage of 9:22, on the need for death and blood and sacrifice to take away sin—contrary to modern, "enlightened" religion, every ancient religion knew this in its bones;
- Hebrews 9:27, a definitive disproof of reincarnation;
- the passage of 13:2, on the sacred nature of hospitality and the disturbing proximity of angels; and

- Hebrews 13:8, on God's opinion of "new" Christianities.

The central theme and thread holding all these pearls together is the center of all reality, Christ. Hebrews' essential message is life's essential message: "Let us keep our eyes fixed on Jesus" (12:2 NEV), for "Jesus Christ is the same yesterday and today and for ever" (13:8). Hebrews goes down to bedrock.

TWENTY

Doers of the Word: James

The author of the Epistle of James was probably not the James who was one of Jesus' twelve apostles, John's brother. That James was martyred very early, probably in A.D. 44 (Acts 12:2). The author was probably the James who was one of Jesus' "brothers" mentioned in Matthew 13:55. (The Hebrew word translated "brothers" can also mean "cousins" or "relatives".)

Since God's people were scattered—or dispersed—over the whole world, James, Peter, John, and Jude all wrote "general epistles", that is, letters "to the twelve tribes in the Dispersion" (1:1) rather than to any one local church, as Paul did in most of his letters.

James' letter is like the Book of Proverbs in the Old Testament: full of maxims and practical advice about living. It is not primarily doctrinal and does not have a systematic outline. But its unifying theme is 1:22: "Be doers of the word, and not hearers."

The most famous and important passage in James is 2:14–26, about faith and works. Martin Luther denied that James belonged in the Bible because he could not reconcile James' emphasis on works with Paul's emphasis on faith.

But faith and works are not opposites. That is James' whole point! They are complementary. James' point is that a faith that does not produce good works is not true faith, but dead faith (2:17), like a tree that produces no fruit.

Actually, James' point is very clear and simple. It is not a contrast between faith and works but between a real faith, a faith that works, and a false faith, one that does not. "Show me your faith apart from your works, and I by my works will show you my faith." We do not see a living plant's roots, only its fruits. Others cannot see your faith, for it is invisible. They can see only your actions, which show your faith as a tulip flower shows you that a tulip bulb has taken root.

The apparent contradiction between James, who says that we, like Abraham, are justified by works (2:21), and Paul, who says that we, like Abraham, are justified by faith (Rom 4), is explained by looking at the context. Paul's context is the relationship between the believer and God, while James' context is the relationship between the believer and his neighbor. God sees your faith; your neighbor sees your works. Faith justifies us before God; works justify us before our neighbors.

A further explanation is that James means by "faith" only intellectual belief. "You believe that God is one; you do well. Even the demons believe—and shudder" (2:19). But Paul means by "faith" (in Galatians and Romans) something more than belief. He means accepting Christ into your soul and thus into your life, where it produces good works as its fruit.

In more technical terms, Paul is contrasting faith with law as a way to be justified, while James is contrasting a faith without works with a faith that works as a way to be sanctified. Paul is asking how to be saved; James is asking how to be holy. Paul is asking how to get to Heaven, James is asking how to live on earth.

In any case, the "bottom line" is that faith and works are two aspects of the very same reality: the new birth, the supernatural life of God, which enters the soul by faith and comes out as the works of love. "You see that *faith* was active along with his works, and *faith* was completed by works" (2:22, emphasis mine).

James also mentions ten other things that faith does: (1) it endures sufferings and trials, (2) it obeys the word of God that it hears, (3) it overcomes favoritism and prejudice, (4) it controls the tongue and gossip, (5) it gives us wisdom, (6) it separates us from the world, (7) it makes us submissive to God, (8) it resists the devil, (9) it puts us in God's presence, and (10) it waits patiently for Christ's Second Coming. James never teaches works *vs.* faith or works *instead* of faith. From beginning to end, the letter is a tribute to faith, but to a faith that works, like the one described in Hebrews 11.

Some unique features of James include the promise of the supernatural gift of wisdom (1:5), the holistic interpretation of the law (2:10–11), a scary verse for teachers (3:1), an answer to what is the most dangerous and uncontrollable organ in your body (3:3–12), the solution to the puzzle of the origin of war (4:1–3), and the scriptural basis for the sacrament of the sick (5:13–18).

Memorable reiterations of doctrines taught many other times in Scripture include the passages of 1:2 (on suffering), 1:17 (on grace), 4:4 (on worldliness), 4:7–8 (on dealing with the devil), 4:8 and 5:8–9 (on purity of heart: see Kierkegaard's great title, *Purity of Heart Is to Will One Thing*), 5:13–15 (on playing God vs. trusting Providence), and 5:12 (on straightforward, simple honesty—if only the "nuancers" would read that and Matthew 5:37).

Each of His apostles emphasized a different aspect of Christ. James, like Mark, emphasized His practicality. This is the epistle theoreticians and scholars like the least and need the most.

TWENTY-ONE

Standing Fast in Christ:
Letters of Peter

Peter's two letters could be called "Rocky I" and "Rocky II", for Jesus had declared Peter to be the Rock on which He would build His Church (Mt 16:18). We see in them not the "sandy" Peter of the Gospels, the Peter with foot-in-mouth disease, but a rock-solid saint. His two letters are full of sound advice and exhortations for daily Christian living. Peter's letters, like James', are practical. Paul's letters, like John's, are more intellectual. Peter and James are exhortatory; Paul and John are expository.

There is no "Rocky III" because Peter was martyred in Rome in or around A.D. 66. The prophecy Jesus had made about how Peter was to die (Jn 21:18–19) was fulfilled when Nero crucified Peter. Tradition says Peter insisted on being crucified upside down because he did not want to seem equal to his Master.

Peter wrote these two "general epistles" to Christians scattered throughout the empire, that is, the civilized world (1:1). Peter had taken the center of Church authority to the center of the world, Rome. He spent the last decade of his life there. He refers to Rome symbolically as "Babylon" (5:13), for Babylon was the traditional enemy of the Jews, the empire that had conquered and enslaved them six hundred years earlier, just as Rome had done again. Now Rome was turning her hatred also to the new Israel, the Church, when Nero and Diocletian began persecuting Christians.

First Peter: Stand Fast in Persecution

Peter writes his first letter to advise Christians in the Roman Empire how to deal with suffering and persecution. The "fiery ordeal" (4:12) endured by these Christians was not yet martyrdom, for Nero's killings were confined to the city of Rome. Only later did Rome begin killing Christians throughout the empire. The ordeal was probably the scorns and sneers of their neighbors, who resented Christians for being different. It was becoming increasingly clear to the pagans, just as it is to the neo-pagans in our contemporary de-Christianized society, that Christians are a dangerously different people with a dangerously different Lord, love, and lifestyle.

This kind of persecution has not ended with the end of the Roman Empire, of course. As anyone knows who has seriously attempted it, *living* the whole gospel in a fallen world can be harder than *dying* for it.

Yet Peter does not blame the state as an institution for its mistreatment of Christians. In fact, like Paul in Romans 13, he tells his readers to submit to its authority as divinely instituted (2:13–14). The state, like the whole world, is seen not as a thing in itself but as relative to God.

Peter's tone is full of grace and encouragement. He practices what he preaches about being a pastor (shepherd) of souls, an example rather than a lord (5:1–3; compare with Jn 13:12–17). Peter had finally learned Jesus' simple lesson and learned it well. Like Paul, he preaches service and submission: of citizens to the state, of servants to their masters, wives to their husbands, and generally of all Christians to each other (3:8).

Christian "submission" makes sense only if the state, master, husband, parent, or friend is seen as an icon of Christ. If we really believed our Lord's words, "Truly, I say to you, as you did it to one of the least of these my brethren, you did it to me" (Mt 25:40), we would not balk at the idea of "submission".

There is a consistent teaching throughout the Bible, especially in the New Testament and the Epistles, that the divine order for human society and relationships involves hierarchy, authority, and obedience. But the rivers that run in these hierarchical riverbeds are rivers of love and humility, not power (5:5; compare with Eph 5:21).

First Peter focuses most especially on the problem of suffering. Peter tells his flock three essential practical truths about Christian suffering:

First, that we should not be surprised at it: "Beloved, do not be surprised at the fiery ordeal which comes upon you to prove you, as though something strange were happening to you" (4:12). If the Head suffers, His body must also suffer, for otherwise it is not His body. Christ never promised us a rose garden without thorns. Instead, He promised that "if they persecuted me, they will persecute you; if they kept my word, they will keep yours also" (Jn 15:20). George MacDonald says, "The Son of God suffered not so that we might not suffer but so that our sufferings might become his."

Second, because of this real incorporation into His Body, suffering can become joy: "But rejoice in so far as you share Christ's sufferings, that you may also rejoice and be glad when his glory is revealed" (4:13). We must not be bitter or resentful to God for allowing us to suffer, but realize that sufferings are God's blessings, not His punishments. As Saint Philip Neri said, "The cross is the gift God gives to His friends."

Third, there is an eschatological dimension to understanding suffering. "After you have suffered a little while, the God of all grace, who has called you to his eternal glory in Christ, will himself restore, establish, and strengthen you" (5:10). Suffering does not weaken us but strengthens us in the long run. The biblical answer to the problem of suffering is not some abstract, timeless truth but two real historical events: the two comings of Christ, one past, one future. The full answer is something that will happen when Christ returns. In this light, read 1:3–10, probably the key passage to the whole letter.

Fourth, in order to transform suffering into joy by its incorporation into Christ, our sufferings must be for good, not for evil. Paradoxically, only unjust suffering is good; suffering justly is evil. "What credit is it if when you do wrong and are beaten for it you take it patiently? But if when you do right and suffer for it you take it patiently, you have God's approval" (2:20; compare with 4:1–16).

Other notable and memorable passages in this little letter include the following:

1. The charter of Christian apologetics: "Always be prepared to make a defense (*logos*, reason) to anyone who calls you to account for the hope that is in you" (3:15).
2. The promise that "love covers a multitude of sins" (4:8)—this is *agapē*, not *eros*, of course—charity, not romance.
3. The unqualified exhortation to "cast *all* your anxieties on him, for he cares for you" (5:7).
4. The exhortation to "be sober, be watchful. Your adversary the devil prowls around like a roaring lion, seeking someone to devour. Resist him, firm

in your faith" (5:8–9). This verse used to be very familiar, in the old days when the idea of spiritual warfare was as commonly taught in the Church as it is in the Scriptures. This passage was repeated every day in the daily Divine Office, prayed by all monks, most priests, and many of the laity.

5. The intriguing passage about Christ preaching to the dead "spirits in prison" (presumably Purgatory) who had lived in Noah's time. This seems to be what Christ did between Good Friday and Easter Sunday. He was busy even then (see Jn 5:16–17)!

6. The simple statement that "baptism . . . saves you" (3:21). This is a very embarrassing one for many Protestants who teach that the sacraments are mere symbols.

Second Peter: Stand Fast against Heresy and Sin

This letter was written just before Peter's anticipated death by martyrdom (1:14–15), between A.D. 62 and 66, from Rome. It is the last recorded words of the first recorded pope.

Peter refers to Paul's letters (3:15–16) as already well-known in the Church, thus proving they were written quite early. By the way, if you find Paul's writings difficult, you are in good company: so did Peter (3:16).

This short letter is Peter's "reminder" (1:12) of the familiar, essential gospel truth and of its solid foundation in two public facts. Only Judaism and Christianity are religions of public record, eyewitnessed facts. All others are (pagan) myths, (Oriental) mysticisms, or (modernist) moralisms.

The two facts are (1) the disciples' and Peter's own eyewitness experience of Jesus (1:16–18) and (2) the written prophecies of Scripture that Jesus fulfilled: "For we did not

follow cleverly devised myths when we made known to you
the power and coming of our Lord Jesus Christ, but we were
eyewitnesses of his majesty. . . . And we have the prophetic
word made more sure. You will do well to pay attention to
this as to a lamp shining in a dark place, until the day dawns
and the morning star arises in your hearts. First of all, you
must understand that no prophecy of scripture is a matter of
one's own interpretation, because no prophecy ever came by
the impulse of man, but men moved by the Holy Spirit spoke
from God" (1:16, 19–21). This passage seems clearly to reject
both the modernist view of Scripture as *human* interpretation rather than divine intervention, and the Protestant principle of *private* interpretation.

Peter's first letter dealt with external dangers to the Church:
persecution and sufferings. His second letter deals with internal dangers: heresies and sins. The early Church and the early
Christians were being confused and harmed by false teaching. This is why the New Testament is so consistently harsh
on false doctrine: down the road it always harms people, and
Christians love people. It's out of liberal-hearted love and
compassion for people that the Church has always been so
hardheadedly conservative about doctrine.

Just as there were false as well as true prophets throughout
the history of Israel, they persisted in the early Church. And
not only the *early* Church. Does anyone really doubt who
they are today? Who can read without embarrassment the
many passages in Scripture denouncing false teachers, and
who can't? Who do and who do not believe there *are* such
things as false teachings because there are such things as objective truth and divine revelation?

Peter points out the connection between false doctrine
and false practice. The saints are always orthodox. They are
the living refutation of all who say orthopraxy alone is

enough—or orthodoxy alone. For just as true doctrine naturally produces true living (since good works are the fruit of faith; see James), false doctrine always produces false living: licentiousness (2:2), greed (2:3), arrogance and the despising of authority (2:10), lust (2:10, 13, 14), and a false "freedom": "They promise them freedom, but they themselves are slaves of corruption; for whatever overcomes a man, to that he is enslaved" (2:19). As George MacDonald put it, "A man is a slave to whatever he cannot part with that is less than himself."

These false teachers were also scoffing at the belief that Christ would return to judge them (3:3–10). Peter writes some very disturbingly strong words against these teachers, just as Jesus used similar words against the Pharisees and scribes—not out of hatred but out of the kind of "tough love" that shouts, "Danger!" when someone is near the edge of a cliff or on thin ice.

For God cannot change His essential nature, which is both love and justice. He delays His punishments to give us time to repent (3:9–15), but punishment for sin is inevitable (2:4–6; 3:9, 12, 17). This is a theme taught on every page of Scripture, yet one hardly taught on a single page of modern books of "religious education". The God of infinite and unchangeable love cast His rebel angels into Hell, destroyed the world with a flood, and rained fire and brimstone on Sodom and Gomorrah. It is not possible that He will wink sleepily at New York or San Francisco.

The best antidote for Christians against heresies is the positive one: understanding the truth. That is why Peter the Rock writes this reminder of the foundations of the faith (1:12–13; 3:1–2). "Reminding" is the business of the Magisterium and the papacy, the Rock. Buildings with a strong rock as their foundation, like those on Manhattan Island, can grow to skyscrapers. A foundation *has* to be conservative, a "stick-in-the-mud", like an anchor.

Also included in 2 Peter is the most explicit passage in Scripture about the high, exalted, and incredible destiny of believers actually to share God's nature: "He has granted to us his precious and very great promises, that through these you may escape from the corruption that is in the world because of passion, and become partakers of the divine nature" (1:3–4). The Eastern Orthodox churches call this *theosis* ("divinization"). It is only in light of this revealed destiny and ultimate identity that the uncompromisingly idealistic, otherworldly, and countercultural moral exhortations found in every book of the New Testament make perfect sense.

TWENTY-TWO

A Spiritual Father Writes
to His Children:
Letters of John

First John: Sharing God's Very Life

This beautiful letter was written by the Apostle John in his old age to his spiritual "children", Christians who were not beginners but already mature in their faith (2:7; 2:18–27; 3:11). Like his Gospel, this letter is profound. Yet it is simple. It is deep, yet clear enough for a child to understand it.

One of John's purposes is to combat Gnosticism. Gnosticism taught that matter was evil, that God had not created the material world, and that Jesus could not possibly be God incarnate. Gnostics believed that their new, super-spiritualized version of Christianity was the superior "hidden knowledge" (*gnosis*). They thought that only the uneducated masses would believe the literal incarnational and traditional faith as expressed in the Gospels and by the Church. They also thought they had a superior morality, which elevated them above the ordinary distinctions between right and wrong, good and evil.

Positively, the fundamental theme of John's letter is the essence of religion: a relationship with God, union with God, fellowship with God, sharing God's life. John wants us to be certain and assured of our relationship with God, of our eternal life: "I write this to you who believe in the name of the Son of God, that you may know that you have eternal life" (5:13). The basis of our certainty is not ourselves but Jesus: "He who has the Son has life; he who has not the Son of God has not life" (5:12). It is as simple as that. John's Gospel also had this simple, absolutely central issue as its point: see John 20:31.

John uses three terms to describe God and the life of God that Christians share through Christ: *light*, *life*, and *love*. These are the three things everyone needs and wants more than anything else in the world. Their opposites, falsehood, death and hate, are the three worst things in the world. Everyone wants to avoid them, but not everyone knows how. Jesus is the answer to that question—the most important question in the world.

Second John: God's Command—Love

This short letter is addressed to "the elect lady and to her children". This "lady" probably refers not to an individual but to a local church. Mother Church is a lady. The letter was written by John "the Elder" (v. 1) in his old age, probably about A.D. 90.

The basic theme is no new command but the command we had from the beginning (v. 5), the same theme we find in John's Gospel and his first letter: the primacy of love. Love is not a new but a very old idea, as old as God.

"Love" means for John not first of all a feeling but obedience to God's commands (v. 6). But God's command *is* to love. "The command, as you have heard from the beginning, is that you must all live in love" (v. 6). Therefore, love and obedience, love and God's commandment, love and law, are one.

Love is also discerning, not naïve. It needs sound doctrine. Love needs truth. John, therefore, writes against the same false teaching he warned against in his previous writing, the denial of the Incarnation of Christ (v. 7). It is false charity to love falsehood. As Saint Thomas Aquinas says, "The greatest charity one can do to another is to lead him to the truth."

Third John: Our Basic Choice

This little letter is the shortest book of the Bible. It is a personal note in response to a situation that had come up in the churches in Asia Minor. John had sent out teachers who traveled from one local church to another with his apostolic authority. One local church leader, Gaius, had accepted them with Christian hospitality and generosity, while another, Diotrephes, had treated them arrogantly and selfishly, denying John's authority as an apostle. He had even driven out those Christians who had accepted the teachers sent by John (v. 10).

John writes this letter to praise and thank Gaius for "living in the truth" (v. 3) and to warn against Diotrephes, who tells "lies" (v. 10). The simple message of this letter is one of the main themes of John's other writings: the real difference between good and evil, light and darkness, truth and falsehood; the simple message, "Do not imitate evil, but imitate good", for "he who does good is of God" (v. 11).

TWENTY-THREE

Warning against False Teaching:
Jude

Jude was the "the brother of James" (v. 1), who was Jesus' "brother", that is, his cousin (Mk 6:3; Mt 13:55). This makes Jude one of Jesus' relatives too. These relatives did not believe in Jesus until after He rose from the dead (Jn 7:1–9; Acts 1:1–14), but they then became leaders in the early Church at Jerusalem (Acts 15:13–21).

There is such a strong similarity between Jude 4 to 18 and 2 Peter 2:1 to 3:4 that one of these authors was probably quoting the other.

Jude's primary theme is false teaching. Most of the letters in the New Testament deal with this theme, but all of Jude is concerned with it. The language he uses is very strong. But as we have noted before, it is not cruel but kind to utter loud warnings when there is real danger and to tell the truth when falsehoods are rampant.

The false teachers Jude opposed taught both false doctrine and false ethics, false practice—two things that *always* go together. These teachers taught that since God was gracious (v. 4), they could live as they pleased. (Sound familiar?) Jude describes their character in a series of five stunning images from nature in verses 12 and 13. Jude reminds them of the aspect of God they forgot: justice and judgment. He recounts past acts of God's judgment on disobedient Israel, disobedient angels, and disobedient Sodom and Gomorrah.

Jude encourages his audience to "build yourselves up on your most holy faith" (v. 20), to stay in spiritual shape, on guard against error, but to "convince some, who doubt" (v. 22). He closes with a great doxology (closing word of praise and glory) in verses 24 and 25. In this little letter as throughout the Bible, the negative is real but the positive outweighs it.

TWENTY-FOUR

The Most Difficult Book in the Bible: Revelation

The Book of Revelation, or the Apocalypse, the only prophetic book in the New Testament, is surely the strangest and hardest to interpret of all the books of the Bible.

Its style is neither the simple, sober eyewitness description that we find in the Gospels and Acts (and in most of the historical books of the Old Testament), nor the straightforward principles and advice that we find in the Epistles (and in most of the wisdom books in the Old Testament). Its closest biblical equivalent is some of the visions of Ezekiel and Daniel.

It is a visionary, highly poetical, even mystical book. It seems to most ordinary Catholics a closed book, even a dangerous book. For it suggests to them images of wild-faced, white-robed, black-bearded fanatics with signs saying, "The end is nigh!" It's true that many "kooky" theologies and sects have used this book to justify their pet ideas. They usually interpret the rest of the Bible in light of their interpretation of this book rather than vice versa. This is backward, of course, for we must interpret the more obscure by the less obscure, not vice versa.

The very strangeness and mystery of this book fascinates some (usually the more curious and poetical minds), while discouraging others (usually the more sober and practical). I don't think God expects all of us to resonate with each of the books of the Bible equally. That's one reason He provided many books, not just one. Not everyone has a poetical bent, especially today. (Look at the shamefully prosaic translation of the Bible that all Catholics have had to put up with at Mass for the last twenty years!) But there are always more poets than non-poets in the world, so there are always many minds that are fascinated by this book.

The author was evidently a poet (I refer to both the human author and the Divine Author); and it takes a poet to understand a poet. I think we can understand this book only when the poetic, intuitive, unconscious, imaginative part of our brain (the "right brain") is used, not only the clear, rational, conscious, controlled part (the "left brain"). Revelation is like a museum of abstract art, not representational or naturalistic art. It is like an Ingmar Bergman movie. Better yet, it is like a medieval illuminated manuscript. If you feel a kinship with medieval illustrations for this book, I think you are closer than most modern people to the mindset that produced it.

It claims to be a divinely-sent vision or dream, not a waking observation. It is not a clever, clear, controlled *allegory*, but is full of mysterious *symbols* with multiple layers of meaning. It is more imagistic than conceptual. That is probably the reason why no consistent, rational, theological explanation of it, however honest and well-intentioned, has ever gained universal acceptance. Just as it is harder to specify the meaning of a painting than a novel, it is harder to be sure what we are supposed to get out of this book than the rest of the Bible. Most of the rest of the Bible is relatively clear. For thousands of years, ordinary people understood it quite well without theology courses or seminary training. Anyone who really wants to know can find what Saint Paul most centrally cares about, or what the Psalms mean. But this book is more puzzling.

Its Main Point

Yet its main overall point is clear from its title. Unfortunately, many modern editions of the Bible include titles added by modern editors, for the original books of the Bible did not have titles separate from the books themselves. The titles were the first words of each book. (For the books were not books with covers, but scrolls.)

The correct title is crucial because it tells us the main, central point of the whole book. If we miss that, then all the details will be misunderstood because their significance is relative to how they serve that main point.

The original title of this book is not simply "Revelation", and certainly not "The Revelation of Saint John". Look it up (1:1). It is "The Revelation of Jesus Christ".

The center of this book—and the center of all world history—is Christ, the same Christ we know from the Gospels. No matter how different in style this book is from the Gospels, its main point is identical to theirs: its point is a Person. The main point is not the end of the world, or even the cosmic battle between good and evil, or the millennium, or the great tribulation, or the Antichrist, but Christ Himself.

The only difference between this book and the Gospels is that it presents Christ in His Second Coming. We see Christ in glory rather than in humiliation. The cosmic Christ reveals Himself universally, not just to the Jews.

When Jesus ascended into Heaven, His disciples, gazing up into Heaven, saw two angels who announced to them the Second Coming: "Men of Galilee, why do you stand looking into heaven? This Jesus, who was taken up from you into heaven, will come in the same way as you saw him go into heaven" (Acts 1:11). Revelation fulfills the third part of our Christian faith about history, which we proclaim each Sunday: "Christ has died, Christ is risen, *Christ will come again*."

The early Church was full of longing—anxious, joyful, operative, expectant longing for Christ's return. Where we see a gray vagueness when we look into the future, they saw golden glory. Why have we lost this? I think it is largely because the doctrine of the Second Coming has been so abused by fringe groups, sects, and theological factions warring over secondary details like the millennium (the thousand-year reign of Christ described in chap. 20). Especially in Protestant Fundamentalism, "premillennialism", "postmillennialism", and "amillennialism" have been bitter battle cries.

But *abusus non tollit usus*—the abuse of a thing does not take away its proper use. We need the Book of Revelation even more than past ages did. For we need to recapture the historic hope it expresses. Even faith and love are not complete without hope.

Its Unity

At first this book seems to be two books, not one. The first three chapters feature seven letters to seven Christian churches (congregations) in Asia ("Asia Minor," modern Turkey): Ephesus, Smyrna, Pergamum, Thyatira, Sardis, Philadelphia, and Laodicea. These churches and cities were real, not visionary. The ruins of some of them can still be seen today. They had real, specific, local problems, just like the churches to which Saint Paul wrote his epistles; and the seven letters address these problems. They give each church a kind of report card.

Though the language is sometimes symbolic, the problems were real. Some were so specific and local that no one knows any more what they were—for example, the problem with the "Nicolaitans".

But then the book suddenly takes off like a rocket ship into the heavens. Visions explode like firecrackers in the mind. Tongues turn into swords. Thunders speak. Burning mountains fall into the sea. Angels blow trumpets. Stars with names like Wormwood fall from the sky. Four horsemen ride across the sky bringing terrible plagues. Giant locusts sting and torture people. The sea turns to blood. No one can unroll a scroll except the Lamb. A dragon battles an angel, a woman, and a Lamb. Angels, elders, and the four living creatures frolic and worship around a golden throne and a sea of crystal. Finally, a golden city majestically descends to earth from the sky. What in the world (or out of it) is going on here?

Revelation is not two books, however great the difference between the first three chapters and the last nineteen. The author wants to show the members of those seven local congregations (and us too) that their little local problems are part of a great cosmic battle that is being fought even now. The real story behind the world's headlines is the battle that will not cease until its consummation at the end of time. What we do in our parishes and homes contributes to what Christ is doing: preparing the Second Coming. *That* is the final meaning of our daily work. Setting up chairs for a parish committee meeting is a contribution, however small, to this greatest of all wars. Our lives are parts of a far greater scenario and significance than the unaided human eye can see, greater even than the unaided human mind can imagine. That is the whole point of juxtaposing the two parts of this book.

Its Author

If a single author can write in two styles as different as those of Revelation 1 to 3 and 4 to 19, there is no reason to think it is impossible that the same John who wrote the fourth Gospel wrote this book too, however different the style. From the earliest Christian writings that mention this book, tradition has always ascribed it to John the Evangelist. Yet since the mid-1700s, a number of Scripture scholars have come to the conclusion that it must have been a different John, largely because the style, form, and vocabulary are so different from that of John's Gospel and Epistles.

Perhaps they are right, but the bottom line is that no one knows for sure. On the one hand, there is the reliability of tradition. On the other hand, there is the reliability of the current crop of scholars. Personally, I would put my money on the Church Fathers sooner than on the Church's new kids on the block until proven otherwise.

Even my gut literary instincts tell me it "smells" Johannine, for the traditional symbol for John is the eagle, and this book, John's Gospel, and 1 John all soar like an eagle. The same Spirit moves over the waters of both worlds, however different the waters and the weather. Also, 1 John and Revelation share some distinctive themes, notably the Antichrist and the vision of a cosmic battle between good and evil, an all-encompassing spiritual war.

Its Purpose

It is often asserted (for example, in short introductions to this book printed in Bibles) that it was written to comfort Christians who were being persecuted. This is probably not untrue, but it tends to leave two mistaken impressions: (1) that the purpose of the book is comfort rather than truth and (2) that its relevance is limited to the second century. (It was probably written between A.D. 90 and 100.)

The book itself says it was written not because John got it into his head to spread around some good cheer to poor souls, but because Jesus Christ revealed Himself to John and commanded John to write down the vision. What better reason did anyone ever have for writing any book? Why substitute a lesser reason for a greater one?

Unless the fundamental claim made by this book right at the beginning is simply false—that is, unless this book is fundamentally a fake—its primary Author is Jesus Christ, just as its primary subject is Jesus Christ. It is a self-revelation, a theophany. If we forget its primary subject matter we misunderstand its content, and if we forget its primary Author we read it in the wrong spirit: the spirit of curiosity and scholarship rather than the spirit of wonder and worship. The most important key to reading this book is profound, interior silence.

Like the Bible as a whole, this book is a love letter from Almighty God to us. It can be helpful at times to peer intently through the spectacles of a scholar at the passages in a love letter, but it is certainly wrong to adopt that as your essential posture instead of lying back and listening to your lover sing beautiful poetry to you.

When we read this book, let us remember that Jesus, not John, and certainly not some contemporary commentator (like me), is its primary interpreter. He is its primary Author, and the Author has the authority to interpret His own work. Authority, after all, means something like "author's rights".

The Symbols in Revelation

Most of the Bible can be understood without paying explicit attention to the principles of symbolism and correct ways to interpret them (though there are a few crucially important passages like "This is my body" where different interpretations, symbolic versus literal, have divided Christendom). But we cannot understand the Book of Revelation without understanding symbolism. When symbolism appears in the other books of the Bible, it appears as a secondary note, or in a few chapters. If we fail to understand the symbolic passages, there is still a lot left that we can understand. Not so in this book. If we don't "get" the symbols, we don't "get" most of the book.

Therefore, in order to understand this book, we need to back up for a moment and review some basic principles of interpretation. This long way around will prove the shortest in the long run because it will block us from many dead ends, many misunderstandings.

A first and obvious question, and the one most often asked, is How are we to know whether we are supposed to interpret any given passage in the Bible literally or symbolically?

There is an extremely simple and commonsensical answer to this question. If the writer claims he has perceived the events he narrates with his physical eyes, in the physical world, or that someone else has done so, then the passage is to be interpreted literally. But if the narrator or his sources do not claim that they or anyone else were eyewitnesses, then it might be possible to interpret the passage symbolically. Symbols express what outer eyes do not see.

For instance, all the language describing God in His own eternal and essential nature, whether in Revelation or in any other book, must be symbolic, not literal, simply because no human being has seen God at any time (Jn 1:18), until He became incarnate in Christ. He has no body, so He cannot literally sit on a golden throne or have a "strong right hand" and a "mighty arm". These are *symbols* for His power.

Another example: the creation story in Genesis 1 and 2 cannot be a literal eyewitness account because there *were* no eyewitnesses before God made any creatures with eyes, that is, until the fifth or sixth day of creation.

This criterion alone does not automatically settle the issue for all passages, for fiction as well as fact may be in the literary form of eyewitness descriptions. For instance, the Book of Job is probably fiction, but its events are visible, except for God appearing to Job at the end. (God appears to the "inner eye" but not to the outer.) There are borderline cases, like Noah and Jonah, which could go either way. But clearly the Jewish exodus and the parting of the Red Sea in the Old Testament, and the appearances of the resurrected Christ in the New Testament, are meant literally, as historical facts. And clearly the flying horsemen and angelic trumpets of Revelation are not—though they may *symbolize* future historical facts that are visible and literal.

A given passage may invite both a literal *and* a symbolic interpretation, on different levels. For instance, Moses was a literal man and also a symbol of Christ. Christ's healing of the blind man really happened, yet it also symbolizes His healing of our spiritual blindness. God can use real events to symbolize other things, while we can use only words.

A second principle of interpretation is even more basic and important. It is frequently violated, for example, when someone says something like this: "You can interpret the Resurrection literally if you wish, but I don't believe in miracles, and therefore I interpret those passages according to my sincerely held beliefs."

This confuses *interpretation* with *belief*. Even great scholars are often guilty of this confusion. We must *never* interpret a book—any book—in light of our own beliefs! We must *interpret* the book in the light of its *author's* beliefs. Then we *evaluate* it according to our own beliefs.

Interpreting a book by your own beliefs is *eisegesis*, "reading into" the book what's already in your own mind. All good interpretation is *exegesis*, "reading out" of the book what's in the *author's* mind.

When a modernist interprets miracle stories as fables, he is reversing the roles of interpretation and belief. When a Fundamentalist interprets symbols literally, he is doing the same thing. For example, the Fundamentalist might interpret the "millennium", the thousand-year reign of Christ on earth (chap. 20), as a thousand literal, historical years. Or he might interpret the 144,000 saved as a literal number, as the Jehovah's Witnesses do. (Get your seats while the tickets last; Heaven's stadium isn't very big!)

The Book of Revelation claims to be a spiritual vision, not a material one, seen by the inner eye, not the outer one. It is a dream sent to John's mind by Sonlight, by Christ, not a sensation sent to his optic nerves by earthly sunlight.

A third principle needs to be added: interpreting a passage symbolically does not necessarily mean not interpreting it *historically*. For instance, the story of the fall in Genesis 3 is clearly symbolic but also historical. The tree, the fruit, and the serpent function in the story not as things in themselves but as symbols of evil, temptation, and Satan. For example, Satan is not literally a snake. Yet the story must be *historical* because its subject, sin, is a historical fact. The story tells us how sin originated. If sin and its origin are not historical facts, then salvation and *its* origin (Christ's death and Resurrection) need not be historical facts either.

The events in Revelation are historical events. Some are past (for example, the birth of Christ and the flight into Egypt, Rev 12:1–6). Most are future. But all are told symbolically rather than literally (for example, compare Rev 12:1–6 with Mt 1:18–2:23).

Many people think that there are only two ways to interpret any passage: either literally and historically, or symbolically and non-historically (as one would Job or the Prodigal Son). But there is a third possibility: symbolically *and* historically, as one should interpret Revelation.

A fourth principle: do not confuse symbolism with allegory. In allegory, each ingredient has one and only one fully definable correct meaning. In symbolism, there may be many correct meanings, and they may or may not be exactly definable. For example, the Antichrist probably means both a single historical individual who will appear at the end of time, and also a spiritual force that was already in the world in the first century (see 1 Jn 2:18, 22; 4:3). The symbol of thunder for God's voice, used frequently in Revelation, is not simply an allegory for power, or fear, or a voice from Heaven; it connotes more than it denotes. You must feel the awe, not just figure out the meaning, to understand such a rich symbol.

A fifth principle in interpreting scriptural symbolism is to compare Scripture with Scripture, to interpret Scripture by Scripture. For example, we interpret the Lamb in Revelation in light of John the Baptist's words about Jesus (Jn 1:29, 36) and the liturgical offering in Leviticus and also vice versa. The sea out of which the Beast comes (Rev 13:1) usually symbolizes death in Scripture (for example, Moses crossing the Red Sea and Noah's flood). Thus, the fact that there is no sea in Heaven (Rev 21:1) is not a threat to surfers and sailors but a symbol for deathless life.

Where, specifically, do you go to find the correct interpretation of a symbol in Scripture, especially in this book, the most symbolic book in Scripture? I think we can divide its symbols into six groups by this standard.

1. Some symbols are explicitly explained in the same passage in which they are given. For example, just as Jesus interprets the parable of the sower to His disciples in Matthew 13, He explains the symbols of the seven stars and seven lampstands to John (1:20).

2. Some symbols are explained elsewhere in Scripture, for example, the Lamb and His Blood, and the sea, as explained above.

3. Some are plain and obvious, for example, the angels (messengers) of the plagues, and the seals (secrets) of the book (God's plan) that no one but the Lamb (Christ) could open (fulfill) (5:1–9).

4. Some *suggest* to the reader a hidden meaning, for example, the number 666, the mark of the Beast (Antichrist) (13:18). The text says, "This calls for wisdom." We are invited to solve the puzzle. The probable solution is that the letters of the blasphemous divine title that the Roman Emperor Domitian (A.D. 81–96) took for himself translate into the number 666 by using standard ancient number code (a=1, b=2, etc.) Domitian began the first virulent persecution of Christians while John was writing this book.

5. Some symbols are intuited with the instinctive poetic imagination, for example, the door in Heaven (4:1), the silence in Heaven (8:1), and the war in Heaven (12:7).

6. Finally, some are not clear from any of the above sources, for example, the two witnesses (11:3) and the number of the horsemen (9:16).

Put all the symbols together and ask what, most obviously and ubiquitously, do they all teach? The answer is spiritual warfare. Revelation describes a cosmic battle between good and evil, light and darkness, Heaven and Hell, Christ and Antichrist.

Every important good has a parallel evil symbol in Revelation. Parallel to the Holy Trinity there is the unholy trinity of the dragon (Satan), the Beast (Antichrist), and his false prophet (for the Holy Spirit is the Spirit of the true prophets). Parallel to the holy city of Jerusalem, the city of God, there is the unholy city of Babylon, the city of the world. (These two symbols were the basis of Saint Augustine's *The City of God*, the all-time classic Christian philosophy of history.) Parallel to the Blessed Virgin Mary (who also symbolizes the Church) is the "whore of Babylon". Parallel to the sea of crystal, there is the lake of fire.

The point is that evil is only an imitation of good, a parasite on good. Nothing is evil in the beginning. Evil cannot win; it is dependent on good. It can do enormous, horrible harm, but it cannot win in the end. If the parasite succeeded in destroying all the good in its host, it would destroy itself as well.

The parasitic nature of evil is shown even in the number symbolism. The number for evil is either three sixes (the number of the Antichrist), or three-and-one-half ("a time, times, and half a time"—12:14). Now seven is the sacred number. There are seven churches, seven angels, seven stars, seven candlesticks. Six is a defective seven, and three-and-one-half is a broken seven.

Twelve is also a sacred number, but an earthly, not a heavenly one. We immediately think of the twelve tribes of Israel and the twelve apostles as the pillars of the Church, the New Israel, the New Jerusalem (21:10–21). The number 144,000—the number of the elect, the saints, the saved (7:4; 14:1)—is twelve (tribes) times twelve (apostles) times one thousand. To the ancients, "a thousand" signified an unimaginably vast multitude.

Probably the most common mistake in interpreting the symbolism in Revelation is to attempt a strict chronology of events, to try to use it to figure out when the end of the world will come. This is a mistake for five reasons. First, the events are not in chronological sequence. Any attempt to interpret them sequentially meets insuperable contradictions. Second, the numbers in Revelation are symbolic, not literal. Third, Christ Himself said He did not know when the end of the world would come (Mt 24:36). How incredibly arrogant to claim to know more than your Lord! Fourth, every single predictor of the end of the world so far has been wrong. How reasonable is it to put any confidence in whatever batter is now at the plate if every batter who has ever tried to get a hit off this puzzling pitcher has struck out? Fifth, and most important of all, it is the wrong focus; it is misunderstanding the central point of the book to seek a strict chronology that points to the end of the world. The point of this book is not *when* but *who*. Its focus is on the One who comes, the Christ. In this, it continues and consummates the central focus of the entire Bible.

Christ the King in Revelation

We find Christ on every page of Revelation. Revelation is no less Christocentric than the Gospels. The only difference is that here He wears not a cross but a crown.

The book is a series of visions. But they have an order. The first, controlling vision (chap. 1) is the vision of the "son of man" (v. 13) who is "the first and the last, and the living one; I died, and behold, I am alive for evermore, and I have the keys to

Death and Hades" (vv. 17–18). This is Christ the King of the universe: of Heaven, earth, and even the underworld, for He has been in all three worlds (see 1 Pet 3:18–22).

The one who sends the seven letters to the seven churches (chaps. 2 and 3) is none other than Christ, as is clear from the last words of each of the seven letters.

The One seated on the heavenly throne (4:2), surrounded by twenty-four elders in white garments and golden crowns, by lightning, thunder, fire, and the sea of crystal (4:2–6), is Christ. The vision of Isaiah 6:1–5 is repeated here (4:8–9) and now finally interpreted and identified as a vision of Christ.

The one, the only one, who can open the scroll and its seven seals (5:5) is Christ. The scroll is history, His-story. The scroll is also our story, our destiny, and our salvation. He alone can fulfill both stories. The one who receives "power and wealth and wisdom and might and honor and glory and blessing" is "the Lamb who was slain" (5:12). The whole story of human history (the scroll) is about Him. He is the hidden key to history. (See G. K. Chesterton's classic *The Everlasting Man* for a brilliant book-length proof of that statement.)

The vision of the "great multitude which no man could number . . . standing before the throne and before the Lamb" (7:9) is again Christ, this time in His Mystical Body, His Church, His people.

History ends in chapter 8. "When the Lamb opened the seventh seal, there was silence in heaven for half an hour" (8:1)—so awful is the sight. The seven angelic trumpets that follow, like the seven seals, are the ending to His story. Finally, "the seventh angel blew his trumpet, and there were loud voices in heaven saying, 'The kingdom of this world has become the kingdom of our Lord and of his Christ, and he shall reign for ever and ever'" (11:15). History ends with the "Hallelujah Chorus"!

The next chapter begins with a flashback vision of Christ and His Mother, the "woman clothed with the sun" (12:1), and continues with a "war in heaven" between Saint Michael the archangel and Satan, the "accuser of our brethren" (12:10), who "have conquered him *by the blood of the Lamb*" (12:11, emphasis mine). Again, we find the gospel, the same gospel and the same Christ, but in symbol rather than in incarnate human flesh, and in glory rather than in suffering.

Christ's defeat of Satan is continued in chapter 13, and chapter 14 begins with another Christ-vision: "On Mount Zion stood the Lamb, and with him a hundred and forty-four thousand who had his name" (v. 1). They "sing a new song"—the gospel. "No one could learn that song except the hundred and forty-four thousand who had been redeemed" (14:3).

There is also a song in chapter 15, "the song of Moses" (v. 3; compare with Ex 15). But this song is now called "the song of the Lamb" (15:3), thus identifying Moses as a Christ-figure.

Three chapters of "the wrath of God" (16:1) follow, under the image of the seven bowls poured out by the angels (messengers) of God. Even this is Christocentric, for His judgment is only the inescapable alternative to His salvation. As the light necessarily makes its own darkness around it, the Savior necessarily makes His own shadow of damnation as the alternative to salvation for those who refuse Him.

After chapter 18's moving and massive mourning for the fall of Babylon (Babel), the great city of the world, chapter 19 contains the triumph song of the winner in the last, greatest, and—in reality—*only* war of all time (see Eph 6:12). This is also Christocentric, for its "hallelujah" celebrates His marriage to the Church, His Bride (19:7).

The latter half of chapter 19 presents Christ again, this time with four names. Three are already known from Scripture:

"Faithful and True" (v. 11), "The Word of God" (v. 13), and "King of kings and Lord of lords" (v. 16). But He also "has a name inscribed which no one knows but himself" (v. 12). There is more, infinitely more, to Christ than we can know. We will learn this new name (identity, dimension) only in Heaven.

We too will have a new name in Heaven, described in the same words: "I will give him a white stone with a new name written on the stone which no one knows except him who receives it" (2:17). Your ultimate identity is a secret known only to you and God.

In a sense the whole Book of Revelation is about Christ's new name. It tells more about Christ than the Gospels tell, but more about the same Christ: glory added to suffering, crown added to cross, Second Coming added to first coming, return added to ascension (see Acts 1:11).

The "millennium" (chap. 20), about which so much controversy has swirled in certain Christian circles, is presented as a thousand-year reign of *Christ* (20:4). Losing the focus on Christ for a focus on time was the first cause of the theological bickering.

Chapter 21 describes the last event in history: the coming of the Church, the New Jerusalem, Christ's Mystical Body, in all its glory descending from Heaven. "And I saw the holy city, new Jerusalem, coming down out of heaven from God, prepared as a bride adorned for her husband" (21:2). Just as God's call "down" to Abraham (Gen 12) comes right after the fall of the "uppity" Tower of Babel (Gen 11), so the descent of the New Jerusalem (chap. 21) comes after the fall of proud Babylon, the successor of Babel, in chapter 18.

This Bride, by the way, is not many cities or many brides but one—not churches but the Church. Christ is no bigamist. When He comes, He will not marry a harem but a bride.

Christ the King is our King *so that* He can be our Bridegroom. The deepest thing is not power but love. Power is only a means to love. Christ exercises His power so that He can consummate His love.

The final cause, end, purpose, goal, ultimate good, meaning of life, point, and conclusion of the whole story that began with the "Big Bang" (Gen 1:1)—providentially steered through every stellar explosion and terrestrial evolution, every molecule and every meeting, every hair's and sparrow's fall—is Christ's marriage to His Church.

The world exists for the Church. The universe exists for the Church, as the raw material the Church is made from. Gases and galaxies are not its point, only its wires and wheels. God went to all the trouble of creation, Incarnation, death, Resurrection, ascension, and this final consummation of history for His marriage to the Church.

Some find Revelation hard, dry, threatening, repellent, cruel, impersonal, and unemotional. But if we belong to Christ, we should read it with a lump in our throat and a leap in our heart, for we are His Bride. Revelation culminates in our wedding night.

The only ones who should find this book threatening are the unrepentant sinners, who call on the mountains and rocks to fall on them and hide them from the face of God, which they fear (6:16). To fear the face of God, which is truth, is, quite simply, to be bound for Hell. To love the face of God is to be bound for Heaven.

Perhaps Heaven and Hell are made of the same thing everything is made of, namely truth, the one thing that is inescapable. To love it and live on it as our food, is Heaven. To hate and fear it and to be tortured by it, is Hell. For truth is inescapable; God can no more turn off the light of His truth than the sun can stop shining.

The book ends (chap. 22) with the invitation to join the wedding feast, that is, the good news (*evangelium*) sent by Christ through His *angelum* or angel (v. 16). This news is the free offer of salvation (v. 17).

"The Spirit and the Bride (Church) say, 'Come.' " Both God and the visible Church have as their primary work on earth the invitation to come to Christ's wedding feast. "And let him who hears say, 'Come.' " The Christian responds, "Come, Lord Jesus!" (22:20). Without this passionate longing for our love feast, our Christian faith is deeply impaired and incomplete. "And let him who is thirsty come. Let him who desires take the water of life [salvation] without price." Our only qualification is thirst, desire. All who seek, find (Mt 7:7).

The one thing we can be absolutely certain of is that we will die. If you were to die tonight and stand before God, and He were to ask you, "Why should I take you to Heaven?" What would you say?

We can argue forever about your answer or my answer, but here is God's answer. It is on almost every page of the New Testament: because of Christ, the water of eternal life is free, "without price". All we have to do is to believe in Him, hope in Him, love Him. Not worthiness but love and desire are our only qualifications. We are bums who have been given clean wedding garments (Mt 22:12) and free entrance tickets to the wedding. The real surprise is that we are not just guests, we're the Bride.

The Second Coming in Revelation

Some time during the first half of this past century—the Christian half, for the event recounted here could never have happened in the *second* half—a question was asked of major American newspaper editors: What would be the greatest headline you could ever hope to write? Many chose something like: "All Wars End" or "Cure for Cancer". But a Chicago editor gave the best answer: "Christ Comes Again".

Of course, when He does come again, we won't be bothering about things like newspapers. Only God will write history's greatest headline.

Revelation is about the last act of our play, the end of history, of time itself. More specifically, it is about Christ's Second Coming. Christ does not come again *because* it is the end of time. It is the end of time *because* He comes again. Christ is not relative to time; time is relative to Christ.

Many readers and interpreters of Revelation are more interested in the *when* than in the *who*. But the only answer He gives to the *when* question is "soon", or "quickly" (3:11; 22:7, 12, 20).

But it's been nearly two thousand years already. That hardly seems "soon". Did He lie?

Not at all. For "the Lord is not slow about his promise as some count slowness, but is forbearing toward you, not wishing that any should perish, but that all should reach repentance" (2 Pet 3:9). How dare we complain about being given extra time before final exams?

Furthermore, God's time is not like ours. "For a thousand years in thy sight are but as yesterday when it is past, or as a watch in the night" (Ps 90:4).

When will you die? "Soon." Whether in sixty minutes or sixty years, death is always soon. Life is always short. Similarly, when will time die? When will the whole world's life end? Soon.

Real time is measured not by clocks but by meanings, not by matter moving across space but by spirit moving across purposes. Real time is qualitative, not quantitative; personal, not impersonal. The Greek language has two different words for these two different kinds of time: *kairos* for the first (real, lived time) and *kronos* for the second (clock time).

All the time between Christ's first coming and His Second Coming is relatively insignificant compared to these two great events. The fall of Rome, the rise and fall of the Middle Ages, the Renaissance, the industrial revolution, two world wars— these are mere footnotes in God's history book, page-two items in God's newspapers. Revelation tells us the headlines.

"When will Daddy come back from Florida?" asks the breathlessly expectant three-year-old. "Soon." Now all the time until Daddy comes will be defined by that event, and it will indeed be "soon", not because it is a certain quantity of clock time but because Daddy is such an important person in the toddler's life.

Expectation of a happy thing before it happens adds to its happiness. Planning a movie, a ball game, or a vacation is part of the fun. But this is infinitely more than a vacation. This is eternal marriage to God. Therefore, this book should make every Christian very, very happy.

For the thing we hope for above all else is here promised, assured, guaranteed. The great King will come to defeat all His enemies and take us, His Cinderella, to His great castle to live happily ever after. The fairy tales are foolish not because they are too good to be true, but because they are not nearly good enough. "What no eye has seen, nor ear heard, nor the heart of man conceived, God has prepared for those who love him" (1 Cor 2:9).

But we would still like to know just how soon that will be. Might He come in our own lifetime? Indeed He might. The end of time and the beginning of eternity, the end of the world and the beginning of Heaven, are symbolized in Revelation by the fall of Babylon, the city of the world (chap. 18) and the descent of the new Jerusalem, the City of God (chap. 21).

It is the perfect finish to the story of clashing symbols that we find throughout Scripture. There is perfect consistency to all the vertical images: all human ways up to God fail, all divine ways down to man succeed. Chapters 18 and 21 of Revelation only complete this consistent pattern.

First, we see God reaching down to create a world that is perfectly good. Then we see a human hand reaching up to snatch the forbidden fruit, and this apparent rise is really the fall.

Next, the Tower of Babel (Gen 11) seems perfectly reasonable and destined for success, but the attempt to reach Heaven by human effort collapses when God confuses human language (*logos*, reason). Then comes the call of Abraham, in the very next chapter. It seems like a perfectly ridiculous way to save history, yet it is God's beginning to the world's greatest success story, the story of redemption.

Later, Job's (Everyman's) attempts to find God seem perfectly right and just, yet they do not succeed. But when God finds Job, even impatient Job is satisfied.

All the false prophets seem to succeed. They are popular, for they measure God by what their hearers want. True prophets, on the other hand, are always unpopular and persecuted since they measure man by God, not God by man. Yet they alone know the truth and survive through the ages.

All human expectations of the Messiah are wrong. He corresponds to none of the ideas our minds conjure up: earthly king, warrior, politician, philosopher, levitical priest, or even merely a prophet. But God's idea is the most brilliant strategy ever conceived. He defeats the devil and redeems us by becoming a crucified criminal. By His death He reconciles earth and Heaven, justice and mercy, at once on the Cross (Ps 85:10).

Finally, at the end, Babylon—all worldly grasping and glory—collapses in one hour. The despair is stunning. Please read the great poetry of chapter 18, not just these thin words about it. After the false ladder from earth to Heaven collapses, the true ladder from Heaven to earth appears: the New Jerusalem is Christ Himself, the Head and His Body, the Church. (He is revealed as the real Jacob's ladder in Jn 1:29–34.)

Revelation preaches the same Gospel in symbols that Jesus preached in deeds and Paul in words: salvation by God's grace, not man's greatness. Other religions are stories of man's search for God. The Bible is the story of God's search for man. Jesus promised us that all who seek Him will find Him (Lk 11:9–13), but that is only because He has first sought and found us. And this divine search-and-rescue operation, which theologians call redemption, is completed only when history itself is completed, when our Divine Lover comes to fetch His Bride to take her home.

OUR LADY STAR OF THE SEA PARISH
1513 6TH STREET
BREMERTON, WA 98337